From

The Women's Press Ltd
34 Great Sutton Street, London EC1V 0DX

Gillian Hanscombe was born in 1945 in Melbourne and read English literature and music history at Melbourne and Monash universities. She has lived in Britain since 1969 and has published work in a variety of modes, including poetry, fiction, polemic and educational texts. Her book on Dorothy Richardson, *The Art of Life* (Peter Owen, 1982) resulted from a D.Phil. thesis completed at Oxford University in 1979. She has one son and currently lives and writes by the sea in Devon.

Virginia Smyers is a rare-book librarian and bibliographer. She recently finished cataloguing the books and papers of the late Winifred Bryher, one of the women in *Writing for Their Lives*. Currently a Reference Librarian at Harvard University in Cambridge, Massachusetts, she is working on a selected edition of the letters of Dorothy Richardson, a project she hopes will allow her to spend more time in London.

GILLIAN HANSCOMBE AND
VIRGINIA L. SMYERS

Writing for their Lives

The Modernist Women 1910–1940

The Women's Press

First published by The Women's Press Limited 1987
A member of the Namara Group
34 Great Sutton Street, London EC1V 0DX

British Library Cataloguing in Publication Data

Hanscombe, Gillian E.
    writing for their lives.
    1. English literature—Women authors—
    History and criticism   2. English literature
    —20th century—History and criticism
    I. Title   II. Smyers, Virginia L.
    820.9'9287   PR116

    ISBN 0-7043-4075-5

Typeset by MC Typeset Ltd, 34 New Road, Chatham, Kent
Printed and bound by Hazell Watson & Viney Ltd,
Aylesbury, Bucks

For my grandmother,
Virginia Thompson Wild,
and for R.E.S.
from Virginia Smyers

To the memory of my mother,
Patricia Martin Hanscombe,
and for Suniti Namjoshi,
from Gillian Hanscombe.

CONTENTS

Acknowledgements

We would like to thank all those whose help and co-operation have made this book possible. In particular, grateful acknowledgement is given to the following individuals and institutions for permission to quote from previously unpublished material and to quote extensively from published sources:

Mrs Perdita Schaffner, (New Directions Publishing Corporation, agents) for permission to quote from the unpublished writings of H.D.; copyright © 1987 by Perdita Schaffner.

New Directions Publishing Corporation and Faber & Faber Ltd. for permission to quote from an unpublished letter of Ezra Pound; copyright © 1987 by the Trustees of the Ezra Pound Literary Property Trust; Carcanet Press for permission to quote from the following works of H.D. and Ezra Pound.

Collected Poems 1912–1944 by H.D., copyright © 1984 by the Estate of Hilda Doolittle;

End to Torment. A Memoir of Ezra Pound by H.D. With the poems from 'Hilda's Book' by Ezra Pound, copyright © 1979 by New Directions Publishing Corporation;

Roger L. Conover and The Jargon Society, Inc., editor and publisher, for permission to quote extracts from *The Last Lunar Baedeker* by Mina Loy (Highlands, N. C.: The Jargon Society, 1982 and Manchester: Carcanet Press, 1985.)

Mrs Perdita Schaffner, (John Schaffner Associates, agents), for permission to quote from the unpublished letters of Bryher; copyright © by Mrs Perdita Schaffner;

Houghton, Mifflin Company for permission to quote extracts from

The Complete Poetical Works of Amy Lowell; copyright © 1955 by Houghton Mifflin Company. Copyright © 1983 renewed by Houghton Mifflin Company, Brinton P. Roberts, Esq., and G. d'Andelot Belin, Esq. Reprinted by permission of Houghton Mifflin Company.

Faber & Faber Ltd. for permission to quote extracts from *Selected Letters of Ezra Pound 1907–1941*, ed. D.D. Paige. Copyright © 1950 by Ezra Pound;

The Estate of Frances Gregg for permission to quote extracts from the unpublished writings of Frances Gregg;

M. François Chapon for permission to quote extracts from the unpublished writings of Natalie Barney;

The Executors of the Estate of Harriet Shaw Weaver for permission to quote extracts from the unpublished writings of Harriet Shaw Weaver;

Mr G. d'Andelot Belin and Mr Brinton P. Roberts, Trustees under the Will of Amy Lowell, for permission to quote extracts from unpublished letters of Amy Lowell;

Mrs Sheena Odle, Literary Executrix of the Estate of Dorothy Miller Richardson, for permission to quote extracts from unpublished letters of Dorothy Miller Richardson;

Mrs Sheena Odle and Virago Press for permission to quote from *Pilgrimage* by Dorothy Miller Richardson (London, Virago, 1979);

Mrs Camilla Bagg for permission to quote extracts from an unpublished letter of Mary Butts;

Catherine Aldington-Guillaume and Alister Kershaw, Executor for the Literary Estate of Richard Aldington, for permission to quote extracts from unpublished letters of Richard Aldington;

Mrs Joella Bayer for permission to quote extracts from unpublished letters of Mina Loy;

The Authors League Fund, N.Y., and Church Preservation Trust, London, literary executors, Djuna Barnes Estate, for permission to quote from unpublished writings of Djuna Barnes and from *Ladies Almanack*, copyright © 1972 by Djuna Barnes;

Mr Robert R. Davis for permission to quote extracts from unpublished writings of Robert McAlmon;

Dr Clive E. Driver, Literary Executor of the Estate of Marianne C. Moore, for permission to quote extracts from unpublished letters of Marianne Moore, copyright © 1987 by Clive E. Driver.

We would like to acknowledge, also, the following libraries for permission to quote from unpublished material in their collections:

The Beinecke Rare Book and Manuscript Library, Yale University; The British Library; The Houghton Library, Harvard University; The Humanities Research Center, University of Texas at Austin; McKeldin Library, University of Maryland; The Rosenbach Museum and Library, Philadelphia; University College, London, Library; University of Pennsylvania Libraries.

Every effort has been made to find copyright holders; we apologise to any whom we have been unable to locate.

In addition, for much-valued help and co-operation given to Virginia Smyers during her research in the US, we are extremely grateful to particular librarians: Ralph Franklin, Donald Gallup, Marjorie Wynne, Steve Jones and Louis Silverstein at Beinecke Library; Rodney Dennis, Roger Stoddard, Michael Winship and Melanie Wisner at Houghton Library; Patricia Willis at The Rosenbach Library; Blanche Ebeling-Koning at McKeldin Library; and Ellen Dunlap, during her appointment at The Humanities Research Center, University of Texas at Austin.

Many of the relatives, friends and literary executors of the women we write about in this book have generously made themselves available for consultation. We are particularly grateful to: Mrs Camilla Bagg; Mrs Joella Bayer; the late Oswell Blakeston; Mr David Kent; Miss Jane Lidderdale; Miss Pauline Marrian; Mrs Sheena Odle; Mrs Perdita Schaffner; and Mr Oliver Wilkinson and the late Margaret Wilkinson.

Both in the US and in Britain, a number of scholars have offered time, interest and comment over a period of some five years. For this help we thank: Dr Diana Collecott, Durham University; Roger Conover; Anne Friedberg and Louis Silverstein. For editorial advice and comment about Ezra Pound we thank Dr Suniti Namjoshi, Scarborough College, University of Toronto.

For support, encouragement, comment, information and practical help we're indebted to friends on both sides of the Atlantic. Among friends in England, we'd specially like to thank Marsaili Cameron, Joan Crawford, Elisabeth Flinspach, Alison Hennegan and Prunella Sedgwick, who variously spoke to publishers, helped with notes, read parts of the manuscript, supplied new information and made a lot of coffee! In the US, Virginia Smyers wants particularly to thank Kathy Tiddens, Gary Hill and Barbara Tiddens for unending hospitality and Kathy Tiddens for reading the manuscript and offering valuable suggestions; Barbara Smyers and Bob Flanders, for providing a home for six months; Barbara Guest, for opening many doors and inspiring fresh avenues of research; James Hallowell, for storing furniture and books and for neverending support of all kinds, Perdita, Elizabeth, Nicholas and Timothy Schaffner for constant interest and kindness during the two years spent with them while working on the catalogue for the Bryher Library; and Leo Abbett, Joe Bourneuf, Deborah Kelley, Anil Khosla, Patrick Miehe; Bill and Beth Meister, Monty Montee, Stephanie Munroe, Hinda Sklar and Zipporah Wiseman.

At The Women's Press we'd like to thank everyone who has guided this book into print; and in particular, Sarah Lefanu, who first read and liked the manuscript and later handled its production; Ros de Lanerolle, whose efficiency and patience make deadlines almost easy; and our editor Sue Gilbert, whose skill and intelligence shaped a manuscript whose unwieldy mass had defeated all others.

Prefaces

I

This book came into being because of another book. In 1979 I
finished work on Dorothy Richardson intended for an Oxford
D.Phil. thesis and in 1980 I used this work as the basis for *The Art of
Life*; a book about Dorothy Richardson and the development of
feminist consciousness. Dorothy Richardson, English modernist, is
avowed by her small following to be a monstrously neglected writer;
and – perhaps consequently – those of us who belong to the
following like very much to meet each other. Genny Smyers and I
met because she was working on Dorothy's letters.

As we talked, she began to tell me more and more about
Dorothy's circle and contemporaries. My own preoccupations had
been determinedly more 'academic'; apart from the rigours
required of a thesis, my disposition was to trace – as well as I could –
the ways in which Dorothy's instinctive feminism had driven her
work. Genny's vast knowledge of the network and ambience in
which Dorothy Richardson lived and wrote excited me in a different
way. She told me about the relationship between H.D. and Bryher,
between H.D. and Frances Gregg, Frances Gregg and the Powys
brothers, H.D., her husband Richard Aldington and the D.H.
Lawrences – and so on. She had read a huge number of their letters
and papers and could conjure each one at will. She detailed the role
played in all their lives by Ezra Pound and his theories and by
Bryher and her generosity.

I remember the talk going on and on and the light fading on the
coffee mugs. I remember becoming instantly obsessed by the sense
of connections: the interdependence of their actual lives and of the

work they produced and provided; the interdependence between 'art' and 'life' which resulted in so much autobiographical fiction; the interdependence between personal bonding and aesthetic theory which resulted in so much new poetry. The 'modernism' of the fiction and the 'imagism' of the poetry began to show their roots in the personalities and lives of their creators.

Another theme emerged in conversation. Most of these writers were women; and most of their partnerships were not conventional marriages. Was there, perhaps, a connection? Might this group – what they did, thought and wrote – have something other than literary experiment to tell us now? Was it for them (and perhaps for us) evident that a woman artist must not only be original in her art but must also (to achieve the art) be original in her lifestyle?

Genny pointed out that, as well as knowing each other and influencing each other's work, these writers also wrote about each other. The role of small magazines, of bookshops like Sylvia Beach's in Paris, of new publishing ventures, was clearly very central. The lives many lived as expatriates explained why – perhaps – it was easier to throw off convention than it is for a native. And the implicit feminism of their compulsive need for independence contrasted curiously with their non-involvement in the struggle for the vote. These strands, among others, entwined my interest as I listened and argued. 'It's another Bloomsbury', I remember saying.

My own obsession, since meeting Genny, has been with the nature of that network and what it might reveal about the modern breaking down of boundaries between 'art' and 'life' which became known in literary history as 'modernism'; and, too, with what might be distinctively female about these interactions and their literary results. I have not, by contrast, been concerned to pursue each biography in the depth and detail characteristic of the biographer's art. That is not to diminish either biography or biographers; simply to say that this book was not conceived as a web of biographies, since it is more a story of connections than a connection of stories.

I have not, either, attempted to pursue the detail relevant to social history. An accounting of this period and of what it was like for women to live and write in it, can be given much more adequately by writers more qualified in historical method. In many ways I have willingly fallen prey to that most a-historical of orientations during the preparation of this book: that is, the imagining of these writers as if they had not lived more than half a century ago, but as if they were still around, since – for me – so much of what interests me about them still seems both current and futuristic.

I apologise, therefore, if there are sometimes mistaken emphases, either of biographical detail which screams in its absence, or of a milieu which may seem impoverished by an absence of contemporary observation.What I want is to persuade you that how these women lived-what-they-wrote or wrote-what-they-lived is part of the jigsaw of women's cultural tradition and part, too, of the conditions we still write in and from.

Our overall purpose is to give an overview which we hope will lead readers first to the great amount of material our writers produced and then to the kinds of detailed studies of their work which it is beyond the scope of one book to provide. The overview we trace presents two themes which seem to us particularly significant: one is the importance of women's patronage, both directly financial – as given by Bryher and Harriet Shaw Weaver – and literary – as given by Sylvia Beach, Harriet Monroe, H.D. and Amy Lowell. The second theme is what appears to be a clear connection between literary endeavour and the shunning of conventionally heterosexual lives: a challenge to what many feminists now call 'heterosexism'.

Patronage provides a key to the loose professional network outlined in the later chapters of our text: how women variously serviced each other's work with funds, encouragement, criticism, recommendations and introductions. The challenge to heterosexism provides a key to earlier chapters, in which we sketch the personal lives our writers led: their different partnerships, friendships and connections. The lesbian alternative chosen by many of them is seen to have direct bearing either on their conditions of work, or on the contents of what they wrote, or both.

Women who want to do things or be people beyond the scope of their expected destinies as wives and mothers, must live differently from other women and from men. How women writers faced that confusing and difficult challenge in the early part of this century is, for us, a constant source of admiration and astonishment.

G.E.H.
London, 1987

II

Lives, the details of lives, what the person looked like, wore, ate, felt like, loved – have become almost obsessions with me. Particularly, the lives of women writers. I first noticed this when packing my books for a move. The man friend helping me suddenly said accusingly: 'But all these books are by women!' He was amazed, I think, that so many books had been written by women – and I was amazed to see that I actually did have very few books by men. It wasn't a conscious decision, not a sudden conversion or a political stand. How, when, had it begun?

Perhaps with Louisa May Alcott, my childhood favourite. I had read everything I could find about her life, I had visited her home – now a museum – and studied her manuscripts in the library where I worked. I wanted desperately to know the woman behind the books I loved. Then at college, there was my discovery of Dorothy Richardson's novels while browsing in the stacks. No one had ever mentioned her name to me and *Pilgrimage* meant nothing until I started to read one of the volumes. From then on, I was deep in my biographical obsession, which spread from Dorothy herself to all her friends and all their writings, and to all the books about them. It spread too, to their manuscripts and letters, many of which are in Beinecke Library at Yale University, in New Haven, Connecticut.

It was in Beinecke one autumn day in 1978 that the Curator of American Literature, Donald Gallup, introduced me to Barbara Guest. 'She's working on a biography of H.D.,' he explained. (This book was published in 1984.) He said that she might be interested to know that I was also looking at H.D. material (her letters to Dorothy Richardson). Barbara was in the tiny typing room, transcribing. Within five minutes we had discovered a mutual passion for Dorothy Richardson – Barbara had even named the main character in her novel 'Miriam' after Richardson's persona in *Pilgrimage* – and our friendship began. Now that I found Barbara had discovered some of the same things I had, we avidly discussed our finds, each bringing up one thing after another: 'And Cournos's

Miranda Masters . . .' 'Then Frances and Ezra . . .'. Excitedly we compared notes and Barbara asked me to help her gather more facts and information for her book. I agreed at once and so, for the next five years, whenever I could get away from my full-time job as a librarian, I researched H.D.'s life. Which meant not only H.D., but all those other women I had come to know, originally through my interest in Dorothy Richardson: Bryher, Sylvia Beach, Djuna Barnes, Mary Butts, Frances Gregg, Marianne Moore, May Sinclair, Amy Lowell, Harriet Weaver, Gertrude Stein, Mina Loy . . . from one life the circle grew larger and larger, and more and more entangled, interwebbed. They all seemed to write to each other, or about each other. They introduced one to the other. They sometimes fell in love with each other or with each other's partners. They were all either writing, or publishing what the others were writing, because they believed in each other's work.

None of them seemed to live conventionally: some were lesbian, some were bisexual, some promiscuous, some seemingly asexual. Those with money used it to help the others live, or publish, or both. Those with time gave it to criticise, or write for, or talk about, each other's work and projects. Men sometimes entered the circles, but usually they were peripheral. Some were catalysts, some were lovers, but few were essential to the women's lives. Why was this? I wanted to find out what these women meant to each other, how they supported each other, in their struggle to establish themselves as writers, usually the privileged sphere of men.

And how had they succeeded? For I felt they had. Going through the periodicals and books of the twenties I saw their names over and over. They were not a sidelight of the literary production of the period; they were as much a part of it as Joyce, Eliot and Pound. That the men's names have emerged since as the stars might have much to do with the perceptions of the predominantly male critics, I said to myself. And besides, where would Joyce, Pound and Eliot have been – where would their work even have been published – without Harriet Weaver, Margaret Anderson, Harriet Monroe, Sylvia Beach, Bryher? I began to question the fact that today everyone knows who the men were, but no one seems to know who Dorothy Richardson was, or H.D., or Mina Loy. I wanted to do something about it.

My own project relating to these women was the compiling and editing of a selected edition of Dorothy Richardson's letters. That was put aside to do this book with Gill Hanscombe, whom I met due to the helpfulness of Mrs Sheena Odle, Dorothy Richardson's literary executrix. We decided to do a book together about this network of writers who fascinated us both. And, in any case, we'd been told that no publisher in London was interested in Dorothy's letters – because so few people knew who she was. We decided that this present book might serve as an introduction not only to Richardson but to the other women writers as well. Consequently, I went off to track down people and places.

As the research progressed, I found my own circle, or network, of friends and connections grew even wider. In fact, I felt I was repeating in my own life the patterns I traced in the lives of the women I was researching. Perhaps it is not so astonishing that other writers, researchers, librarians and literary executors were interested in this book. What did surprise me, and what reinforces my feeling of connection with the women writers we talk about here, was the support and encouragement that all these people, as well as friends not directly involved in the project (who still say 'who?' when H.D. is mentioned) gave to my life during the years I worked on this book. They gave housing, food, entertainment, time and concern in great abundance – they sympathised, wrote letters, made coffee, paid bills, telephoned, visited and had me to visit. Perhaps the fact that I was an American living in London during much of this time brought me closer, too, to those expatriate lives I examined. Being a woman writer is still not easy, and still requires, is made possible by, a connective network of friends, such as H.D. and Dorothy Richardson needed and had. In a way, then, this book is a celebration of friendship; and in particular of friendships formed through and because of writing what one believes in. I've read, transcribed, taken notes, talked to other researchers and librarians and to as many friends or relatives of the writers as I could find. I have tried to track down the places where they lived and worked. All the details of the lives in this book are the result of my biographical obsession, of my need to know the people behind the names and the work. I feel as if I do know them now; and that somehow their lives still have the power to move and – more importantly – to connect us, as women, to our past, to our literary heritage and to each other.

V.L.S.
Boston and London, 1987

Chapter 1

'Another Bloomsbury?'

Ask just about anyone interested in English literature, or women, or both, which women were writing in England just after the turn of the century and you're bound to hear 'Virginia Woolf'. You may sometimes hear added 'Oh, and there was Katherine Mansfield'. Ask more generally what circle seems to have dominated literary socialising and discussion and you'll hear 'The Bloomsbury Group'. Ask, even more generally, who the great writers were and you'll hear 'Ezra Pound, T.S. Eliot, James Joyce, W.B. Yeats, D.H. Lawrence'. Only the name 'Virginia Woolf' consistently straddles these fields of interest. Readers interested in feminism may be led from Woolf to Vita Sackville-West and Violet Trefusis. Readers interested in mainstream literary history may be led sideways from Woolf to Dorothy Richardson and John Cowper Powys. More insistently, however, the Virginia Woolf industry – fuelled with scores of memoirs, diaries, letters, marginalia, unpublished manuscripts and miscellaneous material – leads back to its feted origin, 'The Bloomsbury Group', in whose atmosphere a great number of feminists and literati unusually co-mingled. The fascination exerted by this group seems almost inexhaustible.

And it is surely Bloomsbury's context, after all, that remains the core of its fascination; how the characters lived and discussed and loved and hated together, coupled with the notion that there was something 'modern' about it all. And feminists – whose heroines are nearly always forgotten, obscured or discarded by literary pundits – like knowing that Woolf (and Mansfield) educated themselves in the British Museum Reading Room, being barred, like all other women, from the universities. 'But', some murmur, 'was that all there was?'

Feminists certainly begin to ask 'Were there any other women writing then? Who were they? What did they write? Did they know each other? Was there another "Group", perhaps, like Bloomsbury?'

These aren't idle questions. It's often the case (since traditionalists in the main write our literary history) that some writers are given the centre of the stage at the expense of equally talented (but less sympathetic) players who are kept in the wings. And indeed there is another 'group' or, more accurately, a loose network, who are less well known but who were women living and writing between the 1890s and the Second World War. Unlike Virginia Woolf's set, these women, who knew each other, or each other's work, or both, were often expatriate; many were poor; all were more bohemian than bourgeois; and they were more linked by shared choices and interests than by the tighter ties of traditional background and common blood. Nor were all the women poets or novelists; some were editors and publishers, others ran bookshops, yet others provided patronage of both spiritual and material kinds.

On these and other grounds, the parallel with Bloomsbury is useful mainly as a starting point, at the least to broaden our literary hindsight, but more importantly to locate in time and place the extraordinary radicalism of this more obscured network. There are, that is, two major reasons for beginning an acquaintance with the lives, the writings, and the inter-connectedness, of H.D., Bryher, Dorothy Richardson, Gertrude Stein, Djuna Barnes, Harriet Monroe, Dora Marsden, Harriet Weaver, Marianne Moore, Amy Lowell, Mary Butts, Mina Loy, Margaret Anderson and Sylvia Beach. The first is to learn how they dealt with the anomaly of being 'women writers' or 'literary women'; and the second is to see how they dealt with the consciousness of being 'modern'.

Consider, for example, the environment these women inhabited. It seems to us now, when we study prints and photographs, that Edwardian women were stylish, elegant even, and definitely dressed and posed to look as feminine as possible. The women who stare back at us from such pictures are wearing more layers of long clothing than most of us now can remember the names of. They dress their hair in complex patterns, often (we must assume) suffering agonies from the hairpins and hatpins necessary to keep such head-dressing in place. They wear all kinds of accessories, from collars and cuffs to dangles of every description. Even those who dispensed with as much feminine paraphernalia as they could are still (apart from the cross-dressers) perfectly distinguishable from men, whose attire is very different. The demarcation line between the genders is firm and sharp, its appearance registering the equally clear social, psychological and sexual differences between women and men which society boasted with a confidence few were brave or percipient enough to challenge.

The novelist Dorothy Richardson was only one of several who rebelled; who wanted to belong to themselves and to write in their own voices. Yet if Richardson were to achieve independence, she must question not only the hated petticoats which forbade such an ordinary freedom as riding a bicycle, but also the tradition of the English novel (which she judged explicitly to be a masculine tradition.)

It is less surprising than regrettable that – 80 years on – our impressions of women living at the turn of the century are dominated by images of the gallant, chained to railings, demanding votes for women. We can too easily assume that their cries impinged on every consciousness in the kingdom and that everyone therefore admired their courage. It's easy, too, to forget that attempts to advocate birth control for married women were vigorously prosecuted and that wife-beating was an accepted part of domestic life. We can hardly realise how few in number were those women – supported by even fewer men – who struggled for the vote. Moreover, it is only the vocabulary of the feminism of our own time which can illuminate why then – as now – a large number of women thinkers and writers saw the liberation of women not as a civil matter, to be pursued by campaigns such as demanding the vote or demanding equal representation in Parliament, but as a cultural matter, to be pursued first in the battle zones mapped out in every woman's inner life, next in the social arenas of every woman's personal life, and finally in every painting, poem or piece of prose taking shape under a woman's hand. If many women did not put their hands to the suffragette plough, it was not because their energies lay dormant, but more because they wrestled with those other shackles which were as enslaving as the petticoats: chastity, monogamy, marriage, child-bearing, heterosexual conformity, economic dependence and intellectual infantilisation.

A 'woman writer', in particular, was an anomaly, as indeed she still is. A woman writer, in the context of mainstream culture, has always been a trespasser in men's territory. And she trespasses at her peril. She is as much at home in men's traditions as is a Third Worlder in the privileged landscapes of European society. She has no 'natural' place there. She can either create a new place – a women's sub-culture, with all the derogations the prefix implies – to which the mainstream need give no serious regard, or she can do battle with men to prove she is worthy to be honoured as one of them. (Nineteenth-century women writers who took male pseudonyms were perfectly well aware that they needed to be accepted as honorary men if their work were to be seriously considered.)

It's the word 'woman' used as an adjective which is problematic; and especially so when it qualifies 'writer'. A woman writer, that is, tries to be two different – and incompatible – people at once. On the one hand is the requirement to be a 'real' woman: either beautiful, according to the prevailing taste, or at least good-looking. There is the requirement not to look, or to be, outlandish, unless the woman is so rich, or famous, or both, that she can dispense with what others – especially men – think of her. There is the need, perhaps, to be a good wife: to be supportive of a husband's career, hobbies and feelings, to care for his comforts and to manage his household competently. There is the need to be a good lover: to make her nakedness attractive and to be warm and generous with her sexuality, neither too demanding nor frigid. There is the need, perhaps, to be a good mother: to be kind, caring, nurturant and wise. This woman of the world needs, above all, to be unselfish: to put before her own needs or wishes those of her man, or men, and those of her children. She needs to take second place. And taking second place means being of secondary importance. Whatever she thinks, feels, or sees – if it conflicts with what men think, feel or see – must come second in value. If she persists, as a writer must, in wanting first place, she risks losing out as a woman, since she will be seen by men and by many other women to be an eccentric, or a neurotic, an upstart or a virago, a wallflower or a lesbian. She becomes, in the eyes of the world, unsexed. Most women, writers or not, cringe at the prospect of such a fate; and they do so justifiably. It takes remarkable courage to swim against the current when there are real dangers of drowning.

Given these all too familiar considerations, it is ironical that the other person a good writer needs to be is the exact opposite of her good sister. A writer, by consensus and tradition, speaks with authority about the way things are. A writer never takes second place voluntarily. Writers, like other artists, are supposed to be selfish: to live in ivory towers which protect them from the seaminess of common life; and they are supposed to burn with extraordinary passions, which must have their way. Literary history is littered with stories of astonishing selfishness on the part of writers whose work evokes extraordinary acclaim: Balzac went through women and their chateaux at the exact rate that his purse could thus support his writing; D.H. Lawrence raged his way through every important relationship in his life in the service of his art; Dylan Thomas's alcoholism was cradled for the sake of his poetry; Joyce, Tolstoy, Marx, Freud . . . the list is endless, of men whose thought and writing has been deemed to excuse whatever excesses of selfishness they perpetrated. It is the degree of value we place on a writer's work which measures the extent to which we excuse the way he lives. But can we say 'she' in the same way?

Whatever this artistic stance is called – independence, extravagance, egoism or mere immaturity – it is supposed to be one of the hallmarks of a true writer. As such, it poses dreadful problems for a woman. How can she embody what is required, on the one hand, of a good wife, lover and mother and, on the other hand, of a good writer?

Even if this conflict is made endurable by some circumstance or other, a further conflict arises from received notions about the nature of literature itself. If the writer must be authoritative and egoistic in his living and in his utterance, his writing must be 'universal' in its range and application. This 'universality' is an assumption implicit in men's creative writing and is explicit in their aesthetics; and the assumption is that a writer can – and should – have the power to survey and interpret the entire range of 'human' experience.

Since a man's viewpoint has primacy and a woman's does not, it has traditionally passed unremarked that male writers have subsumed the female half of 'human' experience and that they have done so without qualification. Every female student of literature has heard her professors praise the impeccable characterisation of Emma Bovary or Anna Karenina or even – can she believe her ears? – Ursula Brangwen. These and their myriad sisters – all creations of male novelists – are held to be models of what women are like, the assumption being that a novelist can perceive 'universal' truths about the human spirit and is further able to convey them through embodiments of either gender.

Women students still have trouble agreeing with their professors about Lawrence; that is, if they are not too cowed to confess their true responses to this writer's presentation of women's experience. And all women – students of literature aside – know very well that their experience of the world differs in countless ways from that of any man. If women and men had ever enjoyed equally 'human' status, then their respective viewpoints might well have been complementary and Virginia Woolf's androgynous vision (that great artists are able to rise above the limitations and constraints of being either male or female, thus venturing into the *terra incognita* of what is essentially human) might have been possible. We have no way of knowing. As complementarity has *not* been our shared cultural experience, the taking up of the writer's stance as seer, by people of only secondary importance means presuming to embrace the reserve of male experience. It is a presumption and it does not pass unnoticed.

An androgynous vision entails, for those who argue for it, either complementarity (actual or putative) or similarity. Those who argue against it point to the social and historical evidence of women's different and subordinated actual lives and suggest, therefore, that the possibility of an androgynous vision (with or without inverted commas) must belong to the realms of pure theory. It could even seem to some of us that to argue in earnest that 'art' somehow has characteristics which are the real opposites of the 'life' which gave it birth, or that an artist or writer is somehow beyond the parameters of gender, must be the result of a collusion between men arrogant enough to believe women's lives to be like their own and women servile enough to accept the authority of such men against the evidence of their own experiences. If such a collusion is intrinsic to our cultural tradition, then women trying to write in their own voices are up against even more than the anxieties that they are not proper women and may never be proper writers; and they face, in addition, the anxiety that their writing will be perceived not as 'art' at all, but as 'women's work'.

Given, therefore, the anomaly of there being women who want above everything not just to write, but to be writers – to take to themselves, that is, the authoritative stance that the notion requires – then it becomes of great interest to observe how they went about it. And a network of some dozen women dedicated to the pursuit of writing offers a focus of very powerful interest. A focus of this kind may yield not only further information to add to what we are beginning to uncover about women's real history, but also quite new ways of thinking about literature and about 'writers'. And clearly some characteristics of the Edwardian climate made the emergence of women wanting to be writers more possible than it had been hitherto.

Like the well-known Bloomsbury Group, our more hidden network shared that feature of early twentieth-century *Zeitgeist* in which the traditional chasm between life and art is breached, so that experimentalism and autobiography become inevitably enmeshed and the aesthetic drives impelling the transformation of literature also power the need to live anti-conventionally. The manifestation of the *Zeitgeist* particular to literary creation has become known as 'modernism'.

The use of such a word to designate changes in literary practice which took place at that time betrays more a desperation than a poverty of critical intelligence. 'Modern', after all, means little more than current or contemporary; and all writers, clearly, were 'modern' for their own generation. The designation has stuck, however; and the desperation still resonates within it. How could critics, whose self-appointed task was to measure, and temper, the creative literary current around them, be expected to cope with writers who threw caution to the winds, repudiated convention, scorned tradition, pursued individualism for all they were worth, were no respecters of the 'great', wrote how they pleased and about whatever they thought significant and who, most horrible of all, insisted on writing in entirely new forms? The critic who pronounced Dorothy Richardson's revolutionary 'stream-of-consciousness' style to be neurasthenic voiced more than a personal indignation at a singular new novel; he expressed the outrage of his caste at the prospect of innovations whose anarchic relation to established practice threatened to engulf all that was good in literature: taste, standards, convention, consensus and – above all – the tone of the objective authorial voice. In more ways than one, Richardson's new way of writing a novel was not 'good form'.

Virginia Woolf, however, saw what Richardson was up to. Being herself a 'woman writer' and therefore exiled from a literary establishment which can be expected to protect its vested interests (much though she craved to belong to it), she could not help but perceive truthfully what Richardson's style signified.

> She has invented [wrote Woolf], a sentence . . . of a more elastic fibre than the old, capable of stretching to the extreme, of suspending the frailest particles . . . It is a woman's sentence, but only in the sense that it is used to describe a woman's mind by a writer who is neither proud nor afraid of anything she may discover in the psychology of her sex.[1]

Richardson told H.G. Wells – often – that novels were restricted to male preoccupations, not only in subject matter but also in their form, tone and treatment. She argued that there had never been a female novel and she determined to write one. It took her more than ten years of effort and experiment before she was satisfied. *Pointed Roofs*, the first of her long *Pilgrimage* sequence, was innovatory in form, content and style: it was autobiographical and yet fictional; it was devoid of narrative structure – chronological or any other kind – and it dispensed altogether with the objective authorial voice of third-person narrative. *Pointed Roofs* was published in 1915 when Richardson was already 42 years old.

'Modernism' of this kind did more than challenge convention; it upended it. And women had a special stake in seeing it upended. If literature could be renewed, women might just carve for themselves a legitimate place in the new order. Similarly in poetry, 'good form' was abandoned. Hilda Doolittle, in concert with Ezra Pound, searched for the singing line of pure lyric, a truthfulness of utterance which embraced the direct expression of associations – without logical connection or explanation – and pursued natural speech rhythms rather than the artifice of regular metres and end-rhymes. This *vers libre* style, still most celebrated with reference to the poetry of Pound and Eliot, presented the world as it truly appeared – its fragmentations, its strange juxtapositions, its lack of order . . . warts and all – in the voice of the mind perceiving it, its dreams, half-memories, snatches of knowledge and unpredictable moods and emotions.

All the conventions of literary language were challenged: narrative, discourse, imagery, syntax itself and even punctuation. But it was not only these formal properties which underwent transformations. Subject-matter choices also challenged what had gone before. Mina Loy's poetry, for example, is much more open about sexuality than poetry in English had been hitherto; H.D., Pound and Eliot adopted in their verse direct quotation and allusion taken from the past or from other literatures; Richardson, Joyce,

Mansfield and a host of others reworked parts of their actual lives as fiction.

It isn't that the presence in fiction and verse of autobiographical material was entirely new. Readers are familiar, after all, with the autobiographical sense in what the Brontës and George Eliot wrote. H.D. and Dorothy Richardson, for instance, when they wrote about themselves and called their work poetry and fiction, were not using the material of their lives as mere copy to be changed, elaborated, fashioned. What is startling and different is their pursuit in language of what was taking place in physics and other mathematical languages, and in psychoanalysis: the radical hypothesis that nothing objective exists, that a separation between 'subjectivity' and 'objectivity' is spurious, that the observer (so called) is intrinsic to every phenomenon.

Previous to this time, a welter of intellectual systems – rationalism, nineteenth-century science and natural philosophy, theological discourse and so on – had combined to present a view of nature in which Man, the manipulator, presided over all other phenomena which, in turn, existed independently from him, according to ordered laws which it was the task of knowledge to discover. Many people still, at this late stage in our century, understand this view to be the scientific approach. Notions which were considered unscientific – such as 'the kingdom of heaven is within you' or 'Beauty is Truth' – were called mystical or aesthetic, knowable only through faith or inspiration or some other operation of the spirit, but not through reason.

H.D. and Richardson, like everyone else, inherited this view; but both rebelled against it. H.D., greatly stimulated and fascinated by psychoanalysis, wrote in a language of association. Richardson eschewed 'literature', read mysticism, railed always, in print and in private, against science, mechanism and determinism. She said repeatedly that she could only write best about what she knew best, which was herself. For these women, like the other modernists, it was essential to present not what had *happened* to them, but what it was like *to be* them. Richardson called her work 'realism'; and so it was, for in this new and radical *Zeitgeist*, art and reality could not be juxtaposed but had to be part of each other, interchangeable expressions of Nature, never at rest and perpetually in a condition of creative process, without absolute connections and without parameters.

The male modernists – Pound, Joyce and, in a different way,

Lawrence – wrote and talked extensively about what they were doing, what they thought literature should be like, what kind of poetics they wished to develop. Their views, which mainstream criticism has taken as the modernist map, concentrate on innovations of style, form and aesthetic theory. Pound, like the women, scorned orthodox academic literary values, propounded the supremacy of the poetic image and – to generalise – emphasised the connotative powers of language in contrast to its explanatory denotations. Joyce established inner monologue as a primary narrative device and presented as part of his work – as Pound also came to do – the immanence of literary tradition. Lawrence, not innovative in his use of syntax or narrative technique, presented libidinous energy as the supreme dynamic force directing human lives. (It is, obviously and necessarily, a male view of the nature and meaning of sexuality. Lawrence's work is a definitive instance of gender-specific writing to offer any reader who still maintains that gender is irrelevant to genius and has no bearing on whether literature is 'good' or 'bad', well done or poorly done.)

It's not that male and female modernists shared no common ground whatsoever; nor that readers can say, after seeing a sentence by one of them, that it was definitely written by a woman, or by a man. The differences between them are both more general and more subtle. Pound, Joyce, Eliot and Lawrence, for example, however radical or innovatory or 'creative' their respective literary genius, lived conventionally male heterosexual lives; perhaps wild, sometimes, or eccentric or egoistic, but somehow within the norm. The women, by contrast, in their emotional and sexual lives, in where they lived and how they earned, in everything actual, were just as innovative as they were in their theory and practice of literature. Richardson's remark about a Dostoyevsky in a mean and noisy kitchen having more chance of writing well than a woman in a rich house points up the same theme explored by Woolf in *To the Lighthouse*: that a man can shut out what he wishes, whereas a woman cannot. Joyce believed that the artist must be detached, apart, 'paring his fingernails'. Richardson knew (as did Woolf, and all the other women who have set about being writers) that nothing – including God and art – could exist outside her own lived experience.

H.D., Richardson, Stein, Loy, Barnes, and the others, lived as they wrote, lived what they wrote, wrote what they lived. If the conventions of syntax or of narrative technique must be abandoned,

so too must the conventions of morality, behaviour and expectation. The modernist woman is not unconventional; she is anti-
conventional, wishing her creative energy to take every form of
expression possible to her. Only by this route could the conflict
between being a real woman and a real writer be resolved and the
singular identity be maintained both on paper and in action.
Modernism, for its women, was not just a question of style; it was a
way of life.

It is this simultaneous breaking with both literary and social
conventions which constitutes the radicalism of early twentieth-
century women writers; and it is the radicalism common among
them which makes it possible for them to form a network. There are
those sceptics who might ask whether pursuing the call of high art
and throwing accepted social forms to the wind is anything other
than mere egoism in a female guise. There are others – feminists,
socialists, even Protestants – who may point to an equally obvious
common denominator shared by these women: a rootedness in
middle-class literary values and a devotion to self-expression
available only to the relatively privileged. For our women were not
what we would now call 'politicised'. They inherited – as did the
men – the cultural myth which allows writers to deflect or dismiss
charges of self-indulgence with a magic invocation to Art. Good
writers, according to the myth, are permitted messy, selfish lives,
just as they are permitted self-centred work. The test, the arbiter,
by which this permission is granted or withdrawn is the standard and
quality of the art they produce, a standard agreed by mainstream
cultural consensus. Writers who 'pass' this test are permitted by the
myth to escape moral censure. Casual conversations about writers
are littered with throw-away lines like 'Of course he was a pig of a
man, but . . .'. Writers in general – and those of our network in
particular – would take far more seriously a charge of incompetence
than they would a charge of self-indulgence.

How is it sensible, then, to think of women devoted to High Art,
who were – on the whole – not politicised in our contemporary
feminist sense, as radical? They showed no intention, either in life
or in art, of wanting to 'change the world'. They expressed neither
religious nor revolutionary zeal. They wanted, certainly, to change
literature; but it didn't seem to them that the organic connection
between art and life extended – as it does for those who profess an
ideology – to the shaking of the social foundations on which they
rested. What they did see, or sense, was that changing literature

meant changing their own lives by challenging the conventions set up to contain their social behaviour and by acting as anarchically as possible in the face of tradition.

If they were determinedly, or myopically, not 'political', it is hardly surprising to find these women absent from the ferment for female suffrage which it seems to us now must have been boiling all around them. Those who did have a political temperament, such as Dora Marsden, first editor of the feminist periodical *The Freewoman*, were more feminist than suffragist and, in any case, didn't see themselves as creative writers. (Marsden was a philosopher.)

Political activists are, on the whole, impatient with experimentalism in art when it is hailed as radical by a new and aspirant generation of artists. To activists, artistic radicalism seems all too often traditionalist in its assumptions of the primacy of art over all other workings of the world. It's only in the tiny overlap between the 'political' and 'artistic' visions where the huge conflict between them is seen to subside. This overlap is that relatively small artistic output which issues from an ideological base and which is commonly perceived to be merely propagandist. In the main, the writings of H.D., Richardson, Stein, Barnes, and the others – like the writings of Woolf and her friends – are not propagandist for socialism, for feminism, or for any other recognisable ideology. They are partisan for writing, in and of itself.

This doesn't mean, however, that most of the writers would have greeted radical social change unsympathetically. The difference lies in intention. Those who are 'political' *intend* to effect change, developing an analysis and tactics (which may include art) to bring about desired social and cultural shifts. By contrast, those who consider themselves – or who are considered to be – 'artistic', don't set out intentionally to effect such changes; and may be as astonished as any of their readers if their work turns out to be influential in promoting social change.

What is most striking, both in itself and in relation to their writing, is the shared anti-conventionality of the personal lives of these women at a time when the overwhelming social expectation was that a woman should marry, bear children, and remain both married and monogamous.

If things haven't changed much since then, despite the vote, the pill, attempts at legislative reforms, the establishing of 'Women's Studies', and other forays into the bastions of mainstream, male culture, then women writers now will readily identify with their sisters who, eighty years ago, desired above all else to write and be read and who lived under even greater threat from the problems caused by their gender than we do now. The threats were greater simply because it was harder then for a woman to live independently; but the threats were of the same kind as those which we still face. It's still true that men in our culture enjoy the privileges of the superior class. That Britain has elected a female Prime Minister seems almost accidental, and certainly incidental, when the leadership and control of financial institutions, of academic life, of the legal, medical, educational and ecclesiastical professions, of multinational companies and major industries, of the press and other media – of all the areas which shape and govern our lives – are overwhelmingly in the hands of men.

It follows, then, that a woman who aspires to be anything extra to being a woman, to be someone with power and authority in this vast world of affairs, must still carry the adjective 'woman' before what she does. A 'woman' writer, like a 'woman' doctor, priest or politician, is still an apologist for her gender, whether she likes it or not, whether it makes sense to her or not, whether she colludes or not in the fantasy of a common humanity shared by all.

It's because women writers are anomalous that the lives and writings of 'self-indulgent', unpoliticised, literary innovators are of particular interest. H.D., Richardson, Stein and the rest discovered – and recorded the discovery – that changing literature means changing lives; and that, equally and simultaneously, changing lives means changing literature. In the following pages we shall trace how these women lived, what they wrote, where they published, how they supported each other and, not least, why experimentalism on paper came to have such radical correlations in personal views and relationships.

Chapter 2

H.D.'s triangles

In many respects, H.D. and Dorothy Richardson are exemplars of female modernism. Both have been marginalised by mainstream literary criticism. Both wrestled – with at least as much ardour as any Hopkins or Joyce – with the literary conventions they inherited. H.D., in her Imagist verse, and Dorothy Richardson, in her stream-of-consciousness prose, exploded those conventions. If they have not yet received their due from mainstream critical judgment, it is not solely because they were women writing in their own voices; it is also because their experimentalism presents a complete and profound challenge to the aesthetic idea of what literature is: the idea that a literary work will have a life independent of its creator. H.D. and Dorothy Richardson, in their different modes, wrote about themselves and called their work poetry and fiction.

These two women also shared something else: an emotional ambivalence about the adequacy of men to provide satisfaction and encouragement and about the potential of women to be true accomplices in the dual pursuit of art and love. With respect to sexual and emotional experience, neither H.D. nor Dorothy Richardson (nor, indeed, Virginia Woolf and Katherine Mansfield, whose experience yielded strikingly similar ambivalences) present stereotypes either of the heterosexual or of the lesbian woman. Their passions attach to this or that significant woman or man in ways that seem infinitely more romantic than sexual and with an egoism which clearly has its origins in a desire to create literature rather than babies. The creative energy released and focused by these intense relationships is evidenced in the autobiogaphicallybased fiction the women produced, almost as if there were as organic a connection between love and literature as, in the conventional view, there is between women's sexuality and maternal drive.

These women did not repudiate men, nor show a pathological alarm in the face of men's bodies or emotions. Equally, they did not seek from men those things which women are taught they should seek: home, hearth and babies. They sought parity and partnership; but they sought in vain. The identification necessary to their sense of spiritual fitness came, of necessity, from other women.

'I have the fervour of myself for a presence and my own spirit for light', wrote H.D. in 1917.[1] And her spirit burned with this light, from her youth in the Philadelphia suburbs, through the First World War in London, through Paris in the twenties, through a psychoanalysis conducted by Freud himself, through another world war and through 15 years of seclusion in Switzerland. Emotionally fragile, physically tall and striking with an androgynous beauty that appealed to both women and men, she was a 'grey-eyed goddess', a 'dryad', an inspiration and a muse: not quite of this world, but racked by it. Her life was a constant struggle between 'song's gift' and 'love's gift', as her poem 'Fragment Thirty-Six' suggests.

H.D. was born in Bethlehem, Pennsylvania, in 1886. Her mother, Helen, came from an old Moravian family and her father, Charles, was a professor of astronomy. Owing to promotion, the family moved to a suburb of Philadelphia when H.D. was nine. She and her four brothers (a sister died in infancy) grew up in a large comfortable country house and within a close family atmosphere.

This serene life was interrupted in 1901 by a red-haired explosion called Ezra Pound. He was 16 and he and H.D. had met at a Hallowe'en party. The boy was an undergraduate at the University of Pennsylvania and already cut a flamboyant figure, dressing in capes and velvet jackets, quoting William Morris and writing poetry. It was another four years, however, before they became seriously involved. Their relationship was volatile from the beginning: so much so that H.D. could recall it in vivid detail some 50 years later, in her memoir of Pound:

'You are a poem, though your poem's naught,' quoted Ezra. From what? I did not ask him. We had climbed up into the big maple tree in our garden outside Philadelphia. There was a crow's nest that my younger brother had built . . . He must not miss the last 'car' and the train to Wyncote . . . 'There is another trolley in a half hour,' I say, preparing to slide out of the crow's nest.

'No, Dryad,' he says. He snatches me back. We sway with the stars. They are not far. We slide, slip, fly down through the branches, leap together to the ground. 'No' I say, breaking from his arms, 'No', drawing back from his kisses. '. . . quick, get your things – books – whatever you left in the hall.' 'I'll get them next time,' he says.[2]

The poems he wrote her he typed, had bound in vellum, and called *Hilda's Book*. There were 25 in all, written in different styles but all partaking of the exalted passion characteristic of love lyrics:

> *Sancta Patrona Domina Caelae*
>
> Out of thy purity
> Saint Hilda pray for me
> Lay on my forehead
> The hands of thy blessing.
> Saint Hilda pray for me
> Lay on my forehead
> Cool hands of thy blessing
> Out of thy purity
> Lay on my forehead
> White hands of thy blessing.
> Virgo caelicola
> Ora pro nobis.[3]

They became unofficially engaged and he gave her a ring. 'It was understood', H.D. recalled later, 'but my parents were unhappy about it and I was shy and frightened. I didn't have the usual conventional party-lunch, dinner or announcement dance . . . Mrs Pound brought me an exquisite pearl pendant.'[4]

Planning marriage meant that it was imperative for Ezra to find a job. In autumn 1907 he set out for Crawfordsville, Indiana, to teach at Wabash College. In addition, however, to his correspondence with H.D., he embarked also on a correspondence with a Mary Moore whom he'd met in New Jersey; and then, before long, he was the centre of a scandal, after allowing a young woman to stay overnight in his rooms. He was dismissed, despite his insistence that he'd found her wandering homeless and had merely offered her shelter, claiming that he had himself slept on the couch. The college authorities concluded otherwise; and Pound retraced his steps to Philadelphia. News of the scandal went before him, so Pound chose not to linger in his straitlaced home town. He made up his mind to leave for Europe as soon as possible, with both H.D. and himself unclear about the status of their engagement. She expected to be reunited with him; but when or on which side of the Atlantic was not decided. For Pound, this departure proved to be his major break with America; he never returned to live there.

In Venice, in June 1908, Pound published – at his own expense – his first volume of poems, *A Lume Spento* (he translated the title as *With Tapers Quenched*). Armed with copies, he arrived in London in the early autumn and went to Elkin Mathews' bookshop in Devonshire Street. Mathews was impressed both by the poems and by the poet and, being a publisher as well as a bookseller, soon offered to bring out a new collection by Pound. This was called *Personae*.

Through Mathews, Pound met T.E. Hulme and other poets and began to be asked to dinners and parties where writers gathered. Early in this social round he met Olivia Shakespear, well-known as a literary hostess, and a close friend of W.B. Yeats. Though he couldn't know it then, she was to be his mother-in-law. She introduced Pound to Yeats and the two eventually became close friends. At about the same time, probably at Mrs Shakespear's, Pound met May Sinclair, who was then 44 years old and at the height of her fame as a celebrated novelist. She took to Pound at once, inviting him for tea-parties and beginning a correspondence with him. She introduced him to her friend Ford Madox Hueffer (later Ford), then editor of *The English Review*. Ford recalled: 'Ezra was brought to my office by Miss May Sinclair, who said she wanted to introduce the greatest poet to the greatest editor in the world.'[5] The two men became great friends, playing tennis nearly every day and discussing poetry for hours at a time. Ford described the 24-year-old Pound: 'He would wear trousers made of green billiard cloth, a pink coat, a blue shirt, a tie hand-painted by a Japanese friend, an immense Sombrero, a flaming beard cut to a point, and a single, large blue earring.'[6] And apart from this singular appearance, Pound's manners could also be individualistic; he was known, for example, to spear potatoes with his fork and to eat part of the floral decorations at dinner parties.

By the time Ford published one of Pound's poems in *The English Review* in June 1909, Pound was established as a literary 'character' in London, drawing fire from *Punch*, whose satirist called him 'Ezekiel Tun' (presumably because Ezekiel was a major prophet and Ezra a minor one and because a ton is heavier than a pound, implying that a featherweight was bruiting himself about as if he were a heavyweight).

Pound went on publishing collections of poems. After *Personae* in 1909 came *Exultations*, and then, in 1910, *The Spirit of Romance*. In addition, he wrote articles for *The English.Review* and taught at the Regent Street Polytechnic. In 1910 he planned a visit to Philadelphia to see his family and friends. H.D. had been writing that she wanted to come to Europe, but Pound dissuaded her, explaining that he would soon be back home.

H.D. awaited his arrival with great anticipation, but shortly before he was due she met a young woman called Frances Gregg. 'I think, as the only girl in a very large family,' H.D. later wrote of herself, 'she wanted most passionately a girl child of her own age, a twin sister.' This passage – from an unpublished autobiographical novel, continues:

> This particular yearning for one child, a girl of its own particular temprament [*sic*] was satisfied when Midget had left school, had left childhood, girlhood; was drifting unsatisfied, hurled and baffled out of a relationship with a hectic, adolescent, blundering, untried, mischevous [*sic*] and irreverent male youth . . . She was desparate [*sic*] and tired and weary in her very early twenties. What chemistry and the binomial theorem had not drained from her of avidity and living fervour, the male adolescent had . . . She had failed in her college career, she had failed as a social asset with her family . . . Into this weariness . . . there came as to Paul of Tarsus, light . . . It was not that the girl, Josepha, was beautiful, judged by the ordinary standards . . . It was her eyes, set in the unwholesome face; it was the shoulders, a marble splendour, unspoiled by the severe draping of straight cut rain-proof; it was her hand, an unholy splendour.
>
> Her eyes were the blue eyes, it is said one sees in heaven . . . eyes the colour of wet hyacinths before the spikes have broken into flower.[7]

She read to Frances much that Ezra had read to her:

> I read her some of the poems that Ezra and I had loved together, chiefly Swinburne. 'You read so beautifully,' said Frances. I read

Andrew Lang's translation of Theocritus that Ezra had brought me. I wrote a poem to Frances in a Bion and Moschus mood.

> O hyacinth of the swamp-lands,
> Blue lily of the marshes,
> How could I know
> Being but a foolish shepherd
> That you would laugh at me?[8]

In H.D.'s posthumously published *HERmione*, Frances Gregg appears as Fayne Rabb, while H.D. is both Her and Hermoine Gart. Pound is called George Lowndes:

> Words with Fayne in a room, in any room, became projections of things beyond one. Things beyond Her beat, beat to get through to Her, to get through to Fayne . . . The two eyes of Fayne Rabb were two lenses of an opera glass and it was Hermione's entrancing new game to turn a little screw, a little handle somewhere . . . and bring into focus those two eyes that were her new possession . . . You put things, people under, so to speak, the lenses of the eyes of Fayne Rabb and people, things come right in geometric contour. 'You must see George Lowndes.'

> There was only one thing to read to Fayne; she had read and she would re-read it.
> 'O sister my sister
> O singing swallow, the world's division
> divideth us . . .'
> I promise you I won't ever marry George, my swallow.[9]

Pound's return to Philadelphia, however, disturbed H.D.'s life once again. And of course he met Frances Gregg. An explosive three-way entanglement ensued, with Frances falling in love with Ezra and H.D. continuing to be in love with both of them. When Frances confessed to H.D. that she was in love with Ezra, H.D. came near to breaking down completely.

At the height of the drama, Ezra decided to return to Europe, leaving the two women still involved both with him and with each other. H.D. was devastated by Frances' feelings towards Ezra; but at the same time she loved Frances deeply. Frances, for her part, was besotted with Ezra:

> 'Yes. I love him. Understand this, Hermione. I love him. If I say I love George, it isn't this flimsy thing you call love . . . You never

saw the bright sort of aura that he wore . . . Did you think I was
happy that day, any day, ever when you were with me? Your
beauty lacerated me and I said there is no use Fayne Rabb. I
stood beside you, I dared to stand beside you and say I loved
him.'[10]

Frances Gregg, too, recalled this time; in her memoirs, written in
the 1930s and still unpublished, she recorded: 'That kiss of Ezra's
stirred me to the unsounded depths of my undiscovered womanhood . . . Nothing has ever happened that has borne any relation to
that first kiss . . .'[11] And as if answering, Her Gart, in *HERmione*,
confesses: 'I was not what George wanted. He wanted fire to
answer his fire and it was the tall sapling, the cold Laconian birch
tree, the runner and the fearless explorer (my mind was) that drew
spark from him.'[12]

An untitled poem, written by Frances Gregg on the front flyleaf
of a copy of *Sea Garden* given to her by H.D., expresses something
of the longing she felt for H.D.:

> So, as you touch me, I dream
>   my Hilda
> Ah, in the dusk, are you there,
> heart of the heart of me
> What are you thinking?
> Your hands in my hands
> And the life in me leaps
> to the sound of your dreams
> O my Beauty of Beauty
> Bend me your head –
> dusk, oh my flower . . .[13]

And H.D., in the unpublished 'Paint It Today', tried to set down
her feelings both for Ezra and for Frances:

> The fiancé had shown Midget what love might be or become if
> one, in desperation, should accept the shadow of an understand-
> ing for an understanding itself. Josepha had shown her or she had
> shown Josepha what love was or could be or become if the earth,
> by some incautious legerdemain should be swept from beneath
> our feet, and we were left ungravitated between the stars.[14]

A few months later, in summer 1911, the two friends decided to
leave for Europe. Frances' mother would go with them. They
planned a four-month trip, with the final stop in London. Pound,

when he knew they were due, asked May Sinclair to befriend them:

> Hilda is – in her lucid intervals – rather charming. Will you then, gratia plenis, etc. write to Miss Hilda Doolittle c/o Mrs Symons, 30 Bernard St. WC and ask her to bring Miss Frances Gregg to tea. If you write at once it may be there for her arrival.[15]

May Sinclair duly obliged. H.D. had already read Sinclair's *The Divine Fire* with pleasure and interest and was grateful to Pound for this introduction, remarking later how kind he was to 'anyone who he felt had the faintest spark of submerged talent'.[16] Sinclair was helpful to H.D., inviting her to literary 'at homes' and encouraging her work.

Frances, however, had a more abrasive reaction:

> One party that I particularly remember was at the home of May Sinclair. I had heard much of her devotion to the young artist . . . She was little and mean-souled and repellent, but she could write, and I envied her. And seeing myself against that fine tough woman soul, I learned something of my own destiny that was like a revelation, like a miracle for me in that stuffy room, with its agitated moving of urgent aspiration . . . butter-dripping bits of food stuff, that insane ritual of teacups and iceing [*sic*]. I learned a just proportioning. She knew her stuff, and was no sentimentalist. No woman is, of course, though the false, fair, sidling creatures ape that quality . . . Hilda was far more adroit than I at picking up the patter of this group. It was almost a code that they had evolved from the technicalities of their trade. They spoke as the craftsmen of old . . .[17]

Intimate though they were, H.D. and Frances were competitive in relation to Pound and must have been – to however slight a degree – competitive in their work. Whether Frances suffered mere pique at Sinclair's seeming to prefer H.D. to herself or whether her satirical eye picked up H.D.'s greater need than her own to belong, is open to speculation. For whatever reason, Frances was certainly less easily impressed and did, later, collaborate with her husband, Louis Wilkinson, on a satirical novel called *The Buffoon*, in which in-group 'patter' is greatly derided.

Before long, Frances decided to return to America with her mother. H.D. begged her to stay in London, but Frances insisted – as she would always insist subsequently – that she must stay with her mother:

I saw Hilda's face in the flashes of the street lights as we still plodded round, greatly to the distress of the neighbouring constable. Hilda was putting it to me that she meant never to return to America, and that all was over between us unless I would see that my mother returned alone . . .

'I will return in April' I promised her.[18]

H.D. remained in London, living alone in a boarding house. Her parents acquiesced, themselves planning to travel through Europe some months hence. Her father paid her an allowance, thus removing from her any need to support herself. She spent her time reading in the British Museum Reading Room, talking with Pound in tea-shops all over London and making friends with his friends.

She wrote to his mother in February 1912:

People here are so kind and keep one in such a whirl. I wrote Ezra from Paris that I was coming to London to rest. I remember his scorn 'rest!' I was annoyed at the time but understand it now!

The Rhys' have been very kind – Mrs R asked me to meet Hewlett at her house on Thursday, which *will* be a treat. I heard Mr Yeats at Mrs Shakespear's some weeks ago, and though I was entertained was not hyper-impressed by the poet. Jealousy, on my part, I imagine, since I couldn't get any nearer.

Mrs Shakespear has been most kind and her daughter and I have had some chats together as well! . . . I seem to have written nothing of 'son' and I know how you love to hear. He has been so good to me, introducing me to celebrities and lesser oddities – He always has some under-dog on hand. One Thursday it was a derelict poet named Flint who made the fatal mistake of marrying his landlady's daughter, a hapless little cockney! Ezra thought a dinner party might set them up, and I was flattered by an invitation to see it through. E & I agreed it *had* required tact. The little lady criticised the omlet [sic] (I think she had never dined out before) and informed me that she had a 'baby whose name was Ianthe!' – However, after two years silence, the baby's pappa once more breaks into song!

Next week I am to tea with Monroe [sic] – editor of the 'Poetry Review' – Ezra says M. is depressed. Pleasant prospect![19]

Months passed in like vein. H.D. continued to write to Ezra's mother, describing both her own current life and much of Ezra's. Her circle gradually widened, owing – usually – to Ezra's initiative:

You ask of friends . . .

'Son', of course, figures in the front ranks with a youthful poet –
you saw his songs in November 'Poetry' – Richard Aldington.
Mrs Patmore stands with them, a girl but a little older than
myself, but the dignified possessor of a husband – old Coventry's
grandson – and two boys. We four – that is, E., R.A., and Mrs P.
– *not* her family – were much together during the last year!

There are so many delightful people that come just a shade
lower in the affections . . . May Sinclair was very kind to me,
especially at Christmas time, invited me to the theatre, etc . . .
Mrs Shakespear was very kind. I took tea with her & her
daughter a number of times – and so it goes![20]

Pound had first met the beautiful Brigit Patmore, estranged wife of
Coventry Patmore's grandson, at Violet Hunt's. She in turn
introduced Pound to the 19-year-old Richard Aldington. As he had
done earlier to May Sinclair, Pound asked Brigit to invite H.D. to
tea. She did so and the two quickly developed a great liking for each
other.

Brigit and Aldington were already involved in an affair when
H.D. and the young poet met. The two immediately developed a
rapport, however; both were trying to write poetry and to learn
Greek. In a curious repeat of her earlier three-way entanglement,
H.D. soon found herself keenly interested – both intellectually and
erotically – in this new pair, who were supposedly involved with
each other, but each of whom, in turn, became fascinated by her.[21]

Despite this new absorption, H.D. remained in close contact with
Pound. Years later, recalling this time, H.D. recounted how she'd
unwittingly given birth to the Imagist movement in the British
Museum tea rooms:

We all read in the British Museum reading room. Dark walls and
statues that looked dingy. Frances had gone home. I could wait
till my parents came. My father, at 70, had retired from the
University. My mother wrote, 'We could meet in Genoa.' I had
my own allowance now . . . 'But Dryad,' (in the Museum tea
room), 'this is poetry.' He slashed with a pencil. 'Cut this out,
shorten this line. "Hermes of the Ways" is a good title. I'll send
this to Harriet Monroe of *Poetry*. Have you a copy? Yes? Then
we can send this, or I'll type it when I get back. Will this do?' And
he scrawled 'H.D. Imagiste' at the bottom of the page.[22]

By the time H.D. showed Pound these poems, Harriet Monroe had started her *Poetry: A Magazine of Verse* in Chicago and had written to Pound to solicit contributions. As promised, H.D.'s three 'Imagist' poems were sent to Monroe. They appeared in the January 1913 issue, the first two signed 'H.D.' and the third signed 'H.D., Imagiste'. Two of these – 'Priapus' and 'Epigram (after the Greek)' – were based on Greek originals, whereas 'Hermes of the Ways' was entirely H.D.'s. More than any other single publication, the appearance of these poems announced the birth of the Imagist movement.

Meanwhile, Frances Gregg had, as she'd promised H.D., returned in April, 1912. But she had with her a husband. She'd been introduced to Louis Wilkinson in Philadelphia by John Cowper Powys, who was lecturing there. Powys fell in love with Frances, but wasn't free, having a wife back in England. His solution was to arrange a marriage between Frances and Louis, who was his best friend and a fellow-lecturer. Wilkinson was tall, good-looking, just over 30, sexually open and decidedly eligible. Frances was 28 and wanted to have children. She wanted, also, to go back to Europe and to H.D. She apparently wrote to H.D. about the marriage:

'I am going to marry – I will be married when you get this – a passable person. He gives University Extension lectures. We may get across to Berlin in the spring.' She gave no details, no explanation for her sudden volte-face. She had always repudiated all talk of marriage.[23]

Frances and Louis Wilkinson were married on 10 April 1912; and on the same day, together with Powys, they set sail for England. H.D., Aldington and Pound came to call on the Wilkinsons as soon as they were settled into a hotel near Victoria Station. Frances asked H.D., who accepted the offer, to join them on their Venetian honeymoon; but at the last minute, Pound persuaded her not to go:

I found Ezra waiting for me on the pavement outside the house, off Oxford Circus, where I had a room. His appearance was again unexpected, unpredictable. He began, 'I as your nearest male relation . . .,' and hailed a taxi. He pushed me in. He banged with his stick, pounding (Pounding) . . . 'You are not going with them.' I had seen them the day before at their hotel, off Victoria Station. It was all arranged. Ezra must have seen them afterwards. 'There is a vague chance that the Egg,' (he called her), 'may be happy. You will spoil everything.' Awkwardly, at Victoria Station, I explained to a married Frances, with a long tulle travelling veil, that I wasn't coming. I had changed my mind. Awkwardly, the husband handed me back the cheque that I had made out for my ticket. Glowering and savage, Ezra waited till the train pulled out.[24]

Despite H.D.'s absence, however, the Wilkinsons were not alone for long in Venice. John Cowper Powys and his brother Llewelyn showed up. Llewelyn, like his brother, fell in love with Frances. This odd foursome spent some weeks together, with complex emotions, rather than sex, much in evidence. (Indeed, John Cowper was to remain a lifelong friend to Frances and a book about their relationship is at present being undertaken by Frances' son, Oliver Wilkinson.)

Deserted by Frances, H.D. remained in London with Aldington and Pound as constant companions. All three were now living in Church Walk, Kensington. They met often, usually in Pound's room, for coffee, discussion, poetry readings and the occasional omelette, cooked by Pound over a gas ring. Frances and Louis paid a brief visit to London in the summer of 1912 and sometimes joined them.

In the absence of Frances, Richard Aldington began to assume increased importance in H.D.'s life. In the late autumn of 1912, H.D. left London to meet her parents in Italy; and Aldington soon followed her. With the knowledge of H.D.'s parents, the two went to Capri together, despite their not being married. In May 1913, the four were together in Venice, where they were joined by Pound. Just before he arrived, H.D. wrote to Mrs Pound:

I hear from 'son' occasionally. His usual charming, telegraphic style: – you ask about his clothes? He has a knack of *always* looking well-dressed! I am not laughing! We used to tease him, of course, for being such a bear and doing society so thoroughly – but I assure you, he always looked well. Richard Aldington informs me that E. has appeared of late, in a beautiful new suit, hat, and I don't know what else! Did you know he has grown a little pointed beard? A subject of much contention among his friends. I think it suits his Mephistopolean [*sic*] style of beauty – so does Richard. R. told me that Mr Yeats turned E. to the light 'What have you done with your face, me boy – don't like it!' However, that is a matter of opinion!

. . . I've given up trying to be Kultured (capital k) since I left London. What a whirlpool London is! Awful, if you haven't more than an ounce of brain, comme moi!

Do write me when you can – and rest assured 'son' is 'making good', top of the heap and all the rest; Mr Yeats & Mr Hueffer both say his last book 'Ripostes' is far & away the best. The 'Return' is marvellous – my favourite of the collection![25]

Having temporarily forsaken 'culture', H.D., her parents, Pound and Aldington enjoyed being tourists. H.D.'s mother recorded in her diary: 'Ezra gave a gondola party this evening – sailing for Milano in & out the various canals – light wonderful! Hilda & Richard in one. E & I in other – back 11:30.'[26] By late June, Pound and Aldington had both left Italy. Aldington waited for H.D. to join him in Paris. 'I know H. will enjoy settling down for a time', wrote her mother, 'but we shall miss her.' It was 6 July and H.D. had just left for Paris by train.

By August, H.D. and Aldington were back at Church Walk and had decided to marry. When the Doolittles arrived in London on 4 September, the young pair went to see them at their hotel, where they most probably discussed their marriage plans. The parents went on to Bournemouth, where H.D.'s mother noted:

Eventful day. Richard & Hilda came for the day to talk over the future. Such a lovely time! & I am happy for them both! After our talk went to the pier and had our tea there. They left about 6. I spent the evening down stairs before the cheerful open fire with the guests. Went to bed happy & peaceful![27]

H.D.'s mother was clearly relieved that the two were finally to embrace respectability. If it were hoped, however, that the union would be a conventional one, the hope was vain. In 'Paint It Today', H.D. hints at her feelings about the marriage when she describes Midget answering her mother's queries about allowing Basil to join the family group in its travels around Italy. Her mother wanted to know how things stood:

Of course, I cared. Of course, I cared. I cared from the first. But I couldn't tell you. How could I tell you? After all the mess we all made of everything when I thought I'd marry Raymond. You don't suppose I'd have let him follow us about like that, if I hadn't cared awfully. No, I'm not engaged. After the Raymond fiasco, I couldn't be engaged. I won't be engaged. But I'm going to marry

Basil. No, no, no. Just marry him. No one is to come. *No* one.
We are going to a registrar's or whatever it is's office. *No* one is to
come.[28]

Although, as it turned out, her parents were present at the civil
ceremony, these sentiments are probably closer to how she felt at
the time, after the Pound fiasco and being deserted by Frances, than
those expressed in the light-hearted letter H.D. wrote to Pound's
mother:

Chère Madame –
  Don't faint, but I am going to be married this month sometime!
Am sending forth no announcements – just writing to a few
friends – this will reach you after the event. The courageous
person, as you may suspect, is Richard Aldington! I have no
definite address for the present . . . We want to live in Paris but
will stay here for a few months. I am at present in 6 Church Walk
– most exciting with R.A. two doors above & and the great E.P.
across the way. My mother & father are still here – will return
after the fatal day.
  Ezra looks very well & seems very busy with his two
magazines. He has been very good to Richard & myself – helping
us with our work etc.
  It's a long time, I know, as it always is, since I received your
last letter, & I don't know where to begin. I only know that I am
the usual mad thing, with my head, at present, in a little more of a
whirl. So you will forgive this scanty scratch! – I will write sanely
if ever I find time to breathe . . .
  [A postscript adds about Ezra:] He seems very well, & I don't
think you need worry about the literary 'atmosphere' not being
good for him. He really ought to be here . . . as he is to keep in
touch with magazines, etc. I wish I had time & energy to write
more illuminatingly, but am on the verge of les noces – the 18th
the day![29]

The marriage took place at the Kensington Registry Office, just
around the corner from Church Walk, on 18 October 1913. The
Doolittles and Ezra Pound were witnesses. H.D. and Aldington
returned to their newly rented flat at 8 Holland Park Chambers,
some two blocks from Church Walk. But Number 6 Church Walk
didn't remain vacant for long; Frances and Louis Wilkinson
subsequently moved into it for a while.

H.D.'s first written communication to Frances, telling of her marriage after the event, was in the particular vernacular they always used with each other:

We write to tell Augusta with our auguster compliments *that* –

I.   We have a new house.
II.   An' new tea cups with pictures of cherry blossom on 'em what are blue. But cherry blossom ain't blue –
III. An' a new kettle what shines.
IV.   An' some real blue books, and some poppies in a jug!
V.   An' a new husband–
VI.   An' our name are Mrs Richard Aldington.
VII. An' will Augusta Gregg come to tea one day![30]

Presumably Frances indeed came to tea; but soon she and Louis were off again on lecture tours abroad. About a year later, in 1914, Frances wrote to H.D. from Italy that she was pregnant; and at the same time chastised H.D. again for not having joined their honeymoon. According to 'Paint It Today', H.D. replied, 'I have not forgotten you. I pretend that I have forgotten you because I pretend that I have forgotten everything.'[31]

The Aldington marriage by no means ran smoothly; and the stillbirth of their child in May 1915 was a trauma from which the marriage never recovered. Aldington wrote at that time to the poet Amy Lowell:

I have been rather distressed, because Hilda was delivered of a little girl still-born, about 2 am this morning . . . I haven't seen the doctor, but the nurse said it was a beautiful child & they can't think why it didn't live. It was very strong, but couldn't breathe. Poor Hilda is very distressed, but is recovering physically.[32]

H.D. did recover physically; but emotionally, the stillbirth haunted her for years. Its immediate effect was to make her fear sex with Aldington, especially since the nurses told her not to risk having another child while the war was on. With shattered nerves, H.D. sat in the flat in Hampstead they'd moved to, listening to the feet of soldiers going past. Later she recalled:

London blurred her over, permeated her and she (with London) had forgotten – feet – feet – feet – feet . . . Feet were passing on the way to Victoria Station. Feet were passing on the way to Victoria. Carry on. Carry on. Carry on. She had forgotten. Feet, feet, feet, feet.[33]

D.H. and Frieda Lawrence, whom the Aldingtons had met in 1914 at one of Amy Lowell's dinner parties, were living close by at the time; and Lawrence, in particular, was sensitive to H.D.'s sorrow. When he and Frieda moved away, he began corresponding with H.D. She sent him her draft poems and he sent back fiery letters and criticism.

In 1916, Aldington joined the army and went off to a training camp. H.D., left in the Devon cottage they'd moved to shortly before, became hysterical. Their friend John Cournos, a writer and a fellow Philadelphian, stayed with H.D., promising to take care of her. However, because he was in love with her, he convinced himself that she was in love with him. She was undoubtedly acting strangely, but Cournos – thinking she was leading him on – was outraged when she rebuffed his advances. (Years later he wrote a bitter satire about her, called *Miranda Masters*.)[34] H.D. went off to the town of Corfe Castle to be near Aldington's camp. Here, in the summer of 1916, she wrote anguished personal poems as she waited to see him. He'd been involved in an affair with another woman and the poems reveal her hurt and outrage, as well as her love:

from 'Eros'

> Ah love is bitter and sweet,
> but which is more sweet
> the bitterness or the sweetness,
> none has spoken it.
>
> Love is bitter,
> but can salt taint sea-flowers,
> grief, happiness?
>
> Is it bitter to give back
> love to your lover if he crave it?
>
> Is it bitter to give back
> love to your lover if he wish it
> for a new favourite,
> who can say,
> or is it sweet?
>
> Is it sweet to possess utterly,
> or is it bitter,
> bitter as ash?[35]

All through the next year, Aldington moved around to different camps and H.D. spent time both near him in lodgings and at the flat they had rented in London, 44 Mecklenburgh Square, where their large, first-floor room, with its long windows overlooking the square, became the setting for the final break-up of their marriage.

The story is told, in anguished detail, in H.D.'s autobiographical novel *Bid Me to Live*. The bald facts speak for themselves: H.D.'s fear of sex with Aldington; Aldington's affair with another woman also living at 44 Mecklenburgh Square; H.D.'s turning to Lawrence as a spiritual mentor, and his rebuff of her. Nevertheless, the facts alone cannot convey what these experiences meant to H.D., both at the time and for years afterwards. It was not until after her psychoanalysis under Freud, and after she'd written what would finally be published as *Bid Me to Live*, that she exorcised all the ghosts haunting her.

In the book, as in her life, the struggle for Rafe (Aldington) is a classic one, fought out by Bella (Dorothy 'Arabella' Yorke) and Julia (H.D.):

> 'There was never anyone like him,' said Bella, and she was talking of Rafe Ashton now, apparently, 'He doesn't really love me. He isn't there. When he is with me, he is thinking of you.' This sounded damn familiar, this was simply herself, this was Julia talking, this is what Julia herself had said, or thought rather, having no one to whom she could possibly say it, about Bella.
>
> 'You tyrannize his soul,' said Bella; 'he loves my body, but he isn't all there, half of him is somewhere else.'
>
> How could Julia tell Bella, that exactly the same thing happened in her case? She told Bella, 'But it's the same with me. I never feel he is thinking of me now. It's almost better when he's not with me.'
>
> 'Yes,' said Bella, 'he loves my body but you tyrannize his soul – it's you he cares for.'[36]

Rafe had said it straight out to Julia: 'Listen,' he said, 'it's perfectly clear; I love you, I desire *l'autre*.'[37] Faced with that stark truth, Julia turned to her intense, cerebral relationship with Rico (D.H. Lawrence):

> Rico's flaming letters had been· no ordinary love-letters, they were written to her in 'pure being' as he said . . . Of course Rico did not really want her; he was harassed and distressed and he loved Elsa, his great Prussian wife . . . But it was now as if this

cerebral contact had renewed her . . . Wife, husband. Elsa and
Rico were very near, she and Rico would burn away, cerebralisti-
cally, they would burn out together.[38]

So H.D. envisaged herself with Lawrence, burning cerebrally, in
eternity. Yet she couldn't resist trying to touch him physically, as
well. She might well have sorely needed some affirmation of herself
as a woman, in addition to needing affirmation as a poet. When the
Lawrences were thrown out of Cornwall in late 1917, H.D. invited
them to share the Mecklenburgh Square flat; Aldington was then
still at the front. Lawrence mesmerised her with his talk. 'You are
there for all eternity,' he said. 'Our love is written in blood.' [39] H.D.
took this to be a serious proposal that the three of them would be
together forever. The next night, when she and Lawrence were
alone in the flat, she felt a magnetic communication between them:

> She got up; as if at a certain signal, she moved towards him; she
> edged the small chair toward his chair. She sat at his elbow, a
> child waiting for instruction. Now was the moment to answer his
> amazing proposal of last night, his 'for all eternity'. She put out
> her hand. Her hand touched his sleeve. He shivered, he seemed
> to move back, move away, like a hurt animal, there was
> something untamed, even the slight touch of her hand on his
> sleeve seemed to have annoyed him. Yet, last night, sitting there,
> with Elsa sitting opposite, he had blazed at her; those words had
> cut blood and lava-trail on this air. Last night, with the
> coffee-cups beside them on the little table, he had said 'It is
> written in blood and fire for all eternity.' Yet only a touch on his
> arm made him shiver away, hurt, like a hurt jaguar.[40]

This rejection sent H.D. into shock. When young Cecil Gray, a
composer friend of the Lawrences, started paying court to her, she
responded, though she must have seemed half-hearted at best.
Aldington was at the front; and he desired *l'autre*, Bella, who had
lived upstairs. But Bella, and the Lawrences, all left. H.D. was
alone. Gray was persistent, writing to her from Cornwall, where
he'd rented a house. He pleaded with her to come, whether she
wanted to or not, because – he assured her – he needed her 'very,
very much'.[41]

So she went to Cornwall and to Gray, with whom she spent some
five to six months. She became pregnant by him, but wrote to
Aldington about it before she told Gray. Aldington responded with

sympathetic letters from the front. Nevertheless, H.D. didn't know what to do or where to turn. All her loves began to haunt her afresh and to recur again and again in her writing: Pound, Frances, Brigit, Aldington, Lawrence and Gray. New loves would come. But from now on she would never again be so alone. She would soon have a child. And she would have Bryher.

Chapter 3

Enter Bryher

H.D. had no idea who the young woman was who'd written her a fan letter and enclosed a copy of a pamphlet she'd written about Amy Lowell. She'd signed herself 'Winifred Bryher'. H.D. responded courteously:

> Dear Miss Bryher,
>   I shall look for you and your friend on Wednesday, then, between 3:30 and 4. We can have a little chat over our tea and you can rest before your long walk back to Zennor.
>   Thank you so much for the book! We can discuss it when you come.
>   The house is called Bosigran Castle – a square house standing by itself just below the ruins (with two tall red chimneys) that stand close to the road.[1]

Annie Winifred Ellerman, who later took the name Bryher, was born in 1894. She was technically illegitimate, since her parents – Hannah Glover and shipping magnate John Ellerman – lived together without marrying for many years. They did eventually marry in 1908, in time for the birth of Bryher's brother, John. Bryher was brought up with Victorian rigidity in a large house on South Audley Street in London. Since her father was a self-made man and her mother of middle-class origins, the Ellermans could not be part of London high society, despite John Ellerman's subsequent knighthood. Sir John's world of shipping and high finance involved him in the world's affairs, but his family – wife, daughter and son – were kept more or less secluded in London and

Eastbourne. He did take them travelling, however, all over Europe, Africa and the Near East; travels which the young Annie –or 'Dolly' as her father called her – loved, and which made her a lifelong adventurer.

At 15 she was sent to Queenwood, a girls' boarding school. She hated it virulently; and 'found schoolgirls the slaves of a mass of petty conventions which seemed . . . absurd'.[2] And she hated *being* a girl. She longed to be a boy and run away to sea. She already had her own ideas about education, against all of which Queenwood embodied opposites. Nor did she fume only in silence. Her first novel *Development* (London, Constable, 1920) was based on her Queenwood years and caused something of a stir because of its radical criticisms. Writing this book didn't change her feelings about the school, however. Nearly 60 years later, in her autobiography, she wrote, 'though as age has chilled the emotions I can accept Queenwood as a necessary part of my experience, the impact was a shattering one and it was hell while it lasted.'[3]

It was Queenwood, nevertheless, which gave Bryher her name. Her best friend there, Doris Banfield, took Annie home with her to the Scilly Isles, off the coast of Cornwall, in 1911. Annie fell in love with them and from the island of Bryher took the name that she eventually made her own by deed poll. In the meantime, she struggled with her parents over her future:

What a disappointment I was to my parents! All their friends had liked me as a child but here I was with the raw aggressiveness of a boy, clamoring to be loosed upon a world that had no use for me. My father might have coped with the situation if I had had a mathematical mind but what was he to do with a young savage who was only interested in tearing society apart to see how it worked? It must have been disconcerting when a guest, meaning to be kind, asked me what my hobbies were and got the answer, 'I want to find out how people think.' Once in an unguarded moment I said something about writing. There was a roar of laughter and a visitor answered, 'Oh, no, Miss Winifred, I'm afraid that is a little out of your range but I'm sure you'll run the garden splendidly in a year or two.' Usually I was careful and silent. I prayed to be forty, knowing that as long as I was young nobody would listen to me. I seldom had more than half an hour a day to myself. It taught me concentration because such moments were so precious no noises could disturb them and I usually spent the time memorizing pages of poetry to repeat during our interminable walks.[4]

The Ellermans, who told their daughter that it was 'morbid to read so much' and 'selfish to want to write'[5] reflected the prevailing attitudes of the times. But for Bryher, as for so many others, opposition only made her even more determined to have her own way. She persuaded her father to let her have some of her poems printed (this was *Region of Lutany*, Chapman & Hall, 1914) and to let her take Arabic lessons. She haunted bookshops and bought volumes of poetry and the current little magazines. 'I do not know how I should have lived if it had not been for one of those little magazines,' she wrote years later. In 1913 she found *Des Imagistes* in a bookshop; bought it; and 'flung myself upon its contents with the lusty, roaring appetite of an Elizabethan boy. I was discontented with traditional forms but this was new, it said what I was unable to write for myself.'[6]

Thus Bryher, at 19, discovered the Imagists, just as Amy Lowell – much older – had discovered them in Boston. This new poetry changed both their lives and brought them into contact with one another, although not immediately, since the war intervened and Bryher found herself a helpless prisoner, living with her parents and unable to do anything or go anywhere. She later wrote about World War I that 'none of the survivors ever got over it'[7] and that she would much rather go through the second one than the first. She tried to involve herself in volunteer work, but in the main she longed for it all to be over. In 1917 she managed to have an American friend send her some recent books of poetry and in this way came to have the Imagist anthologies Amy Lowell had put together, as well as Lowell's own volumes of verse and her critical study, *Six French Poets*. Bryher was bowled over and wrote to Lowell: '*Six French Poets* is the primary reason for this letter . . . To me, *Six French Poets* was like having a friend.'[8] Lowell wrote back. Soon, Bryher was sending her own poems for criticism; and then, in 1918, *Amy Lowell: A Critical Appreciation* (London, Eyre & Spottiswoode), a pamphlet she wrote in praise of Lowell's poetry. Amy recommended more books for Bryher to read; and among them was H.D.'s *Sea Garden* and Dorothy Richardson's *Pilgrimage* novels. Bryher had already discovered Richardson; but she immediately bought *Sea Garden*. While her initial reaction to H.D.'s poetry was restrained enough ('from the few I have read,

they enhance by contrast the value of your own poetry', she wrote
to Lowell)[9], she soon became fascinated by this mysterious 'H.D.'
and memorised all the poems in *Sea Garden*.

When Bryher learned from Lowell's *Tendencies in Modern
American Poetry* (1917) that H.D. lived in England, she 'at once
began to meditate an attack on her', she wrote to Lowell. Her letter
continues:

> Mr Shorter with some difficulty got me her address. Curiously
> enough she was staying in the very next village to the place we
> had chosen instead of Scilly this year. I sent her a copy of the
> pamphlet and wrote beseeching I might go and see her.
> Encouragement to a young enthusiasm seems to be a root of The
> Imagist nature for I had a letter back almost at once asking me to
> walk across . . . I found the house without much difficulty – a
> solitary one by the cliff edge and seeing books scattered
> everywhere, I knocked. Mrs Aldington opened the door herself.
> I am afraid my first impression was how magnificently you had
> expressed her and made her live in those few pages of
> 'Tendencies' and my next was that I was a whirlwind disturbing a
> calm Sicilian day . . . I tried hard to keep from asking
> innumerable questions about you – but sometimes they would
> break out . . . Mrs Aldington has promised to come and see me in
> London . . . She was of exceeding interest to me and I owe the
> meeting, the knowledge of her and her poems to you through
> 'Tendencies'.[10]

In *Two Selves*, the continuation of *Development*, Bryher has her
fictional self Nancy anticipate the meeting with the mysterious poet:

> Was something going to happen to her at last? . . . if she had a
> friend something would burst and she would shoot ahead, be the
> thing she wanted and disgrace them by her knowledge. Because
> she would care for no laws, only for happiness. If she found a
> friend, an answer, the past years would vanish utterly from her
> mind.[11]

And Nancy – like Bryher – was not disappointed:

> A tall figure opened the door. Young. A spear flower if a spear
> could bloom. She looked up into eyes that had the sea in them,
> the fire and colour and the splendour of it. A voice all wind and
> gull notes said:
> 'I was waiting for you to come.'[12]

Having met, the two women began a correspondence. 'I trust you will not hesitate to tell me if I can help you in any way and I hope you will have a nice Christmas at Speen. I am so glad you wrote to me',[13] wrote Bryher to H.D., who had taken refuge in a country cottage following her departure from Cecil Gray some months earlier. Although Gray offered to marry her when she told him about the pregnancy, H.D. refused. 'He was, had been, authentic in Cornwall. But she didn't want to marry him.'[14]

Aldington, still at the front, wrote to H.D. that he was willing to take care of her and the baby. From H.D.'s point of view, however – whatever she felt about this offer – Aldington was clearly unable to give any immediate assistance. In any case, he would be returning to his lover, Dorothy Yorke. Bryher's interest and enthusiasm, therefore, were timely and gave H.D. much-needed support, which she didn't fail to acknowledge: 'Your enthusiasm has helped me – and once I hear from R., I will know definitely about my future work and life. I do want your help – I really do!'[15] Indeed the two women helped each other to begin new lives. Bryher came to visit and they made plans to travel to Greece and to America. H.D. offered to help Bryher find a flat in London away from her parents' house. It was not until December, even so, that she told Bryher about the pregnancy:

> You must take pity on me and let me be with you part of the time. We could put aside certain afternoons of the week, and arrange to have people in then to tea, and we could go out together, you with me (as Mr Shorter says 'a good married woman') to chaperone . . . At present, I am a little tied. Three years ago, I had a sad illness & lost my little child. I am expecting to have another towards the end of March . . .[16]

H.D. allowed Bryher to assume that the child was Aldington's; and the two women went on with their plans. They almost moved into W.B. Yeats's flat in Woburn Buildings in Bloomsbury (directly across the court from Dorothy Richardson's old flat). H.D., still in the country, had introduced Brigit Patmore to Bryher; and Mrs Patmore (wrote H.D. to Bryher), would accompany Bryher to look at the rooms.

> . . . [I] have written Mr Yeats about char-woman – there is no trouble with heating as there are gas-fires in all rooms, and I can get our breakfast & simple luncheons, and dinners even if you want to try a month with me . . . I can arrange minor matters –

linen etc. from my old place around the corner at Mecklenburgh Square, if we go into Woburn Buildings. I have written Mr Yeats to send you keys.[17]

This plan fell through; but they made others. H.D. read the manuscript of *Development* and encouraged Bryher to go on with it, although Bryher told Amy Lowell that H.D. had said it would need several *years* of work! H.D. sent Bryher her latest poems, which Bryher typed up for her. H.D. then sent them off to *Poetry* magazine, writing to Bryher: 'I sent off "Hymen" to Poetry. I am really excited now as to what Harriet will write me – a lecture, I know, on my Asiatic abandon!'[18]

In early 1919, H.D. went to talk to Havelock Ellis. She was understandably perplexed about her life and attachments in general and about this latest one in particular, with a young woman so different from herself (and from Frances who had been her 'twin sister'); a young woman so intense, so determined, so devoted to her. Ellis helped her to come to terms with it all. She wrote to Bryher:

I am so eager for more of *Developments* [*sic*] and I want Dr E to see it and Mrs Patmore . . . Mrs Patmore because she is sensitive & feels (knows in another way) and because she is so intensely and vitally interested in women who are more than women, or different from what is ordinarily accepted as such.[19]

Clearly Bryher was 'different from what is ordinarily accepted as such'; she'd always known that. She, too, went to see Dr Ellis and wrote to H.D.:

Then we got on to the question of whether I was a boy sort of escaped into the wrong body and he says it is a disputed subject but quite possible and showed me a book about it . . . we agreed it was most unfair for it to happen but apparently I am quite justified in pleading I ought to be a boy . . . I am just a girl by accident.[20]

Bryher's practical mind accepted the situation and she didn't agonise over the 'unfairness' of her dilemma. Besides, it wasn't such a dilemma now that she'd found the friend for whom she'd longed and to whom she would remain devoted all her life. H.D., more confused by her feelings and about to deliver her child, was having second thoughts about men, which she revealed in 'Asphodel':

Men, men, men and the strange human heart ache. Must she go back to men, men, men? Men could mar or make her. Men could not. Men could do nothing to her for a butterfly, a frog, a soft and luminous moth larvae was keeping her safe. She was stronger than men, men, men. She was stronger than guns, guns, guns . . .[21]

H.D. would, in time, prove herself stronger than the men who had 'marred' her. But just now she needed someone to lean on. Shortly before her baby was due, in March 1919, she came down with influenza. All over London, people were dying from it. Bryher and Brigit Patmore rushed to her side and got her into a nursing home for the delivery. Frances Perdita was born on 31 March 1919. Bryher wanted to do something; but Brigit, a mother herself, was of more practical help, as Bryher acknowledged in a letter to her:

> It has been so kind of you to take charge of the money and get all the necessary things. I should not have known what to get and it was so much better that Mrs Aldington should not have the worry of it. Thank you so much for all you have done.
>
> I am tremendously glad I had the chance of helping a poet and I hope in a few weeks I may be able to take Mrs Aldington away to Cornwall . . .[22]

Bryher had problems of her own. She was becoming desperate to escape from her family's strict rules and regulations. H.D. later projected Bryher's dilemma in 'Asphodel': 'I can't wait much longer. I've thought it all out. I can't have what I want [i.e. to be a writer] . . . I'm going to kill myself – it isn't exactly anybody's fault – but I can't stand it.'[23]

H.D., lying in bed recovering from the flu, asked Bryher to promise her never to threaten suicide again. She wanted Bryher 'to promise me to grow up and take care of the little girl', who, she now told Bryher, was not Aldington's child. Bryher's reaction wasn't surprising: 'The eyes were wide eyes, bluer than blue, bluer than gentian, than convolvulus, than forget-me-not, than the blue of blue pansies. They were child's eyes, gone wild and fair with gladness.'[24] The bond between them was now sealed and would never be broken.

When H.D. had recovered, the two women set off together for Cornwall, leaving Perdita in a London nursery. For the next several years they all lived peripatetically, travelling to Greece, New York,

California, London, Paris, Switzerland, Egypt. Within their first year together, however, a major change took place. Bryher got married.

Robert McAlmon, a 25-year-old writer from the midwest, came into their lives in September 1920. H.D., Bryher and Perdita had sailed to America early in the month, looking forward to seeing Amy Lowell and H.D.'s old friends Marianne Moore and William Carlos Williams. Lowell met them at the dock; Williams invited them to parties; and they had tea with Marianne Moore and her mother. At one of many parties, Williams introduced them to his new friend McAlmon with whom he was starting up a new little magazine called *Contact*. By a strange attraction of opposites, McAlmon and Bryher struck up an immediate friendship. They spoke about their writing. McAlmon was interested in *Development*. But there wasn't much time to get acquainted. Within a couple of weeks H.D., Bryher, Perdita and H.D.'s mother were on their way to California.

McAlmon wrote to Bryher; and she wrote back. When he wrote that he thought he'd get on a ship and work his way to adventurous places, Bryher made a decision. She and H.D. rushed back to New York, where she proposed that they marry. She would then have the protection of being a married woman and thus free herself of her parents' restrictions. She would give McAlmon enough money to live on comfortably so he could write or travel. They would pretend to Bryher's parents that it was a love match but in fact they'd live apart, Bryher spending most of her time with H.D. and Perdita. McAlmon agreed; and they were married at City Hall in New York in February 1921.[25]

At the wedding party afterwards, their friends weren't sure what to make of this new alliance. Marianne Moore and her mother were shocked, thinking McAlmon was taking advantage of an innocent young girl. Williams was disgruntled and perhaps a little jealous. His best friend was deserting him just when they'd started *Contact*.

Within a few days McAlmon, Bryher, H.D. and Perdita set sail for England, after newspaper headlines about a young American marrying an English heiress had hit the stands. Bryher's parents, informed by telegram, were welcoming, eager to meet their new son-in-law. The ocean journey was probably sobering for McAlmon, as he began to realise the complexities of the situation. He got on well with Perdita and was helpful in general; but it didn't take him long to begin feeling stifled by the two women. When they arrived at the Ellerman home, he liked the family, but hated the subterfuge of pretending that he and Bryher had a real marriage. Still, for a while the arrangement worked.

Back in London, H.D. found a flat for herself and Perdita while Bryher and McAlmon stayed with the Ellermans. Before long, however, all four went to Switzerland, where H.D. and Bryher took a flat in the little town of Territet, near Montreux. This would be their base for the coming decade, with McAlmon making occasional visits. H.D. worked on her poems and novels (the unpublished 'Paint It Today', 'Asphodel', then *Palimpsest*), while Bryher took charge of Perdita's education. From the summer of 1921, McAlmon spent most of his time in Paris where, with Bryher's financial support, he started the Contact Publishing Company. Between 1922 and 1928, McAlmon published books by himself, Bryher, H.D., Mina Loy, Mary Butts, Djuna Barnes and Gertrude Stein, as well as Hemingway, Williams and Marsden Hartley, among others. McAlmon's *Contact Collection of Contemporary Writers* (1925) included work by Bryher, H.D., Mina Loy, Dorothy Richardson, May Sinclair, Gertrude Stein, Mary Butts and Djuna Barnes. It was dedicated to Harriet Weaver, with signed copies going both to her and to Sylvia Beach.

By 1923, Bryher and H.D. knew the Paris expatriates through their own forays into the city. Bryher went more often than did H.D., at least in the earlier years of the decade; but when apart, the two women wrote to each other every day. By now they had their own names for each other: H.D. was 'Horse' or 'Kat' to Bryher's 'Fido', while Perdita was 'Pup' and Robert was 'Bobbie' or 'Bob-Cat'. Bryher's letters were sometimes full of gossip:

Dear Baby Horse
 . . . Mary [Butts] has got so drunk it's been too much even for Bobbie!!!
 Djuna [Barnes] and Thelma [Wood] are happy together.
 Williams returns here the middle of May.
 Oncle [Norman Douglas] is in an awful mess . . .[26]

At other times, she simply described her day:

It is 11 pm and I've just escaped the Jockey. Here's a brief list of my day –
 Man Ray's studio, Brancusi, lunch w/Robert . . .
 To Gertrude Stein's who was just going out so on to Ezra's to

find Dorothy awfully upset as her father is very sick . . . Mrs Joyce came in . . . Then we tore off in a taxi to the Boeuf sur les Toits [*sic*], one of the notorious centres of Paris . . . and there I saw . . . the most alluring attractive puma [lesbian prostitute], whom Robert had taken me there to meet . . . she whispered to Bobbie she guessed it was an intellectual marriage rather than . . . Smoke, jazz, scent, drunk Americans, scores of beautiful pumas all dancing *together*. I met Cocteau . . . dinner with Man Ray and Kikki . . . Oh Horse . . . what's the use of seeing funny things if you're not there to be visibly shocked! . . . Then on to Gertrude Stein's who acclaimed me as the pure type of ethical Jewess. It was all right but she is dreadfully pro-French. Very like Amy . . . We talked till eleven and then I insisted on coming back . . . Had a cocktail but thought it beastly. No nourishment and pure fire . . .

Tomorrow lunch with Joyce and Mina [Loy] . . .

An invitation to tea with Dorothy Richardson in October . . .[27]

Expatriate Paris in the 1920s indeed threw together the growing network of innovative women writers and their publishers from both sides of the Atlantic. Many had known each other through correspondence and through publishing in *Poetry* and the other 'little magazines'. Now Paris became the centre where they could meet in person. One of the few people *not* mentioned in Bryher's letter was Sylvia Beach, whose bookshop 'Shakespeare & Company' became a central meeting-place for both English and American writers. Bryher soon became both a friend and benefactor of Sylvia, helping to keep the shop going by giving generously.

Occasionally H.D. joined Bryher on these trips to Paris; but more often she stayed in Switzerland, writing. Both women contributed to the little magazines; and as well as her involvement in Contact Publishing Company, Bryher was also funding several publications from Harriet Weaver's Egoist Press in London.

Increasingly, however, McAlmon became dissatisfied with his and Bryher's marital arrangement. He became lackadaisical about the Contact business. Bryher confided to Sylvia Beach, who was also one of McAlmon's friends:

I am probably very bad for him. I always thought that after he had torn around for a couple of years he would settle into steady work. But I'm now the stumbling block, I think. I've written him if he feels as he did all summer he had better go through whatever legal steps are necessary while he is in the States . . . Maybe if he feels on his own again he will get down to things and will be friendly. I hope he goes ahead for I'm sure he has creative genius back of him.[28]

Earlier, Bryher had complained to H.D.: 'Stayed up till almost two listening to Robert's experiences. Sorry for him as he seems to want a definite friendship much. Perhaps Rhino [possibly a psychiatrist friend] might help him.'[29] The bisexual McAlmon would unfortunately never find a 'definite friendship' with either a man or a woman. He and Bryher did divorce in 1927, but after drifting through a few more years of the Paris connections, he disappeared into the American west.

H.D. and Bryher formed a new attachment however. This was Kenneth Macpherson, whom Frances introduced to H.D. Frances, by 1926 long divorced from Louis, had been living in poverty in the English countryside with her two children. For a while she worked as a journalist in order to send her son to school; but the family, including Frances' ever-present mother, had to keep moving from one old house to another. The Macpherson family lived in the same building as Frances at one point; and Frances fell in love with the young and beautiful Kenneth. Frances and H.D. had not been seeing each other; but some time in 1926 Frances sent Kenneth to meet her old friend. Almost at once, the old pattern of the triangle began to surface. H.D. and Macpherson fell in love. When Bryher realised what was happening, it occurred to her that she, about to divorce McAlmon, could marry Kenneth Macpherson (whom she much liked) and thus regain her British citizenship, as well as maintain the protection of being a married woman. H.D. was, of course, still legally married to Aldington, whom she didn't divorce until 1937, when he wanted to remarry.[30]

Bryher's idea seemed agreeable to all; so, soon after her divorce, Bryher married Macpherson. The personal arrangements between the three were quite complex. Macpherson became 'Rover' to H.D.'s 'Kat' and Bryher's 'Fido'. He got on well with them both; and seemed never put out by H.D.'s nervousness and hysterical tendencies or Bryher's annoying inclination to arrange all their lives. When the romantic affair between H.D. and Macpherson was over, they remained close friends; and when his attention turned to young men friends, the essential threesome remained strong. In addition, he gave Bryher a new interest: the cinema.

In Territet in 1927, Bryher, together with Macpherson, started *Close-up*, the first periodical devoted to the art of film. She wrote for every issue; and contributors included H.D., Dorothy Richardson, and Gertrude Stein. Sylvia Beach sold the journal at 'Shakespeare & Company'. In addition, Macpherson bought a movie camera and started making films. In 1930, Bryher and Macpherson built 'Kenwin', a Bauhaus villa on the lake near Montreux, which would be Bryher's home for the rest of her life. Throughout their association, Macpherson proved a stabilising influence for Bryher, H.D. and Perdita. He and Bryher officially adopted Perdita in the late twenties and he remained a devoted friend to her. H.D. and Bryher still wrote to each other every day they were apart and never failed to send each other special messages on the anniversaries of their first meeting. By now, however, both in their forties, they had begun to grow more independent from each other.

From 1928 till 1939 Bryher and H.D. spent a lot of time apart, although they always shared 'Kenwin' as a base. Together with Macpherson they became deeply involved in film and film-making in the late twenties, an involvement culminating in their silent film *Borderline*, starring H.D. and Paul Robeson. They released the film in 1930. But there was, too, an important new interest shared by Bryher and H.D.: psychoanalysis. Beginning with Havelock Ellis, both women had consulted psychologists. Freudian psychoanalysis, however, proved to be a turning point for both of them. H.D. wrote about her analysis under Freud in *Tribute to Freud* (first published in 1956).

With the outbreak of World War II, all their lives changed. When war was declared, H.D. was in her London flat; Macpherson was in New York; and Bryher, who had been helping Jewish refugees escape from Germany, had left Switzerland at the last moment in order to join H.D. in London. For the next four years they lived together continuously. Perdita, now 21, was on her own and working in army intelligence. H.D. and Bryher worked at their writing: H.D. on poetry later published as *Trilogy* and on several still unpublished novels; Bryher on the first of her historical novels, *Beowulf*. In addition, Bryher continued publishing *Life and Letters To-day*, the literary journal she took over in 1935. H.D. was remarkably calm during this time, but broke down at the war's end. Bryher sent her to a Swiss *Nervenklinik* in Kusnacht, near Zurich. After some months there, H.D. moved to a hotel in Lausanne. For the next few years she divided her time between Lausanne and Lugano, always writing, always in touch with Bryher, but alone. Bryher kept Kenwin, but Macpherson settled in New York, as did Perdita. Bryher and Macpherson were amicably divorced in 1947 and a little later he settled permanently in Italy, where Bryher often visited him.

Travel became more and more of an ordeal for H.D., although she managed to visit Perdita in New York and to see her four grandchildren as they came along. She made her last trip there in 1960 to receive the American Academy of Arts and Letters Gold Medal for Poetry, being the first woman so honoured. By then suffering from various physical ailments, she had settled in Kusnacht, where she could write peacefully and avoid the distractions of everyday life. Bryher visited frequently, making sure that she had everything she wanted. She was with H.D. when she died after suffering a stroke on 27 September 1961.

Their 42 years of partnership gave both H.D. and Bryher the stability they needed in order to work. For H.D. Bryher was a safe haven, a firm foundation, a 'steel-set' star, someone she could depend on totally. She knew Bryher would never fail her or desert her, 'mar' her as the men in her life had done. The only danger was that Bryher's love might be too overwhelming, too stifling, as in their early days it threatened to be. But that, too, worked itself out. Bryher's support, both emotional and material, allowed H.D. to devote herself to her writing, which she did with great intensity and great success. Bryher was never the longed-for 'twin sister' Frances had been; but she was the lover who never left her, who would never say 'I love you but I desire *l'autre*.' In 1926 H.D. wrote this dedication of *Palimpsest*:

To Bryher

Stars wheel in purple, yours is not so rare
as Hesperus, nor yet so great a star
as bright Aldeberan [sic] or Sirius,
nor yet the stained and brilliant one of War;

stars turn in purple, glorious to the sight;
yours is not so gracious as the Pleiads are,
nor as Orion's sapphires, luminous;

yet disenchanted, cold, imperious face,
when all the others, blighted, reel and fall,

> your star, steel-set, keeps lone and frigid trist
> to freighted ships baffled in wind and blast.[31]

For Bryher, in her turn, H.D. was her creative genius, her bright star. She never lost faith in H.D.'s art, in that gift which she knew could never be hers but which she so worshipped. The most important thing in the world to Bryher was that H.D. be free to write; and, to the extent that any other person could, she made that possible. After H.D.'s death, she lived alone at Kenwin with a housekeeper.

Bryher kept writing historical novels and her volumes of autobiography; she continued to travel; she kept up old friendships and maintained her support of many, many writers and friends. Most friends, however, must have agreed with Alice Toklas who said, on hearing of H.D.'s death, 'It is impossible to believe in Bryher without H.D.'[32]

Chapter 4

Dorothy Richardson's life-style of writing

Richardson was born in Abingdon, Berkshire, in 1873, the third of four daughters. Her father Charles, despite his family's success in 'trade', had aspirations to live as a gentleman; so he sold his prosperous business and devoted himself to reading, music, scientific lectures and other cultivated pursuits. His investments, however, proved disastrous and he was forced into bankruptcy in 1893.

Before the bankruptcy, the four sisters enjoyed a middle-class upbringing of relative comfort. When Dorothy was ten, the family moved to Putney in south London, where their lives included croquet, tennis, boating, skating, dancing and musical evenings. After being taught by a governess for a year, Dorothy was sent to Southborough House, whose headmistress was a disciple of Ruskin and where pupils were encouraged to think for themselves. Here the young girl first grew aware of what became her lifelong passion for language and linguistics, discovering 'the fascination of words, of their sturdy roots, their growth and transformation, and the strange drama of the pouring in from every quarter of the globe of alien words assimilated and modified to the rhythms of our own speech'.[1]

During these years, Charles Richardson pursued his intellectual interests with some vigour, frequenting public lectures and libraries and reading an array of papers on science and philosophy. His wife Mary was less fortunate, suffering recurrent bouts of ill-health and nervous prostration. When Dorothy later discovered for herself the availability of talks and lectures for the public, she much resented the fact that her father had never explained that she, too, might have attended them.

Charles Richardson's bankruptcy forced an end to Dorothy's schooling. She resolved to earn her own living (and secretly decided that honour required her to try somehow to settle his debts). There were, of course, only a handful of choices open to her and she took the most obvious, replying to an advertisement for a pupil-teacher in a girls' school in Hanover, Germany. The preparations for the journey, the family leave-taking and her initial impressions of her new life marked for her the beginnings of adult consciousness and provided the opening pages of her experimental fiction *Pointed Roofs*, in which she charts the development of her *alter ego*, Miriam Henderson.

Dorothy's stay in Hanover was short-lived. Owing to a combination of naïveté on her part and diffuse sexual jealousy on the part of the school's director, it was agreed that the young Englishwoman should return home. She took a teaching post in a school in Finsbury Park, north London; and her experiences here gave her the material for *Backwater*, the second volume of *Pilgrimage*. Her last teaching was done as a governess to a family in the country, which time is recounted in *Honeycomb*, the third volume of the sequence.

The closing pages of *Honeycomb* present obliquely the second and more appalling trauma of Dorothy's young life. She had accompanied her mother, who was suffering another mental collapse, on a convalescent holiday to Hastings, on the south coast. Returning one day from an errand she found her mother dead on the floor, her throat cut with a kitchen knife. This horrifying experience, apart from its lasting effects on Dorothy's inner life, precipitated radical change in her external circumstances. The family home was sold and one of her two married sisters agreed to take in their father. The third sister took a post as a governess. Dorothy, at last, faced the prospect of freedom.

She was now in her early twenties. A family friend called John Henry Badcock had just begun working as a dental surgeon in a Harley Street practice. Dorothy leapt at the chance of a job there. It was therefore arranged that she would work in the practice as a secretary for a salary of one pound per week. She began her life there in 1896, poor and alone, but ecstatic at the chance of independence. Her love affair with London – its physical, social and intellectual maps – suffuses the middle volumes of *Pilgrimage*.

Independence on a meagre salary held few horrors for Dorothy. On the contrary, she took to her new life with a curious combination of composure and zest. She took an attic room in a house on the fringe of Bloomsbury and there met other lodgers. She walked to work. Frequently she ate tea in ABC tearooms where a boiled egg, bread and butter and a pot of tea could be had for a few pence; and even more frequently, she sat and read in the British Museum Reading Room. She attended lectures and meetings of all sorts, thus becoming acquainted with the ideologies and allegiances of Quakers, vegetarians, anarchists, socialists, Unitarians and many others. London in the 1890s teemed with emigrés, revolutionaries, feminists – with all manner of radicals. Dorothy determined to find out whatever she could about them.

This strange, serious-minded observer, dislocated from her background, intense – dogged even – in her interests, had nothing neurasthenic either in her manner or in her appearance. She wasn't conventionally beautiful; but she wore a crown of thick golden hair and a skin flawless enough for many who later remembered her to remark upon. Those who were drawn to her were strongly drawn, yet less to her physical appearance than to her intensity and curious inner aloofness. There was something about her that it seemed no one could really touch.

During these London years, Dorothy met the four people who became the central characters both in the drama of her own life and in that of her fictional persona, Miriam Henderson. H.G. Wells (the model for Hypo Wilson in *Pilgrimage*) was already an established novelist when Dorothy met him. He was married to one of her old schoolfellows, Amy Catherine Robbins, whom Dorothy had decided to look up. Invitations to the Wells's country house became regular; and the prolific, successful, confident, womanising Wells became Dorothy's most robust sparring partner. She was unknown, unattached and uncomplainingly a virgin. Wells, according to her account, proposed to her that they have an affair; a credible enough development in a friendship between the arch-advocate of free love and a female companion he found interesting (and exasperating). Wells's son, Anthony West, has written a rather different account of the relationship in his partisan and eccentric account of his father's life.[2] In West's book, Dorothy appears as a dowdy, sexless, egocentric bore for whom his dashing father provided a generous favour in the service of experience. Whatever the psychological truth of the matter, however, it's clear that after ten years of living independently in London and at the age of 32, Richardson began an affair with Wells, for whom she felt an aggravating fondness but hardly a romantic passion.

Richardson's account, given in *Pilgrimage*, of their first sexual encounter must be one of the funniest and least salacious written in English:

> There ought to be homage. There was a woman, not this thinking self who talked with men in their own language, but one whose words could be spoken only from the heart's knowledge, waiting to be born in her . . .
>
> He was incapable of homage . . . But without a touch of it she could not come fully to birth for him. In that sense all women *are* Undine. Only through a man's recognition can they come to their full stature. But so are men, in their different way. It was his constricted, biological way of seeing sex that kept him blind. Beauty, even, was to him beauty by contrast with Neanderthal man – – –
>
> 'The trouble with Miretta [Miriam] is that one can't take liberties with a philosopher.'
>
> She smiled from far away, from where if only he knew and could have patience just to look at what she saw and fully submit himself to its truth, see and feel its truth, she could travel towards him.
>
> . . . 'Now with others than Miretta' – flattery – 'one just takes them in one's arms and immediately there is no barrier.'
>
> . . . He dropped a kiss on her shoulder.
>
> 'You *are* a pretty creature, Miriam. I wish you could see yourself.'

(Obediently Miriam looks at herself with her mind's eye, noticing her ropes of hair, her 'rose-tinted velvety gleaming' of flesh, the 'lines and curves of her limbs, their balance and harmony'.) It is all

> Impersonally beautiful and inspiring. To him each detail was 'pretty,' and the whole an object of desire.
>
> . . . This mutual nakedness was appeasing rather than stimulating. And austere, as if it were a first step in some arduous discipline.
>
> His body was not beautiful. She could find nothing to adore, no ground for response to his lightly spoken tribute. The manly structure, the smooth, satiny sheen in place of her own velvety

glow was interesting as partner and foil, but not desirable. It had
no power to stir her . . .

The impulse seemed reckless. But when she had leaned
forward and clasped him, the warm contact drove away the idea
that she might be both humiliating and annoying him and brought
a flood of solicitude and suggested a strange action. And as gently
she rocked him to and fro the words that came to her lips were so
unsuitable that even while she murmured 'My little babe, just
born,' she blushed for them, and steeled herself for his comment.

Letting him go, she found his arms about her in their turn and
herself, surprised and not able with sufficient swiftness to
contract her expanded being that still seemed to encompass him,
rocked unsatisfactorily to and fro while his voice, low and shy and
with the inappropriate unwelcome charm in it of the ineffectual
gestures of a child learning a game, echoed the unsuitable words
. . .

'Lost lady. Your reputation's in shreds, Miriam, virginal
though you be.'[3]

A subsequent encounter makes even clearer the alienation Dorothy
experienced as an intrinsic part of their sexual relationship.
Unbidden, her lover comes to her room in the middle of the night
while she is on a visit to him and his wife. He complains artlessly of
the cold and she submits to the subterfuge:

It was uncanny, but more absorbing than the unwelcome
adventure of her body, to be thus hovering outside and above it in
a darkness that obliterated the room and was too vast to be
contained by it. An immense, fathomless black darkness through
which, after an instant's sudden descent into her clenched and
rigid form, she was now travelling alone and on, without thought
or memory or any emotion save the strangeness of this journeying
. . .

His relaxed form was nothing to her. A mass of obstructive clay
from which the spirit had departed on its way to its own bourne.
Its journey, foolishly undertaken through her fault in hiding,
failing to communicate their essential unrelatedness, had been
through a familiar pleasure into restful nothingness that presumably would bear the fruit he sought therefrom.

The robed figure stood over her like a short doctor: flattering,
warning, trying to edit her mind . . .

. . . she awaited the welling of appropriate emotion. But the power she felt the presented facts ought to wield, and might possibly yet attain, failed to emerge from them. Within her was something that stood apart, unpossessed. From far away below the colloquy, from where still it sheltered in the void to which it had withdrawn and whence it had set forth alone upon its strange journeying, her spirit was making its own statement, profanely asserting the unattained being that was promising, however faintly, to be presently the surer for this survival. Joining forces with it, using her will to banish the lingering images, she felt herself sink towards sleep.[4]

The basis of the bond between these two was neither sex nor romantic passion, but discourse. The flavour and quality of their debates, arguments, banter and quarrelling occurs through many pages of *Pilgrimage*, Miriam, prosecutor of materialism, challenges Wilson, advocate of science; Wilson, believer in rationalism, spars with Miriam, champion of mysticism; Wilson, hooked on biology and 'nature', attacks Miriam's notions of individualised rates of human evolution. In life, too, Richardson and Wells argued for years about the nature of reality and never found agreement. His faith in objectivity and the provenance of scientific law was for Richardson reductionist and deterministic, inimical to her view that only consciousness itself was knowable and that the details of the physical world, the constraints of time and the events of history, were all disposed according to the individual's perceptions of them. Richardson did not believe that there could be any facts about anything.

Most striking of all in these never-resolved disputes – and possibly the most telling reason for the fascination they held for both protagonists – was the feminist perspective shaping Richardson's convictions. She often denied that she was a feminist, since she associated the term with the campaign for the vote and she had flirted only briefly with that campaign. More significantly, she never advocated either the equality or the supremacy of women in relation to men since, she was convinced, women and men were utterly separate species. She has Miriam state unequivocally that by every word they utter, men and women mean different things.[5] And from Miriam's mouth, too, comes one of the most feminist cries in all twentieth-century literature: 'I wouldn't have a man's – *consciousness* for anything.'[6]

Between 1912 and 1922 Richardson contributed articles and a

column to the professional journal *The Dental Record*. In much of this writing, her anger towards men and their science is directly expressed. In a comment on a book by a certain Dr R. Murray Leslie, for example, she writes:

> His very human, or, perhaps more strictly speaking male fear [of a relatively unified personality] leads him to what is at once the most amazing psychological blunder in the whole book, and also an acknowledgement of the real truth . . . Dr Leslie hopes 'that the acquisition of intellectual knowledge may not be at the expense of certain feminine passive qualities, such as sympathy, tenderness and common sense.' . . . But the besetting sin of the average amateur male psychologist is very strong. His tendency is to exaggerate the angle of intellect and call it active and male, and to put the angles of feeling and wilfulness in the shade and call them feminine and 'passive'.[7]

In Richardson's view, women constituted 'the synthetic principle of human life', whereas men had a 'mental tendency to departmentalize, to analyze, to separate single things from their flowing environment'.[8]

Marriage predicated on such assumptions and expectations about what women are like (or should be like) was impossible for Richardson to contemplate. She has Miriam reflect on her rejection of a very acceptable suitor, a young doctor:

> Farewell to Densley is farewell to my one chance of launching into life as my people have lived it. I am left with these strangers – people without traditions, without local references, and who despise marriage, or on principle disapprove of it. And in my mind I agree. Yet affairs not ending in marriage are even more objectionable than marriage. And celibates, outside religion, though acceptable when thought of as alone, are always, socially a little absurd. Then I must be absurd. Growing absurd. To others I am already absurd.[9]

Nor did she change her mind. When she was well into middle age, having married unconventionally a man very much younger than herself, she gave this advice to a young friend contemplating marriage to an eligible suitor:

> As I see him, he needs only the home-life that is usually discoverable filling out & supporting the public life of a keen

professional man. Such a man's engrossments & interests, including the speculations & scientific technicalities which are so large a part of the mental life of an investigator, his wife must either share, or leave alone & live, as do so many professional men's wives, more or less in loneliness, aware only, for their comfort, of the necessity for their man, of the serenity & quietude they provide. Very rarely, & perhaps never for very long, can an intense, emotional personal relationship flourish side by side with a real life professional existence. I saw a good deal of professional ménages during my time at Harley Street & my rather narrow escape from marrying into a medical ménage was perhaps helped thereby.[10]

If romantic passion had no place in Dorothy's relationship with Wells, it was certainly central in two other relationships which ran more or less concurrently: one with Benjamin Grad and the other with Veronica Leslie-Jones. Grad, on whom the Michael Shatov of *Pilgrimage* is based, was a Russian Jewish emigré and a fellow-lodger, who approached Dorothy initially in order to have help with his English. They quickly fell into fevered exchanges about books and opinions. Grad wanted to explicate to her his views of Russian culture and his preoccupations in general; and Dorothy willingly complied, wanting in turn to extend her mental map of Europe.

Dorothy Richardson was a gifted linguist, later earning much of her meagre livelihood from translating books from French and German; and was fascinated always by the nature of language: by etymology, grammar, semantics and comparative linguistics, far more than she ever was by works of literature or corresponding aesthetic theories. Grad shared her enthusiasm for linguistics. (Much later, when he was a prisoner of war, he asked Dorothy to send him a Welsh Bible so that he could tackle yet another language.) They shared, too, a fascination for philosophising and associational (rather than logical) theorising. Unlike Wells, however, Grad fell in love with this earnest Englishwoman and wanted to marry her. In spite of her own attraction towards him, she was shocked and disorientated by this development, finding his efforts to embrace her too generalised and inappropriate to her sense of identity, her 'egoism'.

Richardson presents this realisation in *Pilgrimage*, placing it in the context of a conversation about revolution which marks the end of their courtship. Miriam says:

'Women know that humanity is two groups. And they go into revolutions for the freedom from the pressure of this knowledge.'
'Revolution is by no means the sole way of having a complete sense of humanity. But what has all this to do with *us*?'
'It is not that women are heartless; that is an appearance. It is that they know that there are no *tragedies* . . .'
'Listen, Mira. You have taught me much. I am also perhaps not so undiscriminating as are some men.'
'In family life, all your Jewish feelings would overtake you. You would slip into dressing-gown and slippers. You have said so yourself. But I am now quite convinced that I shall never marry.' She walked on.

He ran round in front of her, bringing her to a stand-still.
'You think you will never marry . . . with *this*' – his ungloved hands moved gently over the outlines of her shoulders.
'Ah – it is most – musical; you do not know.' She thrilled to the impersonal acclamation; yet another of his many defiant tributes to her forgotten material self; always lapsing from her mind, never coming to her aid when she was lost in envious admiration of women she could not like. Yet they contained an impossible idea; the idea of a man being consciously attracted and won by universal, physiological facts, rather than by individuals themselves.[11]

Shatov's erotic response to her is, for Miriam, identical with the erotic response of the male in general to the female in general. The paradox is ironic, since Shatov intends his approach to be personal and consistent with his response to her as an individual; but for Miriam it projects their relationship into an abstraction of the depersonalised conjunction of male and female.

Parallel with her relationship with Grad ran Dorothy's involvement with Veronica Leslie-Jones, who appears in *Pilgrimage* as Amabel. This dynamic and idealistic woman, younger than Dorothy, was living away from home in a London club called the Arachne, where Dorothy was a non-residential member. Veronica was intent on becoming an actress and was leading a risqué life pursuing, among other matters, a love affair with a much older married man. The immediate attraction and subsequent intense friendship between the two women are recounted in the later volumes of *Pilgrimage*, where the extravagant Amabel and the phlegmatic Miriam counterpoint each other in a curiously satisfying way. Unlike her disputatious and highly verbal encounters with Wilson and Shatov, Dorothy's relationship with Amabel is almost wordless. After initial almost silent but profoundly satisfying and disturbing meetings, Miriam finds herself – alone in her room – staring at her mirror, half turning to look into it to exchange 'a smile of congratulation with her reflected image'. But the image given back to her is obscured:

> The glass was not clear. Across her face, that should have shown in the reflected candle-light, was some kind of cloudy blur. Holding up the candle she found lettering, large and twirly, thickly outlined as if made with chalk or moist putty, moving with a downward slope across the centre of the strip of glass. Mystified – for who in the wide world could have had access to her room, or, achieving it, should be moved to deface her mirror in a manner suggesting it was for sale? – and disturbed by the unaccountable presence that had been silently witnessing, unpardonably mocking, it seemed to her as she pushed away the chair and stood aside to let the candlelight fall upon the strange apparition, her private rejoicings.
> 'I love you,' it said.[12]

Amabel's next communication is likewise unspoken, coming in a letter:

> Forgive – I watched you – in your little English clothes – go across the square – oh, my lady – my little – you terrified my heart – I hold it out to you – my terrified heart – in my two hands –[13]

Though the social meaning of such an attachment may be unclear, its existential meaning is not. Miriam tells Wilson that she is 'perpetually preoccupied' with Amabel who is treasure beyond his or anyone else's 'power of diagnosis'. She explains, more to herself than to him:

> There was in the whole of her previous experience . . . nothing that could compare with what Amabel had brought. Nothing could be better. No sharing, not even the shared being of a man and a woman, which she sometimes envied and sometimes deplored, could be deeper or more wonderful than this being together, alternating between awareness of the beloved person and delight in every aspect, every word and movement, and a solitude distinguishable from the deepest, coolest, most renewing

moments of lonely solitude only in the enhancement it reaped by being shared.[14]

The sharing continued for the rest of their lives, despite the marriage of each of them. Veronica as an old woman recalled:

> I do know that even after she married Alan we were still part of each other – even in these last years after we both had shingles and I had to go on being active & she gave up it was still a queer kind of partnership that briefly she recognized when I visited her & now I've a bit lost
>
> Once down at Hillside [in Cornwall] we were talking & I said 'You know Dorothy I suppose I've always been a bit jealous of you of your life' & she said 'But Vera, I've always been jealous of you!' . . . We were in some way I don't understand more "lovers" than we ever could be to any man – & Dorothy loved Alan & I loved someone too – but it wasn't I know to either of us what *we* were . . .[15]

The level of commitment required, however, to sustain this level of intensity was too much for Dorothy (or Miriam) to contemplate. Nor was the choice a simple one, between man or woman lover, between Grad or Veronica. It was a more troubling choice between independence and compromise. Soon a solution began to take shape in Dorothy's mind:

> as though it had prepared itself while she was refusing to take thought, there passed before her inward vision a picture of herself performing, upon an invisible background, the rite of introduction between Michael and Amabel. It slid away. Joyously she recalled it, supplying time and place, colour and sound and living warmth. And it stood there before her, solving the mystery of her present failure to suffer on Michael's behalf, filling so completely the horizon of her immediate future . . .[16]

The two friends are duly introduced to each other; and Amabel's response is startling. She says afterwards to Miriam, 'you *must* marry him', whereupon Miriam replies, 'then marry him, my dear, yourself.' Amabel responds gleefully, 'I would. I would tomorrow.'[17]

In letters written after Richardson's death to her literary executrix and sister-in-law Rose Odle, Veronica Grad confirmed the actual sequence of events to have been precisely those given in the analogue provided in *Pilgrimage*:

The night the man I loved died v. suddenly – we slept in the same
bed & I wept & wept & towards morning – both of us exhausted
Dorothy suddenly said 'Vera, *now* you can marry Benjamin' and
I remember saying 'Yes' – because what I had really said when in
the book she makes me say – 'I would I would & have his
beadyeyed children' I had added 'but not while Philip is alive' – It
was half in jest but she knew I would for *her* – if she asked me &
she did, & I did, & Benjamin knew why I married him . . . & so
you see in a way she was quite right in feeling David [the Grads'
son] was hers in a way he was – Benjamin loved Dorothy, but he
wanted to marry anyway & above all he wanted a son – I never
pretended – to be in love with my husband – but in the end he
grew v. jealous of Dorothy & me – & then our lives seperated
[*sic*] because she went to live at 32 [St John's Wood, London]
. . .[18]

The solution certainly suited Dorothy; but the Grads became
embittered by it. Still responding to Rose Odle, Vera wrote:

I have at last seen her as she really was – I loved her but Dorothy
never for one moment 'loved' anyone but herself. Not even Alan
[Odle] – not anyway as I see love – Dorothy never paid any
prices. She took an avid interest in other people their lives, their
misfortunes, their successes, but she never – looking back I see –
gave either sympathy or help – or let herself become in any way
involved – I am not thinking only of myself. I call to mind a dozen
examples of utter self-protective ruthlessness – Her own sisters –
Florence Daniel – Jane Wells – Lissie Beresford – Benjamin – my
own children. Maybe it was all worth it as a sacrifice to her 'Art'.
I can't judge of that . . . You know she was rather like a
vivisectionist in her attitude to us all – but, I cant [*sic*] see myself
that the handful of pioneer books makes it any less ugly.[19]

Clearly, a bond with this kind of power signified no commonplace
friendship. Nevertheless, in spite of the intimacy and identification
between the two women, there is hardly a hint anywhere, either in
the documentation surviving them or in the pages of *Pilgrimage*,
that the basis of their mutual attraction was sexual, as usually
understood. What is more interesting is the way Dorothy solved her
need for closeness by separating her satisfactions so that she could
retain her independence. Wells gave her access to a literary–
intellectual circle. He gave her himself as a sparring partner for

argument and as a guide to an unproblematic experimentation with sex. Benjamin Grad gave her insights into different cultural perspectives, and shared interests in philosophy and linguistics. In addition, he offered her the prospect of romantic attachment and marriage. Veronica gave her the excitement and ecstasy of spiritual recognition and identification without the constraints of sex-role typing or the possibility of a socially sanctioned commitment. The combination of these people and their gifts suited both her development and her consuming thirst for autonomy. Even more, they suited her gradual realisation that she wanted to be a writer and that she must write about what she knew best: herself.

Urged and encouraged by Wells and other friends, she began writing 'middles' (occasional literary sketches) for the *Saturday Review*; but the pressure of trying to stay unattached while at the same time engaging with her three intimates, was taking its toll. After a pregnancy scare, the cessation of her affair with Wells, and the bringing together of Grad and Vera, Dorothy suffered a physical and mental collapse. She convalesced in Sussex at the farm of Quaker acquaintances, experiences recounted in *Dimple Hill*, the second to last *Pilgrimage* volume. After she'd recovered, she returned to London but resigned from her job with the dental practice, to begin what would be an even more precarious existence as a writer, earning as best she could from journalism and translation. She was now over 40. A chance encounter with a fellow-lodger, a young artist called Alan Odle, now began the last significant relationship of her life.

Alan Odle, to the scorn of his respectable banker father, who paid him a tiny allowance, was a perfect aesthete, devoted to drawing and the importance of art and taking no heed of practical matters. He neglected his physical needs inordinately; and indeed had so dissipated his health that the army rejected him on medical grounds at the height of its need for manpower during the First World War. The army doctor informed him that he had six months to live. With this knowledge, he asked Dorothy to marry him; and with this knowledge, she agreed, later commenting that if she could have known that he would survive the six months and might outlive her, she would never have married him.

Dorothy tended Alan with maternal solicitude, made him eat nourishing food, took him to Cornwall for the clean air and bracing climate, and assumed the responsibilities of running their frugal household and managing their accounts. As they grew older, the thought of how Alan might cope or not after her death preyed on her mind. To her intense relief, a friend offered to take Alan in, if it turned out that he survived her:

> Peggy, my dear, you have lifted from my heart its worst load. Sympathy real, I knew you would give, for I know the great power of your sympathetic imagination. But I did not envisage you rising up, with a flaming sword in your hand, between my helpless darling & all I saw confronting him . . . and, for ought [*sic*] you knew, the poor lamb would not be only helpless but penniless! Well, that is not quite the case. A tiny income will be his, about £150 a year. Thus: Bryher, who has been endlessly good to us, when she started, in memory of Sir John Ellerman, a trust-fund for the benefit of artists & authors & nominated me as one of the beneficiaries, made over to me, by deed, the capital sum producing my annuity, absolutely, & this of course goes to Alan under my will . . . Since I had my Civil Pension in '39, reckoned retrospectively to cover '38, I have scraped & saved all I could in the hope of covering rainy periods. Our bank account has been transformed in a 'Joint & Several', so that A can draw on it & am learning him, whenever a few certificates can be bought, to write a cheque. It takes him nearly as long as a small drawing. The annuity, of course, is fully taxed at source & I have done my best to explain the rebate business, the tax vouchers from Coutts to be carefully cherished & sent in with income-tax returns & the resultant treasury cheque to be banked & held to spread over the following year to make up income. My Civil List pension is tax free, so there will be nothing to claim from the last of that. In a note-book labelled 'Data for Alan' I have set down all this lore, including the way to fill up income-tax returns. But the poor lamb cannot do compound addition & although it was a relief to get these data set down, it is nothing to the relief of communicating them to you, &, when the time comes, he shall know to whom to turn for advice . . .
>
> Worry drains away from me as I write. Even the prospect of his being landed down here alone – he can't pack & is lost in railway stations – with everything to attend to, is less daunting than it was. I'm leaving what instructions I can, in case the war is still on . . .[20]

Clearly in Dorothy's eyes – if in no others – her 'poor lamb' was unworldly to such a degree that his survival without her seemed problematic in the extreme. This maternalism towards Alan explains more than can any other indications, that it was such an adaptation of the maternal role which gave Dorothy her only access to an intimate relationship with a man.

Fortunately for her peace of mind, she did outlive Alan, who collapsed and died suddenly while out walking near their cottage in Cornwall. He was 60 years old. Dorothy was devastated but grateful as well, obviously considering herself better equipped than he to carry on alone. Typically, despite more than 30 years of companionship, she never complained about loneliness, writing late in her life to a young friend:

> Certain of your personal feelings distress me, the more deeply because at one time I occasionally experienced one of them, falling headlong into a pit of 'loneliness'. Easy it is to say that this pit is imaginary. But I think you will know what I mean. When one is within it, one is apt to exaggerate the quality of human 'belongings', particularly, whether in the case of 'love' or of 'friendship', or of the two combined. These relationships are perpetually on the move, like all else, & unless at their centre there is some common faith they cannot endure save as conventions or conveniences. The idolators of such things, describing them from outside, fill our literature with falsities. Solitude is neither loneliness nor lovelessness.[21]

Dorothy's independence – what she called 'egoism' – was as clearly enacted in her life as it was in her work. Her rejection of tradition was due largely to this organic connection, a connection more feminist than literary, since she felt unable as a woman either to identify with the literary past or to attest its values. Her referential framework was psychological rather than ideational; unlike other novelists she diagnosed the conventions she inherited to be not merely cultural, but quite precisely masculine. The corresponding feminine vision, which she designated often as 'life-as-experience', she found lacking in all novels before her.

Any woman persuaded of such a view and already motivated to write would be prompted to redress the balance. Of all the reviewers and commentators who had passed judgment on *Pilgrimage* by 1950, only one satisfied her that her original impulse had been perceived and understood:

Ford saw what without-realising-its-effect-upon-the-development-of-the-novel (odious word) I was moved to do. Monstrously, when I began, I felt only that all masculine novels to date, despite their various fascinations, were somehow irrelevant, and the feminine ones far too much infl [*sic*] by magic traditions, and too much set upon exploiting the sex motif as hitherto seen and depicted by men.[22]

Richardson felt she must shape a 'woman's sentence' and if that attempt involved, or resulted in, a restatement of the novel as a literary form, then that was accidental and unpremeditated. Fidelity to the rhythms of her own life demanded an exactitude which meant that even minutiae must be carefully selected and patiently realised.

In spite of the voluminous correspondence she left behind, the memoirs written by friends and acquaintances, the research amassed by her biographers, Richardson's personality remains strangely inscrutable. The Grads' son, in later life, explained that in his view the key to understanding what she was like was to realise that she had a 'man's mind', capable of a ruthless pursuit of logical discourse in any and every social setting. Young relatives remember her as an awesome presence, not to be trifled with or engaged with in too familiar a manner. Anthony West's cruel portrait outlines a dowdy, humourless, sexless, tedious and uncompromising egotist. John Cowper Powys thought her a great genius. Friends with whom she corresponded through the years of the Second World War were as likely as not to get letters from her with recipes for eggless cakes or butterless scones, mixed in with descriptions of landscape and domestic life, together with speculations about the nature of time or consciousness. Original and serious she most certainly was, fighting shy throughout her long life of all authorities: academic, literary–critical, political and polemical, insisting to the last on the primacy of the individual vision.

Richardson seems never to have exuded the fey qualities of an H.D., the refinement of a Virginia Woolf, the practical wisdom of a Bryher, or the wide-ranging warmth of a Sylvia Beach. She could never have exhibited the generosity of a Harriet Weaver. Placed alongside all of them, she can appear infuriatingly stolid, more imperturbable, less flamboyant, less 'artistic'. And yet it is Richardson – more than anyone else, with the possible exception of Gertrude Stein – who never faltered for any cause, person or purpose from her single-minded pursuit of the truthfulness and integrity of her own existence and her recording of it.

Chapter 5

Amy Lowell's garden

Amy Lowell's name – if it means anything to readers now – perhaps conjures up images of poppy seeds, lilies, spring days and faintly remembered poems in the Imagist style. Or it may recall stories that made her a legend in her own time; stories about her obesity, her eccentric habits, her cigar-smoking. The prevailing image handed to us is one of a fat, frustrated woman who penned the famous line 'I am a woman sick with passion.' But the image is wrong; and the line was not written about herself. Amy Lowell was a vigorous, outspoken and indefatigable supporter of the new poetry, a generous and warm friend to other writers, an important benefactor of the little magazines, and a poet whose best and most personal work reflects the deeply satisfying lesbian relationship she enjoyed with her partner, Ada Russell.

Born in 1874 into one of Boston's oldest and wealthiest families, Amy was the youngest of five children. She was brought up on the Lowell estate 'Sevenels', in a suburb of the city. Her father continued the family business – cotton mills – although he was also a horticulturalist and an active civic leader. 'Sevenels' became a garden showplace, with its ten acres of beautiful grounds decked with exotic flowers, greenhouses and grape arbours. It isn't surprising that she inherited the Lowell love of flowers and that gardens play such an important role in her verse, symbolising love in poem after poem.

Amy's father Augustus was a rigidly disciplined man who rose at 4 a.m. for brisk swims in the summer and deskwork in the winter. Her mother Katherine was never really well after Amy's birth and spent little time with her youngest daughter. At eight years old, Amy was sent to a private day school. She was already overweight and her family already joked about it; for the rest of her life this problem remained with her. In adolescence it caused her much pain and made her an easy target for ridicule. As a defence, she became the class clown. But she was also witty and clever, writing stories from an early age; by the time she was twelve there were enough stories for her mother to collect and have privately printed as a little book called *Dream Drops by a Dreamer*, copies of which were sold at a charity bazaar.

This staid Victorian childhood reads rather like Bryher's English one, some two to three decades later. Amy, like Bryher, escaped as best she could by reading boys' adventure stories and by being a tomboy, trying to rebel in matters of dress and conduct. Beneath the rebellion, though, Amy was painfully aware of her appearance, recording in her diary, 'Really, you know, I am appallingly [*sic*] fat' and 'I am ugly, fat, conspicuous and dull; to say nothing of a very bad temper.'[1] Even so, she had to endure the torments of being a debutante: the dancing classes, teas and parties at which she felt stupid, awkward and ugly. Although she had schoolfriends, there was no one close enough for her to confide in. 'I feel very much in need of a *very* intimate friend' she wrote in her diary in 1889 at the age of 15, 'a friend whom I should love better than any other girl in the world, & who would feel so toward me. To whom I could tell all that is in my heart, and she would do so to me. We should love to be alone together, both of us.'[2] This wish – like the one Bryher records in *Two Selves* – remained with Amy until she was 38 years old, when it finally came true. In the meantime, she endured her loneliness stoically, and kept hoping.

In 1894, when Amy was 20, her mother died. She was left at 'Sevenels' with her father, since her brothers and sisters – much older than she was – had long ago left home. For a year or two she did her best to fit into Boston society and she even hoped for marriage. A young man did propose to her in 1897; but after she accepted, he withdrew his offer and disappeared.[3] Soon after this, Amy decided to do something about her weight and embarked, with several women friends, on a trip to Egypt. Sailing down the Nile in a comfortable boat, she stuck to a diet of nothing but tomatoes and asparagus. This regime, called 'banting', was supposed to shed pounds quickly, with the heat helping to sweat them off; but it didn't work for Amy. Instead, though she did lose some weight, she became seriously ill on her return to Boston. Her weakened physical condition, a combination of gastritis and hyperacidity, led to what she called 'nervous prostration', as she wrote later to H.D. in 1916: 'You see, my Dear Girl, I know what it is to have shattered nerves, I had nervous prostration for seven years once, and it is not a nice condition.'[4] In a letter to another friend she described it as 'the real thing, the kind where you live with a perpetual headache and the slightest sound jars you all over'.[5] At the time, she set out for California for the winter of 1897–8 to try to recuperate, but this venture met with little success. The following summer she decided to go to Devonshire in England, where the heavy cream and moderate climate were considered healthy. Gradually she got better and regained her old energy. The Egyptian trip did have one permanent effect, however; she swore she would never diet again.

In 1900, after her return from Devonshire, Augustus Lowell died. This left Amy, at 26, alone at 'Sevenels'. She wanted to keep the house and to remain living there, so she bought out her brothers' and sisters' shares. From now on the house would be associated only with her; and she began to make changes. Her major renovations were on the main floor, where she joined two large rooms in order to make an enormous library, with oak panelling, floor-to-ceiling bookcases, well-stuffed chairs and sofas, and two huge fireplaces. This room was large enough to use for amateur theatricals, another of Amy's interests. On the main floor, too, she turned the old billiard room into a music room decorated in dainty eighteenth-century French style. Her bedroom, which she called 'Sky Parlour', remained on the top floor; here she'd slept since she was a tiny child. Here, too, she had an enormous bed with 16 pillows always propped up behind her.

With control of 'Sevenels' and a considerable income, Amy Lowell began at last to feel like an adult. From now on she could create the kind of life she wanted. She was still plagued by her self-image; and she still hadn't found the friend she longed for; but she was a woman of means and she began to act like one.

Poetry had always been important to Amy; but she hadn't started to write verse herself until she was in her late twenties. In 1902, after watching the famous Eleanora Duse in *La Giaconda*, she noted:

I just knew that I had got to express the sensations that Duse's acting gave me, somehow. I knew nothing whatever about the

technique of poetry, I had never heard of vers libre, I had never
analyzed blank verse . . . I sat down, and with infinite agitation
wrote this poem . . . it loosed a bolt in my brain and I found out
where my true function lay.[6]

This determination never wavered, though it would be several years
before she attempted to have any of her poems published. She spent
her time on amateur theatricals, entertaining, and generally acting
as the squire of 'Sevenels'. In 1910 she sent off some poems to *The
Atlantic Monthly*, a prestigious Boston literary magazine, which
published 'A Fixed Idea' in the August issue. At the age of 36 she
was finally a published poet. By 1912 she was putting together a
collection in order to make a book. Then, that March, she met Ada
Dwyer Russell.

Born 11 years before Amy, in Salt Lake City, Utah, Ada Dwyer
was already an established actress when she married Harold Russell
in 1893. She kept on acting, even after the birth of her daughter
Lorna in 1894. In March 1912, when she was 49, she was playing in
The Deep Purple, which was a great success in Boston. Amy Lowell
was in the audience on the opening night and was immediately
taken with Ada.

When the two women met, during the run of the play, at Amy's
luncheon group, the attraction – at least from Amy's side – was
instant and sure. Like Bryher's immediate recognition of H.D. as
the friend she'd sought all her life; like Sylvia Beach's first
encounter with her lover Adrienne Monnier and Gertrude Stein's
with Alice Toklas; Amy's meeting with Ada Russell changed her
life at once and for ever. She would be alone no longer.

Ada, too, loved poetry. Amy invited her to dinner at 'Sevenels'
to hear Amy read her verse. Soon afterwards, Ada had to be back
on the road; but she promised to visit Amy's New Hampshire house
that summer. During their brief Boston acquaintance they'd
discovered mutual enthusiasms for flowers, long drives and – best of
all – for Amy's 'children', her sheepdogs. Ada's daughter was
grown up and her husband was a shadowy, background figure. She
seemed quite free; and she did come to the farm that summer. Amy
did her best, then and in the following two years, to persuade Ada
to give up the stage so they could live together. Ada wasn't yet
ready to do so – though she visited frequently – since she was still
much in demand.

During Ada's first summer visit, Amy received the prospectus of

Poetry: A Magazine of Verse, from its editor Harriet Monroe, in Chicago. Harriet had seen Amy's poems in *The Atlantic Monthly* and wanted her to contribute to the new magazine. Amy responded by sending $25 and a promise that poems would follow soon. In 1912, too, Amy's first collection of poems, *A Dome of Many-Coloured Glass*, was published in Boston. Unfortunately the book was reviewed badly, as a result of which Amy took to her bed with an attack of gastric neuralgia. She longed to have Ada with her; but as Ada was on tour, Amy recovered enough to join her in Atlantic City. She returned alone to 'Sevenels'; but soon had a fascinating new interest to pursue: it was 'Imagisme'.

Amy Lowell read H.D.'s first Imagist poems in *Poetry* in January 1913 and – so it's said – put down the issue exclaiming 'Why I too am an Imagiste!' She'd been struck immediately by the form of H.D.'s work; and by Pound's article on the 'Imagiste' method. She was so intrigued by both that she fired off an enquiry to Harriet Monroe, whom she'd met in Chicago earlier that year. Who was this Pound; how could she get in touch with him? She decided to go to London to find out and asked Harriet for an introduction. 'I enclose a check at our usual rate of $10 a page for your two poems', Harriet wrote back. 'Also a card of introduction to Mr Pound, who I think will be in London when you are there.'[7]

Having failed to persuade Ada to accompany her, Amy sailed alone for England in late June and installed herself at the Berkeley Hotel in Piccadilly. She met Pound; and at first they got on well. 'Miss Lowell is back from Paris, and pleasingly intelligent', Pound wrote to Harriet Monroe that August.[8] Pound placed Amy's poem 'In a Garden' in *The New Freewoman*, which had just been launched and for which he was acting as literary editor; and after Amy's return to America, they kept up a friendly correspondence. He asked her to keep sending him poems to place; and they discussed the idea of an Imagist anthology which Pound was putting together. They agreed that she should visit again the following summer, to talk and so she could meet the other Imagists, H.D. and Richard Aldington, who'd been travelling in Europe while she'd been in London. In addition, in one of his typical attempts at literary manipulation, Pound suggested that Amy might like to buy into *The New Freewoman* (which became *The Egoist* in 1914) when Dora Marsden gave up control. Amy wasn't interested, however, in trying to run a London magazine from Boston; and in any case Harriet Weaver soon stepped in to take over the London periodical.

Nevertheless, Amy was eager to return in the summer of 1914 to discuss Imagism and the proposed anthologies. This trip was to be important for many reasons; but perhaps the most important for Amy was that Ada at last agreed to come with her.

Ada had been taken ill while on tour during the winter of 1913–14; and Amy hurried out to Chicago to be with her. She persuaded Ada to come back with her to 'Sevenels' and to stay on a business basis, to help her with the books she was planning to write. Ada agreed; and their life together began in the spring of 1914. Amy was soon calling Ada 'Peter' or 'Mrs Pete', perhaps as an allusion to her belief that at last she had found her rock, her lifelong companion.[9]

In July 1914, the two women sailed to England with a maid, a car and a chauffeur; and settled in at the Berkeley. This time they met H.D. and her husband Aldington, as well as the Lawrences and John Gould Fletcher, all of whom became close and lasting friends. Pound, as usual, was busy organising everyone's social life; and gave a dinner which they all attended at the Dieudonné restaurant. Amy and Ada returned the gesture with a dinner in their rooms on 30 July. War was in the air, but was not much spoken of that night, except by Lawrence, who brought ominous rumours. Pound was in one of his ill-tempered moods and made fun of Amy's poetry. H.D. and Aldington rallied to Amy's support; they liked her and were tired of Pound's outbursts and machinations. The schism between the Imagists had begun; and Pound dissociated himself from the others' plan for an Imagist anthology.

With the others, however, Amy continued to get on famously, particularly with Lawrence, whom she saw as someone who could 'express in words the real throb, and misery, and gusto which [life] has'.[10] Towards H.D. and Aldington, she felt maternal, taking upon herself the task of trying to place H.D.'s poems in American magazines. On her return to America she began to give lectures about the new poetry to clubs and groups in Boston, New York and Chicago. In late 1915 she wrote to H.D.:

> I think we are gradually having a distinct effect upon poets and people here. It is slow and it is hard work, but it is coming . . . I have two lectures in New York next week: one before the Cosmopolitan Club, and one before the American Poetry Society . . . But I think that the most important thing of all is that this coming Anthology [the second *Some Imagist Poets*, 1916] should be a great advance on the last one . . .[11]

On a more personal note, she continues: 'I cannot tell you how I long to see you both. There are no two people in the world whom I miss so much and whom I feel it such a loss to be parted from.'[12] Soon she was sending them their share of the royalties from the first Imagist anthology, and, in addition, a little extra, knowing they were hard up. 'Please do not think anything about it,' she commented, 'and do not dream of paying it back. Take it as the most natural thing in the world, as I do.'[13] She was never-failing, too, in her encouragement of H.D.'s work, writing to her in June 1916:

> I know you are fearfully lonely, my Dear. I wish I were anywhere near, it would be so good if Ada and I could drop in on you at intervals and cheer you up, and it would be so good for us to have you near by. But you are a brave woman, Hilda, and a good poet, and I believe those two qualities are the ones necessary to make a great artist. I have no words to describe my admiration for your poems . . .[14]

Amy's support meant a lot to H.D., who was, at the time, trying to cope with the stillbirth she'd suffered, with her favourite brother's death and with Aldington's imminent departure for the front. Amy herself had come a long way from her years of nervous prostration and loneliness. Her relationship with Ada gave her the security she needed in order to reach out to others; as well as giving her the inspiration for her best poetry. From her second collection – *Sword Blades and Poppy Seed* – onwards, many of her poems celebrate Ada and their love:

> from 'Christmas Eve'
> You have lifted my eyes, and made me whole
> And given me purpose, and held me faced
> Toward the horizon you once had placed
> As my aim's grand measure.[15]

It's true that Amy Lowell's love poems suffer from self-censorship, since she disguises that she's writing about two women. Yet it's fair to say, too, that the intimacy of lesbian life could hardly have been openly depicted in the poetry of the time, not only for the obvious reason that social opprobrium would result, but more seriously because the masculine tradition of lyric writing had not then been questioned or even come under scrutiny. While Dorothy Richardson was quite clear about the masculine nature of the novelistic

tradition in European literature, the women poets were not yet
consciously aware that the same masculine precepts also controlled
and constrained lyric utterance.

In many of the love poems, Ada, the beloved, is associated with
gardens and flowers:

> When I think of you, Beloved
> I see a smooth and stately garden
> > 'Mise en Scène'

> You are quiet like the garden
> And white like the alyssum flowers
> > 'The Garden by Moonlight'[16]

An undisguised portrait of Ada and their domestic life together is
given in 'Madonna of the Evening Flowers' from *Pictures of the
Floating World* (1919):

> All day long I have been working.
> Now I am tired.
> I call: 'Where are you?'
> But there is only the oak-tree rustling in the wind.
> The house is very quiet, the sun shines in on your books.
> On your scissors and thimble just put down,
> But you are not there. Suddenly I am lonely:
> Where are you?
> I go about searching.
> Then I see you,
> Standing under a spire of pale blue larkspur,
> With a basket of roses on your arm.
> You are cool, like silver,
> And you smile.
> I think the Canterbury bells are playing a little tune.
>
> You tell me that the peonies need spraying,
> That the columbines have overrun all bounds,
> That the pyrus japonica should be cut back and rounded.
> You tell me all these things.
> But I look at you, heart of silver,
> White heart-flame of polished silver,
> Burning beneath the blue steeples of the larkspur,
> And I long to kneel instantly at your feet,
> While all about us peal the loud, sweet Te Deums of the
> > Canterbury bells.[17]

Amy and Ada spent most of their time at 'Sevenels', but spent the summers on the New Hampshire farm. Because of Ada's support, Amy was able to work well, keeping to her chosen routine of working all night and sleeping until three each afternoon:

> Mrs Russell made it possible for Miss Lowell to devote her entire time to writing. It was Mrs Russell who preserved the morning silence, quelled kitchen quarrels, got books from libraries, did bits of research, read proofs, informed guests they must leave when they were intruding on a creative period. In the evenings she criticized the latest poems; she listened to every composition before it was pronounced finished, standing proxy for the public; and so well did she act as comrade in art that Miss Lowell once suggested they put out a sign: 'Lowell & Russell, Makers of Fine Poems.'[18]

That Amy depended on Ada's critical judgment is evident all through her correspondence. In 1915 she wrote to Harriet Monroe, 'I have decided to leave in the last part of 'May Evening in Central Park.' Mrs Russell and I have read it over several times, and, although we see your point perfectly, to stop at the end of the first page makes a different poem of it . . .'[19] And Ada's role in the creative process is referred to in Amy's poem 'April':

> I will lie among the little squills
> And be delivered of this overcharge of beauty.
> And that which is born shall be a joy to you
> Who love me.[20]

Home life ran smoothly; and there was an established ritual for entertaining. Guests were invited for 7 p.m., but were left alone in the library to read the newspaper until 8, when Ada entered and invited them to the dining-room. Everyone was seated, and dinner was served, without Amy. At some point during the invariably large and old-fashioned meal – typically of oysters, soup, fish, meat, salad, dessert, fruit and appropriate wines – Amy would appear, together with her sheepdogs. Preceding courses were brought back for her while the guests continued. After dinner, they all moved to the library and gathered round the log fire with coffee, cigarettes, liqueurs and cigars. Amy smoked her favourite small, light Manila cigars, delighting in the procedure of unwrapping one and cutting off its tip. When the First World War threatened to cut off her supply, she ordered 10,000 of them.[21] The maid brought towels for the guests' laps as the dogs would sprawl on them; and Amy talked: brilliantly and at length. At 11 p.m. Ada would retire and a maid would put a cold supper on the table for Amy to eat during the night. At midnight the guests would leave; then Amy would settle down to work, in front of the fire in the library. Usually she worked until dawn, leaving a pile of manuscript for a secretary to type up in the morning.[22] During her day (which began at 3 p.m.), she would garden, play with her dogs, and go for walks and drives with Ada, as well as discuss her poems.

After 1914, time not spent at 'Sevenels' was mostly spent on the lecture circuit. Amy spoke in New York, Chicago, and elsewhere, always on poetry and always promoting the work of her friends H.D., Aldington and Lawrence, as well as her own. On her trips to New York before 1920 she became acquainted with the literary avant-garde that already included Djuna Barnes, Mina Loy and Marianne Moore. Because she was putting the Imagist anthologies together, she wanted to meet as many poets as possible. By 1917, *The Little Review*, with its editors Margaret Anderson and Jane Heap, had moved from Chicago to New York, so Amy renewed her friendship with them. Anderson had written to Amy in 1914 before beginning her new magazine, much as Harriet Monroe had done two years earlier: 'Yes indeed, I know your work – particularly 'The Forsaken' which we groaned over not having ourselves. I hope you'll please come to see us when you're in Chicago . . .'[23] Later that year, Amy contributed a considerable sum to *The Little Review* and Anderson wrote to thank her, calling her a 'Fairy Godmother'. As well as sending Anderson her own poems, Amy was, of course, still trying to place H.D.'s during these war years; and she succeeded in getting Anderson to accept several.

Whenever they visited New York, Amy and Ada stayed at a grand hotel, taking a five-room suite and a separate room for their maid; and at Amy's request, all the electric clocks were stopped and all the mirrors and other shiny objects were covered in black. Ada took all the telephone calls and entertained visitors, friends and reporters while Amy prepared or went over her lectures.[24] On one of these New York visits, in 1917, Amy ruptured some of her abdominal muscles while trying to move her bed. This led to a series of operations over the next several years, which eventually wore down her health. She kept up her active correspondence, however, with Harriet Monroe, H.D., Margaret Anderson and others; and of course kept writing verse.

The year 1917 wasn't all bad luck; it was then that Amy first heard from a young English admirer who signed herself 'Winifred Bryher'. Amy's critical study *Six French Poets* (1915) had first aroused her interest; and then, in reply to Bryher's letter, Amy sent her *Tendencies in Modern American Poetry*, which, as we've seen, introduced Bryher to H.D.'s poetry. Amy was a generous correspondent, writing to Bryher, 'I shall be very glad to hear from you whenever you care to write and to give you any advice in my power.'[25] Before long, Amy offered to try to place some of Bryher's poems in American magazines, which offer Bryher gratefully accepted. Next, Bryher sent part of the manuscript of *Development*, for which Amy eventually wrote a Preface. Harriet Monroe was one editor whom Amy successfully approached on Bryher's behalf; she wrote to Bryher: 'I had a letter from Miss Monroe yesterday, and she told me that she has just decided to take the three poems, 'Wakefulness' 'Rejection' and 'Waste', just as they are . . .'[26]

In her turn, Bryher was helping Amy's reputation in England, not only with her pamphlet *Amy Lowell: A Critical Appreciation*, but also with articles in London papers. Amy responded:

> You are doing wonderful work in the cause of poetry by your critical articles. Even Miss Monroe, who does not care very much for my work and who is one of the ones jealous of me because I have enough money to live on outside my work . . . has quoted your 'Saturday Review' article as extremely important . . .[27]

Bryher confided to Amy her desire to 'run away to America, live on what I can earn myself, and have adventures'.[28] When this dream came true in September 1920, Amy was there in New York to greet Bryher, H.D. and Perdita. Bryher related how it was, in her autobiographical novel *West* (1925):

> [Miss Lyall (Amy Lowell)] To-morrow I am going to drive you round the city, I want to feel you get the streets, the pulse of the machinery, the beauty, the barbaric splendour of it all. For it is barbaric, but I'm proud it is.
>
> [Nancy (Bryher)] I think it will take me a month to feel I've arrived.
>
> Haven't hitched my poems onto me yet. Am I a terrific disappointment?
>
> You couldn't disappoint anybody.
>
> Ah, so many think I'm the creature of my poems, young and in shot silk waiting for the sun to rise.

> I had seen your photograph, you know. But I can't imagine
> people. I have to meet them for them to become real to me.
> But your books were real. For five years now. It's three, isn't
> it, since I first wrote you?
> And that was a marvellous letter . . . I've been glad of your
> letters, you know, Nancy. And glad to meet you.
> It was awfully nice of you to come to the boat.[29]

After Bryher and H.D. returned to England, the correspondence
went on, although Amy remained closer to H.D. than to Bryher. In
1922, Amy was still trying to have H.D.'s work printed in America.
On her own account, she was still hard at work on her own poetry,
as well as researching a biography of John Keats. She began to have
hernia attacks; and soon after the biography was published in 1925,
she had such a serious attack that an operation was planned. At
least she had the satisfaction of seeing the Keats biography carry the
dedication she wanted: 'To A.D.R., This, and all my books. A.L.'
For years she'd wanted to dedicate each book to Ada, but
previously Ada had never allowed it.

Before the operation could be carried out, Amy suffered a
stroke. Ada was, as usual, at her side. 'Pete', said Amy, in a low
voice, 'a stroke.' After that, she lost consciousness and died the
next day, aged 51.[30] Ada was treated as a widow by all their friends;
and as literary executrix of Amy's estate, she took her job seriously.
Amy had kept meticulous files, including carbon copies of all her
outgoing letters. All these papers were given to Harvard University,
with one exception: Amy had asked that all Ada's letters to her be
burned, with which desire Ada complied.[31]

If no letters remain as testimony to their love and companionship,
many poems do, such as this one:

'In Excelsis'

You – you –
Your shadow is sunlight on a plate of silver;
Your footsteps, the seeding-place of lilies;
Your hands moving, a chime of bells across a windless air.

The movement of your hands is the long, golden running of light
from a rising sun;
It is the hopping of birds upon a garden-path.

As the perfume of jonquils, you come forth in the morning.
Young horses are not more sudden than your thoughts.

Your words are bees about a pear-tree,
Your fancies are the gold-and-black striped wasps
buzzing among
red apples.

I drink your lips,
I eat the whiteness of your hands and feet.
My mouth is open,
As a new jar I am empty and open.
Like white water are you who fill the cup of my mouth,
Like a brook of water thronged with lilies.

Do I tease myself that morning is morning and a day after?
Do I think the air a condescension,
The earth a politeness,
Heaven a boon deserving thanks?
So you – air – earth – heaven –
I do not thank you,
I take you,
and live.[32]

Chapter 6

French connections

Gertrude Stein's face looms like a monument out of all the histories of the expatriate twenties. With her short-cropped, iron-grey hair, sandalled feet, long robes and 200-pound frame she sat, like a Buddha, in her studio, receiving painters, writers and admirers. Truly convinced of her own genius, she wrote prolifically in an individualistic, experimental style. Exasperating to some, terrifying to others, a legend in her own time, she became as much part of the Paris landscape as Notre Dame. And always beside her was her partner Alice B. Toklas.

The two women met in 1907 in Paris when Gertrude was 34 and Alice 30. Gertrude's journey there had been more indirect than had Alice's. Born in Allegheny, Pennsylvania, in 1874, the youngest of five children, Gertrude spent her first five years in Europe with her parents. Her father was a successful businessman who eventually moved his family to San Francisco, where the children grew up in a large house with servants and a governess, although they all attended ordinary schools. When Gertrude was 14, her mother died; and then three years later, her father died also, leaving 26-year-old Michael in charge of the household. Gertrude, now 17, was sent off to an aunt in Baltimore and from there applied to the Harvard Annexe (now Radcliffe College). Her brother Leo, two years older, was also at Harvard; and they continued an already close relationship.

For the next four years Gertrude lived in a Cambridge boarding house and studied, principally philosophy. Her favourite teacher was William James whose courses motivated her to plan further study in psychology. She was advised that further progress would require a medical education, so after graduation from Radcliffe in 1897, she entered Johns Hopkins Medical School in Baltimore. Leo, who had been travelling, also came to Baltimore to pursue independent research at Hopkins.

Despite four years spent in medical school, Gertrude didn't graduate. Replying to a friend who urged her to graduate so as to further the cause of women in medicine, she said wryly, 'You don't know what it is to be bored!'[1] Indeed, having lost interest, she failed several of her final examinations and became disenchanted with medicine. In 1902 she sailed to Europe to join Leo. They planned to spend the winter in London. Leo had befriended Bernard Berenson and his wife Mary in Italy; and the Steins now became part of the circle at Friday's Hill, the home of Mary's parents outside London. Bertrand Russell, too, was there; he was married to Mary's sister, Alys Pearsall Smith. Gertrude and Leo rented a cottage nearby and Gertrude began to match wits with Russell and Berenson in long discussions, frequently about America versus Europe. From these exchanges grew the idea for her monumental work *The Making of Americans*.[2] Berenson, a small and fastidious man, was rather frightened of Gertrude, who was already, at 28, an imposing figure. She looked, said Berenson, like a statue from Ur of the Chaldees.[3]

After some weeks, Gertrude and Leo moved back to London to a boarding house at 20 Bloomsbury Square. During the dark, damp winter Gertrude spent long days in the British Museum Reading Room; but although she felt the effects of London quite as intensely as the English experimentalist Dorothy Richardson, she found them by no means as intoxicating:

> The time comes when nothing in the world is so important as the breath of one's own particular climate. If it were one's last penny it would be used for that return passage.
>
> An American in the winter fogs of London can realise this passionate need, this desperate longing in all its completeness. The dead weight of that fog and smoke laden air, the sky that never suggests for a moment the clean blue distance that has been the accustomed daily comrade, the dreary sun, moon and stars that look like painted imitations on the ceiling of a smoke-filled room, the soggy, damp, miserable streets, and the women with bedraggled, frayed-out skirts, their faces swollen and pimply with sordid dirt ground into them until it has become a natural part of

their ugly surface all become day after day a more dreary weight of hopeless oppression.[4]

The London winter sent Gertrude straight back to America; arriving in New York, she moved in with three friends, only to hear from Leo that he, too, had left London. He'd decided he wanted nothing more than to be a painter and to collect paintings; and had consequently found somewhere to live in Paris. This was 27 rue de Fleurus, near the Luxembourg Gardens, where Gertrude joined him in the summer of 1903.

A studio, or atelier, was attached to the two-storey apartment where Gertrude and Leo lived; and the studio soon became the focus of their lives. Its walls were hung with modern paintings and drawings by Cézanne, Matisse, Picasso and others, many of whom became friends, grateful that someone was buying their paintings at last. On Saturday evenings the Steins were 'at home', although the painters and other friends often came early to join Gertrude and Leo for dinner. Picasso, in particular, became a lifelong friend. The Stein evenings began around nine o'clock and generally went on till two or three in the morning.

Gertrude, too, had found her vocation. During her first summer in Paris she wrote her first novel, *Q.E.D.* (first published as *Things As They Are*, in 1950). Based on her relationships with two women she'd known in Baltimore while she was in medical school, the writing was astonishingly frank about the lesbian experiences shared by the three main characters. In this love-triangle there are no graphic sex scenes nor explicit mention of lesbianism; but neither is the language obscure or self-censored. The secret code-words and experimental style of her later work is not yet developed and the implications of the women's relationships are clear. Possibly for that reason, Gertrude chose to 'forget' this novel and didn't 'find' it again until the 1930s.

From now on, her main occupation was her own writing; but before long, something happened that made everything infinitely easier and happier for her. She fell in love with Alice Toklas. Tiny, dark, Alice Babette Toklas, who dressed in flowered print dresses and elaborate earrings, had just reached her own critical thirtieth year when she walked into the Paris apartment of Gertrude's brother Michael and saw Gertrude sitting there:

a golden brown presence, burned by the Tuscan sun and with a glint in her warm brown hair. She was dressed in a warm brown corduroy suit. She wore a large round coral brooch and when she talked, very little, or laughed, a good deal, I thought her voice came from this brooch. It was unlike anyone else's voice – deep, full, velvety, like a great contralto's, like two voices.[5]

Alice had just arrived in Paris during that autumn of 1907. Born in 1877 in San Francisco and brought up there, she'd begun training at the University of Washington for a career as a concert pianist. Her studies were interrupted, however, by her mother's death; and she returned home to care for her father and younger brother. She didn't give up her hopes of a concert career and therefore kept up her work at the piano, as well as pursuing her interests in art and theatre. She also read a great deal, was an accomplished cook and needlewoman and had a circle of interesting friends. She felt no attraction for men, but enjoyed romantic episodes with women, although she'd never become involved in the agonising situations Gertrude shows in *Q.E.D.*

In 1906, after the great earthquake had ruined much of San Francisco, Gertrude's brother Michael and his wife Sarah returned to see if their property had been damaged and were introduced to Alice by a mutual friend. Alice was fascinated by their descriptions of life in Paris, especially by their talk of modern art and painters. Sarah liked Alice so much that she invited her to return with them, but Alice declined, instead suggesting that her old friend Annette Rosenshine should go. Annette did go with the Steins and, through her, Gertrude began to hear about Alice.

Gertrude was still interested in individual psychology and became fascinated by Annette as a case in amateur psychoanalysis. Annette was a rather unhappy young woman, who suffered from a cleft palate. She agreed to confide all her fears and problems to Gertrude, who also asked to see all her correspondence. From the letters Alice wrote to Annette, Gertrude learned of Alice's romantic attachments to two other women friends, knowledge which would be important when she and Alice finally met during the following year.

Back in San Francisco, Alice thought more and more about Paris, and finally made plans to go there, together with her friend Harriet Levy. They arrived in the late autumn of 1907, checked into a hotel, and almost immediately went to call on Michael and Sarah Stein. Having now met Alice, Gertrude invited her to call at rue de Fleurus on the following day, to see the paintings and go for a walk.

Alice heard bells; signifying, she said later, that she'd met a genius.[6]

Alice indeed visited Gertrude on the following day and they went walking in the Luxembourg Gardens. It was the first walk of many. Their attachment was intense from the beginning. It was a critical time in both their lives; Gertrude had just finished another novel (*Three Lives*) which was about to be printed at her own expense, and had started on *The Making of Americans*, her grand epic. Leo, her once-adored brother, had no interest in her writing and even seemed opposed to it, telling her that her *Americans* was no good. Gertrude, of course, intended to go on; but she needed support, encouragement and approval.[7] Alice, for her part, was already 30 and without a vocation. Gertrude's need, and her genius, could provide one. She would be the beloved 'wife', helping Gertrude not only in domestic matters, but as editor, sounding-board, typist, manager and secretary.

By December 1908, Alice had assumed most of these tasks. She was still living in an apartment with Harriet Levy, but went every morning to rue de Fleurus to type up the latest manuscript of *The Making of Americans*.[8] Soon their days took on a routine pattern: Alice arrived early in the morning to type; Gertrude rose at about 1 p.m. and took coffee with Alice while Alice ate lunch, during which time they would discuss the writing; then Alice returned to her apartment and Gertrude worked on her manuscript; and finally Alice would return in the evening for several hours before going home for the night.[9] Day by day they became closer, although they were not yet lovers. In the summer of 1909, when *Three Lives* was published, Alice took over distribution problems and subscribed to a clippings bureau to keep track of reviews. Gertrude then wrote the first of her pieces in which Alice appears. The 'Ada' of the story is Alice, who takes care of her widowed father, then leaves, then falls in love:

> Trembling was all living, living was all loving, some one was then the other one. Certainly this one was loving this Ada then. And certainly Ada all her living then was happier in living than any one else who ever could, who was, who is, who ever will be living.[10]

By the time of this story, Gertrude had proposed to Alice and Alice had accepted. Gertrude's piece 'Didn't Nelly and Lilly Love You'[11] tells, in the cryptic style Gertrude adopted, how the proposal was made. Although the narrator is referred to as 'he', it is clearly

Gertrude who is the husband. As Lillian Faderman has suggested,[12] Gertrude's use of 'he' and 'husband' for herself and 'wife' and 'bride' for Alice is as much a device to deceive the censors as a real description of their respective roles. The husband issued the orders:

> May I say, I passionately may say, can you obey.
> Remember the position. Remember the attention that
> you pay to what I say.[13]

But it is also the husband who realises what good fortune has arrived in the person of Alice: 'I am a husband who is very very good and I have a character that covers me like a hood and must be understood which it is by my wife whom I love with all my life . . .'[14]

In this, and many other poems and stories, Gertrude told about her private life with Alice, from cooking and walks and conversations, to their most intimate sexual practices. In order to do this, and have her work published, Gertrude invented a secret language as well as a cryptic style, characterised by repetition and deletion of key words.[15] The most obvious sexual allusion in her work, occurring over and over again, is the word 'cow', which seems synonymous with orgasm. 'As a Wife Has a Cow A Love Story', for instance, is a two-page description of love-making. It was written in 1923 and included in *The Selected Writings of Gertrude Stein*, published in 1946. The piece ends:

> Have it as having having it as happening, happening to have it as happening, having to have it as happening. Happening and have it as happening and having it happen as happening and having to have it happen as happening, and my wife has a cow as now, my wife having a cow as now, my wife having a cow as now and having a cow as now and having a cow and having a cow now, my wife has a cow and now. My wife has a cow.[16]

Alice finally moved in with Gertrude in July 1910, after her friend Harriet left for America. For the next 36 years, until Gertrude's death, they were together; and more together than any other partnership in their circle, either lesbian or heterosexual. They never took separate vacations, separate apartments or entertained separately. Soon after Alice moved in, Leo moved out; and by 1912 it was Gertrude and Alice who hosted the famous Saturdays.

The First World War interrupted life for everyone. Gertrude and Alice spent part of it in Spanish Mallorca, where Gertrude continued her writing. After returning to France, they volunteered for war work and by the end of the war were helping refugees in Alsace.

Back at rue de Fleurus after the war ended, the two women found that life didn't resume as it had been before. English and American expatriates began to flock to Paris, and Gertrude found herself something of a cult figure within the expatriate community. Her work had been appearing in numerous of the little magazines; had been praised in New York; and her friends Mabel Dodge and Mina Loy, whom she'd known in Florence before the war, had been publicising her work in the literary milieu of New York's Greenwich Village. Gertrude and Alice began visiting the new American bookshop 'Shakespeare & Company', run by Sylvia Beach, who became a good friend. Sylvia directed admiring young American writers to rue de Fleurus; and it was possibly Mina Loy who introduced her friend Robert McAlmon to Gertrude soon after his arrival in 1921.

McAlmon was impressed by Gertrude and her work and agreed to try to publish *The Making of Americans* at the Contact Publishing Company. Through him, Gertrude and Alice met Bryher and H.D. Bryher in particular became a devoted friend, later asking Gertrude to contribute to *Close-Up* soon after she and Macpherson had started it. Gertrude obliged with a story. 'The rue de Fleurus,' wrote Bryher, 'if I were not with Adrienne [Monnier] and Sylvia, was the only place in Paris where I felt at home.'[17]

The Little Review was one magazine that had published Gertrude's work; and when the editors Margaret Anderson and Jane Heap came to Paris in 1923, they called on Gertrude and Alice. Gertrude liked Jane immensely and the two remained close friends until Jane's involvement with Gurdjieff became too much for Gertrude.

Alice and Gertrude went, too, to Natalie Barney's Friday afternoon salons, where they heard the latest lesbian gossip. Gertrude, however, relied less on her friendships with other women than did any other women writers in our network. By contrast, throughout the twenties she created her own circle of followers, who were mostly men, some of whom – Carl van Vechten and Thornton Wilder, for example – were a tremendous help to her career. From her point of view, Alice gave her everything she needed for her personal satisfaction and growth:

Little Alice B. is the wife for me . . .

Little Alice B. so tenderly is born so long as she
can be born along by a husband strong who has not his hair
    shorn . . .
You are my honey honey suckle.
I am your bee.[18]

The couple lived contentedly together in Paris and in their country house, with their white poodle, Basket. Alice kept her roles as protectress, editor, typist, cook, companion and general manager. People flocked to see the famous 'monument'; but very often Alice made an equally strong impression. In 1933, Gertrude published her most popular book. *The Autobiography of Alice B. Toklas*; and Alice, too, became a household word. They went through another world war together, spent mainly in the country at Bilingin where – now aged 66 and 63 – they survived rationing and the threat to them as Jews of being sent to concentration camps.

In the autumn of 1944, after the liberation of France, they moved back to Paris. They were busy after the war. Gertrude spent time speaking to American troops in Germany and Belgium, as well as in France. Within a year, however, it became obvious that Gertrude was very ill. She was in the American Hospital in Paris with an intestinal problem waiting for a scheduled operation when she died of cancer on 27 July 1946.

Alice, at 69, was a widow. She devoted her remaining 20 years, as she had her previous 38, to Gertrude's work, organising her papers for Yale University, helping numerous Stein scholars, and corresponding with many people about Gertrude and her writing. She found time, too, to write two cook-books and the memoir *What Is Remembered*.[19] When she died at the age of 89, she was buried, as she'd wished, with Gertrude in Père Lachaise Cemetery in Paris. Both their names are carved into the granite block marking the grave.

Gertrude and Alice had met many women couples, some since more celebrated than others. But just as Gertrude needed to function autonomously as a writer, so, too, there were those who needed to function autonomously in their chosen areas. Not least of these were two women who played an immense part in servicing the literature created in the Paris of the twenties: Sylvia Beach and Adrienne Monnier. Sylvia's English language bookshop and library 'Shakespeare & Company' was both a meeting place and a melting-pot for the host of writers and painters who crowded there.

Sylvia Beach, too, was an American expatriate. She was born in 1887 and grew up in Princeton, New Jersey, although she travelled a great deal in Europe with her mother and three sisters. Her mother preferred to live separately from her husband, a Presbyterian minister, reputedly because she didn't like sex. Sylvia went to Europe during the First World War and helped the Red Cross in Serbia just after the war ended. She then decided to settle in Paris. Her mother supported her, giving her the funds she needed to open the bookshop and, although she wasn't wealthy, she continued to send her daughter money, sometimes selling her jewellery and other possessions in order to do so.

In 1917 Sylvia met Adrienne Monnier who had a French language bookshop selling works by modern French writers. The two became close friends, especially so when Sylvia opened her own shop in 1919 and after Adrienne's partner, Suzanne Bonnière, died in the same year. Sylvia's first shop was on rue Dupuytren, but in 1921 she moved it to the street in which Adrienne had her shop (and living quarters above), rue de l'Odéon. Before long, Sylvia moved in with Adrienne and they lived together until 1937, when Sylvia moved to live above her own shop after Adrienne became involved with Gisèle Freund, the photographer.

Through 'Shakespeare & Company' Sylvia got to know virtually every one of the American and English writers living in, or passing through Paris in the years her shop was open, 1919 till 1940. She is best known for publishing the first edition of Joyce's *Ulysses* and for years of devoted service (and funds wrung from her meagre resources) given to Joyce and his work. She became a good friend of Harriet Weaver in the 1920s because of their shared support of Joyce; and she made friends, too, with Gertrude and Alice, Natalie Barney, Djuna Barnes, Mina Loy, Margaret Anderson and Jane Heap, Kay Boyle, Mary Butts, and of course Bryher, who helped to support the shop. After Adrienne died in 1955, Sylvia wrote, 'My loves were Adrienne Monnier and James Joyce and Shakespeare and Company.'[20]

Margaret Anderson, who founded *The Little Review*, also spent time in Paris. Born in Indianapolis, Indiana, into a middle-class family, she grew up to be extremely romantic and idealistic. In 1906 she went to Chicago where she worked on newspapers, writing book reviews and later becoming literary editor of a religious paper in 1913. By this time, however, she'd decided to start her own magazine. She had no capital of her own, but was a very successful fund-raiser. One friend, Dewitt Wing, gave most of his salary to the new venture; and others provided advertisements and donations. In 1916 she met Jane Heap, who became her companion and associate editor. After another struggling year, they moved with the magazine to New York in 1917, the year in which Pound became its foreign correspondent. From the connection with Pound flowed contributions from Joyce, H.D. and T.S. Eliot, as well as from Pound himself. In New York, Margaret and Jane became friendly with the Provincetown Players group, and therefore met Djuna Barnes, Mina Loy, Alfred Kreymborg, William Carlos Williams, Robert McAlmon, and others. In 1922 and 1923, they took the *Review* to Paris, where they met Gertrude Stein, Sylvia Beach and Pound, as well as already established friends who had also gone to Paris, including Barnes, Loy and McAlmon. Through Robert McAlmon they met Bryher and H.D.

Before long, Margaret handed over *The Little Review* to Jane Heap, to go off with her new love, Georgette LeBlanc, a singer, with whom she lived for the next 20 years until LeBlanc's death. She remained friendly with Jane Heap and indeed both women became involved together with Gurdjieff. Margaret Anderson edited the last issue of the magazine in 1929. After LeBlanc's death in 1942, Margaret lived with Enrico Caruso's widow, Dorothy, until she, too, died in 1955. From then on Margaret Anderson lived mainly in France until her own death in 1973.

Chapter 7

Djuna Barnes: 'A most extraordinary and unusual time of it'

Djuna Barnes, the dashing cape-lady of the Paris café twenties, was tall, red-haired and striking. Best known for her experimental novel *Nightwood* (and T.S. Eliot's championship of it), she was also an experimental playwright, successful journalist, artist and poet. She died at 92, an embittered recluse, in New York's Greenwich Village where her career had begun in 1913.

Born in 1892 in rural New York state, her unconventional family life and her reaction to it provides a key to her personality and her choice of lifestyle and friends, as well as to her writing. Unconventionality began with names in her family; her father, Wald Barnes, had been born Henry Budington, but when his parents divorced, he stayed with his mother and assumed her maiden name (as did she also), which was Barnes. He changed his first name a number of times before settling on 'Wald', when he was in his twenties. His mother Zadel was a convinced feminist long before feminism became fashionable, and was, too, a prolific writer, publishing stories and poems in major American magazines throughout the 1870s and 1880s, as well as a number of novels and journalistic articles, often on feminist themes. After divorcing her first husband, she married again but soon left her second husband, with whom she'd moved to London, and returned to America with Wald and his new wife, an Englishwoman named Elizabeth Chappell.

Djuna's grandmother Zadel stayed with her son's family as it grew. Wald built a house for them on the country estate of his older brother Justin Budington, who had become a wealthy New York eye doctor. It seems that Zadel was in charge of her grandchildren's education; both she and Wald believed strongly in individualism and both disapproved of formal schooling. Besides Djuna, there were four brothers, all with unconventional names: Thurn, Zendon, Saxon and Shangar.

Even more unconventional than their names, however, was the Barnes lifestyle. Wald Barnes made what amounted to a religious cult out of sex; he had numerous mistresses and various illegitimate children, some of whom lived with his wife and legitimate children for periods of time. According to Djuna, Wald Barnes would carry a wet sponge with him when he went horseriding, just in case he might meet some woman or other with whom he could have sex (which apparently he often did).[1] Djuna's childhood was so traumatic that it haunted her for the rest of her life; it is even thought by some[2] that she was raped – on her father's instructions and with her mother's collusion – by a farmhand when she was fourteen or fifteen. Scenes of rape, incest, sodomy and bestiality occur frequently in her work, which – taken as a whole – often creates a twisted nightmare world where sex and sexual identity lie at the centre. Certainly her attitudes towards men were shaped to some extent by her father. In an early play called *To the Dogs* she shows a relationship between a 35-year-old woman, Helena Hucksteppe, and her neighbour, Gheid Storm, who is 'decidedly masculine. He walks deliberately, getting all the use possible out of his boot-leather, his belt-strap and hat-bands. His face is one of those which, for fear of misuse, has not been used at all.'[3] This man 'vaults the window-sill', lands in Helena's living-room and proceeds to try to seduce her with compliments. Helena, however, is more than a match for him:

> Storm: [Without attempting to hide his admiration] I've watched your back: 'There goes a fine woman, a fine silent woman; she wears long skirts, but she knows how to move her feet without kicking up a dust – a woman who can do that, drives a man mad.'
> In town there's a story that you come through once every Spring, driving a different man ahead of you with a riding whip; another has it, that you come in the night –
> Helena: In other words, the starved women of the town are beginning to eat.
> Storm: [Pause] Well [laughs] I like you.
> Helena: I do not enjoy the spectacle of men ascending.[4]

Neither did Djuna Barnes. Helena's cryptic conversation, with its heavy sarcasm, quick wit, and scorn, defeats Gheid's attempts at seduction. From all accounts, it sounds much like Djuna's own sharp-tongued repartee. It reflects, too, her hostile attitude towards the 'masculine' man of her father's type.

Djuna lived on the farm with her parents, brothers and grandmother until she was 16. All the children helped with the farmwork: milking, ploughing, and planting; and were taught at home by grandmother Zadel. It was Elizabeth, Djuna's mother, who finally made the break with Wald in 1908, when she and the children moved to a farm in Huntington, Long Island, at the opposite end of the state. After helping her mother on this farm for a while, Djuna began to plan a literary career. She started sending poems off to magazines before she was 18. By 1911, at the age of 19, she had had her poem 'The Dreamer' published in *Harper's* (24 June 1911) and was trying to have others accepted. Her grandmother's literary contacts helped her reach editors; in particular, to reach Robert Davis at Frank A. Munsey Company in New York, which published a number of popular magazines: *Munsey's Magazine*, *The Argosy*, *The Scrap Book*, *The Cavalier*. Davis took an interest in the young writer:

> Dear Miss Barnes,
>   Thank you for Harper's containing 'The Dreamer'. There is much fine imaginative work in these twelve lines, and I am glad indeed to have read it . . .
>   I hope you found something pleasant in the books I lent you.
>   Under separate cover I am sending you another entitled 'In the Midst of Life.' Ambrose Bierce, the author, comes nearer to understanding the English language than any other writer of fiction I know . . . Some of his stories are very harsh and brutal and will wound you. But that, after all, does not amount to very much when one considers that the ability to recover even from pain is measured out to all of us.
>   Please give my compliments to Mrs Gustafson [Zadel] . . .[5]

That this advice was important to her is evidenced by her own later work, which could well be described as 'harsh and brutal'; as well as by the fact that she kept this letter with her until she died. It is indeed one of very few early letters that she did keep.

Soon after this exchange with Davis, Djuna left Long Island and moved into New York City. She was 20 years old. No longer did young women necessarily sit at home waiting for marriage offers;

and in any case, Djuna had already witnessed the collapse of her parents' marriage and the resultant financial uncertainty. By 1913 she was making a living as a freelance journalist, writing for the big daily New York newspapers *The Press*, *The World* and *Brooklyn Daily Eagle*. A talented artist, she often illustrated her own feature articles, and she wrote on controversial topics. In 'How It Feels To Be Forcibly Fed'[6] she described what happened to her after she'd volunteered to undergo this horrible process. The imprisoned English suffragettes who were suffering forced feeding were in the news at the time and there was talk of using the procedure on women labour agitators in American prisons. Djuna went to a hospital, where she was fed pea soup through tubes forced into her nose. The story and photographs are graphically dramatic; every minute of the ordeal is described in detail.

Djuna Barnes lived alone in Greenwich Village, where she met many other young writers and actors. Rather like London's Kensington in the same years, the Village was a definable neighbourhood, known for its bohemian inhabitants. Anyone who lived there and frequented the local cafés and bars, in particular the Brevoort Hotel bar on lower Fifth Avenue, sooner or later was bound to meet everyone who was involved in writing and theatre. And so Djuna Barnes, in her turn, was taken to Mabel Dodge's[7] 'evenings' where she mingled with radical activists, poets, painters and socialites. She joined the Provincetown Players group on Macdougal Street; and in her spare time, wrote poetry. Soon she came to the attention of the infamous Guido Bruno, a literary entrepreneur with a reputation as a ladies' man. He published a variety of short-lived periodicals and pamphlets by Village writers, hawking them from his apartment above Washington Square, the centre of Village life. Bruno published Djuna Barnes' first 'book', the pamphlet *Book of Repulsive Women*, in 1915.

The overtly lesbian *Repulsive Women* became an underground hit in the Village. At twenty-three, Djuna was exploring her own sexual identity and was in love with the beautiful red-haired poet, Mary Pyne. They probably met through the Provincetown Players group, which included – at one time or another – John Reed, Louise Bryant, George Cram Cook, Susan Glaspell, Hutchins Hapgood, Mary Heaton Vorse, Mabel Dodge, Neith Boyce, Eugene O'Neill, Alfred Kreymborg, Mina Loy, Laurence Vail and Edna Millay. At the time of their meeting, Mary Pyne was married to the poet Harry Kemp, also a Player, while Djuna herself was involved with an older man called Courtenay Lemon, another writer and Player. In spite of these attachments, the two women fell in love; and it was Djuna who nursed Mary until she died, in that same year, from TB. One letter from Djuna to Courtenay survives to describe that grim situation:

> Dearest Courtenay,
> Mary has been given up by 2 nurses, 2 doctors & a score of others at least 10 days back, but she still breaths [sic] – lies on her left side for the first time & is living on oxygen . . . Harry [Kemp] seems restive . . .[8]

After Mary's death, Djuna wrote and dedicated to her memory a group of poems which she sent to Harriet Monroe at *Poetry*. They were rejected and remained unpublished until 1923:

SIX SONGS OF KHALIDINE
To the Memory of Mary Pyne

The flame of your red hair does crawl and creep
Upon your body that denies the gloom
And feeds upon your flesh as 't would consume
The cold precision of your austere sleep –
And all night long I beat it back, and weep.

It is not gentleness but mad despair
That sets us kissing mouths, O Khalidine.
Your mouth and mine, and one sweet mouth unseen
We call our soul. Yet thick within our hair
The dusty ashes that our days prepare.

The dark comes up, my little love, and dyes
Your fallen lids with stain of ebony,
And draws a thread of fear 'tween you and me
Pulling thin blindness down across our eyes –
And far within the vale a lost bird cries.

Does not the wind moan round your painted towers
Like rats within an empty granary?
The clapper lost, and long blown out to sea
Your windy doves. And here the black bat cowers
Against your clock that never strikes the hours.

And now I say, has not the mountain's base
Here trembled long ago unto the cry

'I love you, ah, I love you!' Now we die
And lay, all silent, to the earth our face.
Shall that cast out the echo of this place?

Has not one in the dark funereal
Heard foot-fall fearful, born of no man's tread,
And felt the wings of death, though no wing spread
And on his cheek a tear, though no tear fell –
And a voice saying without breath 'Farewell!'[9]

After Mary's death, Djuna lived with Courtenay Lemon and – it is assumed – married him, though no legal record of the marriage has as yet been found. They shared a large Village apartment within an even larger house, with a number of other writers and artists from the Players group. Edmund Wilson described this apartment, located at 86 Greenwich Avenue, years later:

> that cavernous old house, where Fitzy, Stark Young, Dorothea Nolan and Djuna Barnes once all lived at the same time – with its wastes and stretches of linoleum, its steep staircases and rambling halls, its balustrades, its broken skeleton hatrack in a marble-framed niche, its high square-topped radiators, its enormous vestibule doors, its mysterious inside windows covered over with cloths from within, the desolation of its corridors, the interminable and exhausting climbs of stairs, the yellow plaster and yellow woodwork, the smell of bathrooms, the sound of dripping bathtubs and defective toilets.[10]

Djuna continued to write articles; but also worked more and more on plays, short fiction and poetry. At first she was awed by Lemon's mind:

> My husband was a scholar, he really had a fine mind . . . He works on the *American* to earn a living – and uses his money to buy books . . . He's writing a book on the philosophy of criticism – but it'll never be finished. He's been working on it seven years . . . He had me absolutely stunned so that I didn't know whether I was coming or going . . . Oh, you couldn't pry me away from him . . .[11]

Nevertheless, by 1919 the marriage was over. Djuna's joking explanation to Edmund Wilson explains in part – 'He thought earrings were very foolish; he couldn't understand why I should want to wear earrings . . . But I couldn't stand it any longer!'[12] – but letters between Djuna and Lemon written at the time are more illuminating. In a postcard stamped 28 July 1919 from Woodstock, N.Y., and addressed to Lemon at 86 Greenwich Avenue, Djuna writes, 'Haven't made up my mind yet when I'll come back – Have you read my poems over – Be good & sleep – '[13] And in an undated letter written later in 1919, she says:

> Dear Courtenay,
>   You promised that you would not trouble me again – I have nothing to say & nothing which I want to listen to.
>   I know this sounds unkind – but it is final – I can't be tortured any more.
>   Djuna[14]

There is, too, part of the story from Lemon's side, in an undated letter presumably written in late 1919 or early 1920:

> Dear Djuna –
>   Forgive me – I can't help it – Please do not blame yourself – it is all simply an unfortunate accident, for which fate is more to blame than you or I. After all, what's the difference – I simply don't exist any more – & there's an end to it. Try to regard it simply as if I had been run over by a trolley-car. I would like to write more but I can't. Forgive me & forget – or remember only the happiness you gave me before I retired to the nothingness where we must all go soon anyhow. I no longer blame you for anything – you did not & cd not know – & I wrecked everything by not making sufficient allowances. I love & bless you & trust to yr strength of intellect to pull you through to the interesting, fruitful life that this false start should not be allowed to blight.[15]

It's easy enough to speculate about Lemon's 'you did not & cd not know – & I wrecked everything by not making sufficient allowances.' Was he referring to her lesbianism? To her frigidity? To something – an affair – he had had? It remains unclear; but from this time on, with the exception of one relationship, Djuna was a loner. She did not try marriage again.

At the age of 27, her personal life was a shambles but her literary career had taken off. She published a play in the avant-garde magazine *Others* in 1918 and was accepted as a member of the group who published there: Alfred Kreymborg, William Carlos Williams, Man Ray, Marianne Moore, Mina Loy. This same group often met for evening parties which turned into poetry readings.

And by 1918, a new magazine had arrived in the Village, one that would shortly make Djuna Barnes' name; *The Little Review*.

Djuna met Margaret Anderson and Jane Heap soon after their arrival in New York with the fledgling *Review* in 1917, and befriended them. Many years later, in her autobiography, Margaret Anderson pointed to an 'intense maternity' in Djuna Barnes, a characteristic others also singled out in her;

> You two poor things, she would say in her warm laughing voice. You're both crazy of course, God help you. I suppose I can stand it if you can, but someone ought to look out for you. She looked out for us by bringing in the first strawberries of spring and the last oysters of winter, but to the more important luxuries of the soul she turned an unhearing ear. Djuna would never talk, she would never allow herself to be talked to. She said it was because she was reserved about herself.[16]

However, Margaret never became truly close to Djuna; and the reason may well have been Jane Heap. Some suggest that during this time Djuna and Jane had an affair. Certainly Djuna was extremely fond of Jane and kept a picture of her on the mantelpiece.[17] In any case, the *Review* editors' style – flamboyant, outgoing (gushing, on Margaret's side), openly lesbian – never really suited Djuna, who was – even then – more reserved and solitary. Personal differences, however, didn't prevent Margaret from admiring and publishing Djuna's work. They kept up a correspondence, too; and remained friends, if at a distance, all their lives. When Djuna heard of Jane Heap's death in 1964, she wrote to Margaret:

> Dear Martie,
>   Arlie has just phoned me of the death of Jane . . . I never get the American papers, so I do not know why or how; death bringing everything full circle, she's at home again; and that house being yours, I send my sympathy.
> Always affectionately,
> Djuna[18]

Whether or not Djuna had an affair with Jane in 1918–19, she was certainly experimenting with sex. On her own account, she had nineteen male lovers during this period; and then gave up dealing with men and took on a woman lover.[19] Some of the men linked with her at this time were the bisexual artist Marsden Hartley, the

rich writer–playboy Laurence Vail, the young publisher Horace
Liveright, and Provincetown Player Jimmy Light.[20] She was,
though, never attracted to the 'masculine' kind of man, the Wald
Barnes type. Such men she treated with scorn, both in her life and
in her writing. Her close male friends – some of whom were lovers –
were, on the whole, either bisexual or homosexual: Hartley, van
Vechten, McAlmon and Charles Henri Ford, for example.

During this time, too, Djuna was making the contacts that would
lead to her joining the Paris expatriate circle in the twenties. She
probably met Mina Loy in 1917, when Mina was in the Village and
publishing in *Others*. Man Ray photographed them both in that
year; and both were active in the Provincetown Players at the time.
They became firm friends, though after Mina began her affair with
Arthur Cravan, they didn't see so much of each other. Their
friendship resumed when Mina returned to the Village in 1920 after
Cravan's disappearance; and they became even closer when they
shared the same apartment building in Paris, later in the decade.
McAlmon, who met them both in 1920, has left a vignette of the two
women in his autobiographical novel *Post-Adolescence*, written in
1920 and published by Contact in 1923. The Mina Loy character,
'Gusta Rolph', opens a conversation with the Djuna Barnes
character, 'Beryl Marks':

> 'I intended going out this afternoon to see if I couldn't get some
> fashion designing work to do, but my will seems paralyzed for the
> time being. What's the use of any kind of movement', she said
> hardly. 'Don't mind me, Miss Marks; I'm just not up to being
> anything but wearing upon your nerves at the moment until I get
> a cup of coffee within me. My mind will keep wondering about
> that husband of mine – whether he's really drowned or not. If it
> had only been my first husband so he couldn't pester me about
> the children.'
>
> 'You have children – and in the plural – were they accidents?'
> Beryl asked.
>
> 'No, not quite. The third, who is only two, I wanted because I
> liked her father so much. The other two I rather wanted because I
> detested their father so much, and thought they'd keep me from
> reflecting on that all the time. I married so young that it took me
> some years to have sense enough to break away, and we lived in a
> horrible conventional English environment in Florence. One got
> to thinking there might be nothing else in the world.

'My children ain't. I took well care to see that they weren't, though one operation nearly did me in', Beryl commented, and laughed raucously. 'And there's some tell me that I'm all mother and should have seventeen, but who'd keep them? I, like a poor boob, have spent most of my young life supporting men, brothers, one husband, and lovers through some periods. I've no luck at all.'

'We'll have to form a union of women to show the men up, and make ourselves exhibits A and B of horrible examples.'[21]

Both Djuna and Mina were emotionally worn-out, disillusioned with men, and ready to change their lives. Djuna was 28 and making a living from writing, was part of an avant-garde crowd, but was restless. She may well have said, as McAlmon's Beryl Marks does (in conversation with the McAlmon character, Peter):

'Ho, ho, for God's sake? Me have energy? I've been dragging my hips around New York for the last five years ready to be taken away to the dump heap, and still these male editors I want to sell special articles to try to feel my figure, or comment on my shape, when I go to market with my literature. You'd think they'd have learned there are mirrors in the world by now, but no, they think it's the great compliment for them to insinuate they're ready to play with you.'

'Have another drink' Peter said.

'Asti spumante, dearie. Oh dearie, what asti spumante can do for one?' Beryl talked. 'Sure; my gut's in a hell of a shape already, but order me some more of that firewater – what is it? I was interviewing Loraine Dale, that show girl, about her divorce yesterday, and she dearie-d me all over the map, talking about the Asti Spumante she used to get in Italy, and what a glass of it could do for her life. She got real chummy with me, and showed me 600 photographs of herself in the nude or near nude. She wanted me to understand just what it was that made her so appealing to the various husbands she's grabbed out of the rag bag. Buh-lieve me dearie, but buhlieve me, you don't mind my calling you dearie, but buhlieve me, why should I go on the stage again, when that big stiff I'm divorcing has ten cold million bucks. I ain't the kind of woman to be treated like a bauble. I make them pay, buhlieve me dearie. I do wish I had some asti spumante to offer you . . . That's the kind of thing I have to write refined interviews from; can you see me?'[22]

McAlmon's rendering of Djuna's conversation is probably accurate; he had a good ear for dialogue. And, without a doubt, the sophisticated, fast-talking, wisecracking Barnes made a lasting impression on the 23-year-old McAlmon, who remained a lifelong friend.

Soon Djuna was on her way out of New York. The war was over; the word was that American dollars went a long way in Paris. Armed with introductions to Pound, Joyce and Stein, Djuna set sail for Europe in the summer of 1920.

The Hotel Angleterre on rue Jacob, the Left Bank, was a haven for Americans that year. Man Ray, Marsden Hartley, Berenice Abbott, Alfred Kreymborg, and others, all turned up there. Djuna spent most of her time there writing, 'in bed, and particularly in the mornings',[23] a habit she would keep throughout her life. Her breakfast was brought in every morning by the hotel chambermaid, so she had no need to leave her room until lunch time. Her old friend Laurence Vail turned up in Paris and introduced her to his bride-to-be Peggy Guggenheim. Peggy, a young American heiress, became an important friend and patron of Djuna, as well as of Mina Loy, partially supporting both of them in later years. Djuna also met Pound, recently moved to Paris from London, and already rushing about as usual, looking for writers and backers. Djuna recalled how he looked at the time:

> With his red head and beard, smocked in blue velvet, sashed in red and trousered in workingmans corduroys [*sic*] . . . used to appear walking up the Avenue de l'Opéra in broad daylight carrying a basket of lonster [*sic*] aubergines and fruit . . .[24]

By the late summer of 1921, McAlmon – now married to Bryher – had settled in Paris and was looking up old friends, including Djuna. Thanks to his arranged marriage with Bryher, he now had the money to travel and have fun. That year, Djuna joined him in Berlin, the wicked cabaret city; years later, recalling that time, he wrote to her: 'I've been writing something, maybe memoirs, I don't know, but remember you of the early Paris days, and Berlin, and the Russian jewellery, the orchids, not to speak of the absinthe, at the Adlon . . .'[25] And again, telling her how he'd come across her old letters:

> and am damn glad I saved them, because they are mainly from Berlin, of the old In Den Zelten, 18, Tiergarten, Berlin, when

Harrison Dowd was holding forth at the Eric Borchard nightclub
– whatever its name – and Thelma, Berenice, Marsden, and who
in hell else, were around and around, rounding the Adlon and tea
with absinthe, and your holding up a fork to ogle an old dame
who had lorgnetted you, your trodding on orchids, and your love
for brocaded velvet, and the Old Russian jewelry to be had for
nothing. What in hell did you ever do with the iron necklaces, no,
bracelets, maybe even earrings, we bought. Your cape-throwing
gesture, my throwing myself with every step, your sinking in the
pit of the stomach and the depth in the iris of the eye as you
strove to look into infinity so far as infinity permitted . . .[26]

(We know from McAlmon that drugs were plentiful in Berlin that
year; especially cocaine.)

The 'Thelma' of McAlmon's letter was Thelma Wood, the great
love of Djuna's life. They met in Paris in the autumn or winter of
1920, both newly arrived from America. Thelma was nineteen, an
artist and sculptor from St Louis, Missouri, who had an allowance
from her well-off family. By the time they were in Berlin with
McAlmon, their affair had already begun. Djuna's first year in
Europe must have passed in a kind of dazed abandon, considering
the travel, drugs, drink and sex she undertook. Yet she never
stopped writing. In 1922 she went briefly to New York to try to get
commissions and to place a collection of her stories and plays with a
publisher. Her old friend Horace Liveright agreed to publish the
collection as *A Book* in 1923, by which time she was back in Paris
and settled with Thelma.

The early years of this partnership were idyllic. The two women
created their own family; Thelma was 'Simon' or 'Papa'; Djuna was
'Junie' or 'Momma'. Their cat Dilly was the child. While Djuna was
in New York, Thelma joined a cruise to Bermuda and Jamaica,
from where she wrote Djuna loving letters, some of which have
survived:

Dear little angel
This is where I have finally gotten to . . . I have a nice room –
great big – and great big bed – for $5 a week . . .
Old Papa begins to feel like a new papa – don't *forget me* –
because I'm really sort of a nice kid.
I dreamed last night you ran away with Bob Chandler – and I
nearly died . . .
I love you sweetheart – I want you here. I would like to ride

with you. I love you, love you, love you, ever and ever and ever
and Dilly too – I kiss your precious sweet face –
Simon
Kiss Dilly[27]

And again:

It will be so long now before I can hear from you angel. I will
cable you as soon as I arrive at Kingston – can't tell just when it
will be but don't worry about me sweet –
I love you
Simon[28]

Finally, there is the following note:

Junie angel –
Such a sweet letter from you – but Dilly he no write he pappa.
When I get back – he will get a good birching – he hitting he
mozza! Pappa will take the huming bird out of he . . .
I wish I could bring you pretty things from here – but maybe
she'll be pretty glad to see Simons silly old mug again –
I adore you Junie –
Always
Simon[29]

They were, by all accounts, a striking pair; both tall, imperious,
striding down the boulevards arm in arm, feet moving in time,
tossing their heads and their capes. Everyone noticed Thelma's
huge feet, but otherwise she was beautiful. They lived together –
between travels – from 1922 on, at 173 Blvd St Germain; and then
at an apartment Djuna was able to buy at 9 rue St Romain. Both
addresses were in the heart of the Left Bank, where they became
fixtures at Natalie Barney's weekly lesbian salon, held at her rue
Jacob house with its Temple of Friendship in the back courtyard.
They frequented the local cafés and bars: the Flore, the Dingo, the
Select. Djuna later immortalised the Barney circle, which included,
among others, Radclyffe Hall and Una Troubridge, Romaine
Brooks, Janet Flanner and Solita Solano, in the funniest book she
wrote, *Ladies Almanack*. Djuna and Natalie Barney became good
friends and corresponded throughout their lives, Natalie coming to
her financial aid many years later and reminding Djuna that even
then, in the early twenties, her friends had doubts about the future
of her relationship with Thelma; 'Do you remember', wrote

Natalie, 'when we tried in vain to carry you off from Thelma?'[30] And indeed, by 1924 or so, the idyll was over; and there were from then on very few quiet fireside dinners with just the two of them and their beloved Dilly.

Their relationship was volatile in the extreme; and they both drank a lot. Thelma was notoriously promiscuous and often went on drinking binges while looking for women to pick up.[31] Sometimes, when she was approached by men, she led them on, only to strike out at them physically, later on. John Glassco, in his *Memoirs of Montparnasse*, has Thelma appear as 'Emily Pine'; a 'tall, beautiful, dazed-looking girl . . . who had the largest pair of feet I had ever seen'.[32] When the 18-year-old Glassco took her away from her women friends to have a drink, she 'all at once gripped my hand and ground the knuckles viciously together; her strength was remarkable and I felt such pain that I impulsively raised my heel and drove it back against her shin.'[33]

When Thelma was off on a binge, Djuna would set out looking for her, going from bar to bar and becoming more and more drunk herself. They would fight and make up, again and again. In 1926, after several years of Paris life, Djuna wrote to an old friend from Provincetown Playhouse days, Eleanor Fitzgerald:

I lay awake last night & could not think what in the world the world is about – old women starving (my aunt) Elsa out of a mad house – my mother soon to be left sonless – you without your love – and all I could think of was how many pairs of gloves were bought last week by wealthy bitches without a worry!! And then peoples charactors [sic]! My God, their awful states of mind, their dreadful pettiness – their ghastly ghastly souls – the best of them occasionally think up things too incredible to believe! . . .

Now – Fitzi darling – I have a tiny appartment [sic], 2 rooms – small, a kitchen – and am going to try to finish my work – I expect to be in Paris until October, there are many books I *must* read, etc – and I must try to get some short stories & articles over, or after this summer I'll be no better off than the Baroness [Elsa von Freytag-Loringhoven], & not as well – rich people come admire, & part!

Taking their millions with them – I heard that you got 2 thousand five hundred for Jane [Heap], & immediately – for now such is my nature – wished her in the bottomless pit, and myself with the sum . . .[34]

Despite her bitterness and complaining, she ends with 'Love from Thelma and a big kiss', seeming happy in love, if in not much else. But drinking, especially Thelma's, began to take its toll on the relationship. In 1927, their first major break occurred; Thelma sailed for America and wrote from on board ship:

> Dearest one – You said something just as I was leaving that makes things seem a little less terrible . . . that we could meet in New York and maybe Simon would be different.
>
> But you see how silly Simon must clutch on anything to make him stronger – you see I can't think of anything ahead that doesn't mean you.
>
> I keep saying – Simon, you've got to be a man and take your medicine – but then always in my head goes – There is no Simon and no Irine [Djuna] and I can't bear it and go crazy . . .
>
> I feel so shy at saying any thing for fear it sounds like excusing which God knows I don't – but I've thought over it all and I think if I didn't drink maybe things wouldn't have happened – as that is usely [*sic*] when I get involved –
>
> Now Simon will not touch one drop till you come to America and I'll have my exhibition done . . . Perhaps we could try it a new way – . . . if you will I will never again as long as you love me take one small drop of anything stronger than tea.
>
> If this sounds like bunk to you precious – drop me a little note and say no use. But if there is any slight chance for Simon if he bucks up let him know that too – I tell you angel darling the only reason your Simon doesn't drop off that boat is because I've made you sufficiently unhappy as it is –[35]

They did come together again later in the year when Thelma returned to Paris. Soon afterwards, Djuna was able to buy the lease of the apartment at 9 rue St Romain, from the proceeds generated by her first novel, *Ryder* (dedicated to Thelma), which was a best-seller in America. The two women decorated the new apartment: the main room had many mirrors, ecclesiastical pillows and yellow curtains with red flowers. Glass chandeliers were scattered throughout; and there was an old oak dining-table surrounded by tapestry-covered chairs. The bedroom had a large double bed, two satin-covered chairs, more than 60 pictures, mostly religious ones, a large Venetian mirror, a dressing-table, another glass chandelier and a fireplace. It was a crowded, eccentric and warm environment. Besides Dilly the cat, Djuna and Thelma had a doll they treated as a child. In her masterpiece, *Nightwood*, which she wrote after their final break-up, Djuna wrote: 'when a woman gives it [a doll] to a woman, it is the life they cannot have, it is their child, sacred and profane.'[36]

The cause of their final break-up was another woman. At first Thelma tried to integrate her new love into her life with Djuna, but with bad results. She wrote to Djuna:

> I did not want such a thing to be known between us – something I did not care about – It seemed a shame for foolishness to spoil us – I wanted no *acknowledged* disloyalty and after you came back from N.Y. I loved you so terribly – and my one idea was to wipe out the fact I'd been stupid – I tryed [*sic*] desperately – with her I wheedled and raved I was cruel and sweet – and no good – always if I did not see her or call she sent something or a note – and it made you unhappy – and I did see – Till I thought I'd go mad . . .
>
> I saw I was losing you – and felt I could save it if I came to you – and again I listened to her – She swore it would be alright she would meet you and become friends as I had always begged her to.
>
> Then she played tricks and sent a note – and you were going out and asked me to come with you and I wanted so to – and didn't dare – and you were so beautiful – and we got you a flower – then I went to her and cried and raved for two hours – and again she promised to be good and friends. But she's mad . . .
>
> I will not be different for your sake or hers – She can kick up the dust as much as pleases her – I have nothing to lose – and I've lost what sympathy for her I had –
>
> As for the rest of our eight years you seemed to have had a pretty rotten time – with my brutishness and I'm sorry – sorry – You say you 'know me now so terribly well'. Something is undoubtedly wrong with me – I lack perhaps a conscience or sensibility or memory or logic or all – when I left France I felt as you say just unfit for human dignity . . .[37]

A few weeks later she wrote again:

> at times Djuna things get very terrible – something will happen and I go to pieces – for instance I dream of you every night – and sometimes Djuna I dream we are lovers and I wake up the next day and nearly die of shame – taking advantage in my sleep of something I know so intimately – and something you do not wish

me to have – Its [*sic*] like stealing from you and I feel the next day like cabling 'forgive me' . . .[38]

The two women had one more reconciliation, living together in New York during 1930–31, but Djuna returned alone to Paris in the autumn of 1931. Thelma, for her part, lived with the 'other woman' for years, keeping in touch with Djuna through letters and phone calls until she died. Djuna told Mina Loy that the affair was finally over and that there was nothing else to take its place in her life.[39] After ten years spent in the grip of passion, Djuna had had enough. She was 38; and alone, as she would remain for the rest of her long life. She sat in bed (where she always wrote) and began to put down the story of these ten years in *Nightwood*.

For the next decade, Djuna Barnes moved restlessly about while keeping 9 rue St Romain as her base. After an operation for appendicitis in late 1931, her young friend Charles Henri Ford, an American writer she'd met in the Village during the previous year, moved in with her to help with the typing of *Nightwood* (then called *Bow Down*). Ford, a homosexual, got on well with Djuna and for a while her emotional life seemed stable. She spent the summer of 1932 at Peggy Guggenheim's English country house, working on *Nightwood*. When Ford joined Paul and Jane Bowles in Tangiers in January 1933, Djuna decided to go too, but found she hated being there. Then, to her dismay, she found she was pregnant as a result of a brief affair with a French painter.[40] After an abortion in Paris, she went again to Peggy Guggenheim's country house to recover and to continue working on *Nightwood*. Peggy was now divorced from Laurence Vail and living with the writer John Holms. In the house, too, were Emily Holmes Coleman, a writer, and her young son. She and Djuna became close friends. Her time here was comfortable and relaxed; she wrote to Ford, soon after her arrival:

> my life is very quiet here, tho there were a number of people about the first few days & will be again at the end of the week – I do not leave my room (writing) until lunch hour – one o'clock, after which I read, or go motoring – I can't ride horseback so when horses arrive I wander about . . . tea at 5.
>
> Then after dinner games – including Emily's ever adored one of 'truth', arguments & slight insults & deadly earnestness until 12 or so – when I go to bed . . .[41]

At the end of the summer of 1933, Djuna left for Paris and then New York, where she stayed with her mother and brother Saxon, for a short time, in the Village again, working in bed. She tried, unsuccessfully, to get a job; and went on rewriting *Nightwood* and trying to have it accepted for publication. Finally, Emily Coleman almost forced the manuscript on T.S. Eliot in the Faber office in London. When Faber took it, Djuna rented a flat in London and moved her furniture there from Paris. By this time she had begun an affair with an Englishman and had begun drinking heavily again, which resulted in her going in and out of hospital.[42] After the publication of *Nightwood* in 1936 she was at a loose end again, now in her mid-forties and still not settled anywhere. She went back to Paris and was considering whether or not to move back into her old apartment when war broke out. Peggy Guggenheim paid for her passage back to New York. It was not a happy homecoming. Djuna had to stay with her elderly mother in a small Village apartment. She started drinking again and had to be hospitalised. Finally, in the autumn of 1940, she moved into a one-room apartment of her own at 5 Patchin Place, in the Village.

She was 48, poor, alcoholic and alone. Although she was forced to spend time with her mother, she hated doing so; and spent more and more time by herself. She began to have health problems with her eyes, her teeth and her breathing. Mina Loy was also living in New York by now, but was more or less unavailable; 'Mina is in the last stages of depression and won't let me come to see her,' Djuna wrote to McAlmon in 1940.[43] Desperately short of cash and facing falling royalties, she relied mainly on periodic assistance from Peggy Guggenheim. She was forced to ask McAlmon for $20 to settle a dentist's bill, telling him, 'I live on less than $20 a month for food – in fact $25 is all I have for *everything.*'[44] *Nightwood* had had some excellent reviews, but it brought in little money. Nevertheless, Djuna Barnes kept writing. After her mother's death in 1945, she began to write about her family, the result of which was *The Antiphon*, a play published in 1958, as if her mother's death had left her free to explore in excruciating emotional depth the Barnes family story. It was not a pretty story. One commentator writes:

> [Djuna's mother] had declared that it was like a coil of snakes around her neck having her children still alive. Her daughter saw her as a Mrs King Lear who took breaks to read passages of Mary Baker Eddy to her. Djuna thought she had the capabilities of a devil. Elizabeth [her mother] had said that Djuna was full of self-pity and the rotten Barnes ego.[45]

The play did not enjoy much success, although a few critics praised it at the time. Its obscurity went too deep for most of its audience. And as the years went on, Djuna became more and more reclusive and money became an increasing problem. Piggy sent her a little, but never enough and, in any case, they sometimes quarrelled. Natalie Barney, still unquenchable in her late eighties, came to Djuna's rescue, writing, 'What are your resources? Has Piggy Goosenheim let you down? I enclose another cheque that may prove useful . . .'[46] From this time on, Natalie sent regular, generous cheques. Janet Flanner, another old friend of Paris days, sent money for a typewriter. Marianne Moore arrived on the doorstep of Patchin Place with a large cheque from a wealthy patron.

Djuna was all too aware of the restrictions placed on her life. She wrote to Natalie in 1966:

> What am I doing with my time? But I thought I had gone into all that! Certainly *no* 'little friend' and if I saw one I would jump into the river . . . I live in complete isolation. I have no door-bell, and at one time had no telephone. I have bars at the window, and a police-lock on the front door . . . and all of this not from any additional ferocity to my nature, but merely as means to enduring. Living? no, enduring yes. Physically I was too ill (my emphysema etc etc better) and entirely too fed up with the horror of what people turn out to be, to be pleased to see or talk with anyone. So I swept my doorstep clear. It is, at times rediculous [*sic*], because one would like to talk to someone, now and again, but *not* unless they are 'one of ones people'. How often do such go by? And then I write, or try to, and of all good things, at the point in life when poetry is *not* written, I write poetry. It pleases me not very often, but you can't just sit and read all day and all night . . . and then after that, I go out and spend a bit of your charming money. Thank you, it is a pleasure to have a little longer rope.[47]

She lived on, in the same way and with the same attitudes, at Patchin Place until 1982. Sometimes she seemed shocked herself by her lifestyle:

> I am dreading winter. I fear that I've got myself too much cut off. I see absolutely no one. I have to be alone to work, but the French and the Italians etc etc, have the answer to the whole

thing, the cafe . . . you go when you want, you stay away when you want, and therefore people do not intrude on you, nor are you so completely sure that, on going out, you'll meet with nobody, but *no body*.[48]

Djuna Barnes judged the world by harsh standards. She maintained tight control over her emotions and over her writing, with the one exception of Thelma Wood and the resulting novel *Nightwood*. But, embittered and scornful, she later wrapped herself in silence, devoting herself to the language. In her last years, she wrote mostly poetry: 'But the work! The poetry – how difficult it is, and how strange an occupation in our times . . . how fortunate is anyone who still finds the English language fascinating . . .'[49] People were too risky to take chances with; and yet sometimes her guard could fall: 'There's no doubt that all of us, of the "Lost Generation," had, when thinking it over, a most extraordinary and unusual time of it . . . not all of it was "wasted"!'[50]

Chapter 8

Mary Butts, Mina Loy, and the dead language of amor

If she appears at all, Mary Butts is usually glimpsed in histories of the twenties as ever-present in the cafés and bars of London and Paris. Her work is even less often mentioned, making her one of the most neglected of the female modernists. Carrot-coloured hair, pale blue eyes, nearly translucent white skin, a single white jade earring – she was described by one friend as a 'storm goddess'. Her unorthodox personal life, in which she more often sought out what was curious than what was virtuous, has – perhaps – overshadowed her work, since references to her tend to concentrate on her more notorious escapades: black magic with Aleister Crowley; opium-smoking; pub-crawling; flagrant borrowing; and abandonment of her only child. Her writing, nevertheless, is far from insignificant. Ezra Pound, Ford Madox Ford, Bryher, Robert McAlmon and Marianne Moore were only a few of those who thought highly of it and who helped her career.

At least on the surface, Mary Butts' life differs from the lives of the other women in our network. Instead of creating an atmosphere, situation or relationship that could allow space and peace for working, she seems to have chosen a life pattern which looks more like a series of disruptions of working conditions. Indeed, her friend the composer Virgil Thomson said that she called herself an 'unrest cure'.[1] Nevertheless, in the 17 years of her writing career, she managed to publish six novels, three collections of short stories, an autobiography and numerous short pieces; and to leave a substantial amount of unpublished material at her death at the early age of 47.

Born in 1890 near Poole in Dorset, Mary was the child of her father's second marriage to a much younger woman. On her father's side, the family was descended from Thomas Butts, a friend and patron of William Blake; and Mary grew up on the comfortable family estate 'Salterns'. Her autobiography *The Crystal Cabinet* describes her first 20 years, spent mainly at 'Salterns' in the milieu of English country life. After her father's death, the estate had to be sold, an event which would always haunt her and which is often represented in her fiction. Her strongest family attachment was to her younger brother and only sibling, Tony, a relationship which would also haunt both her and her work. Mary and Tony often quarrelled, however, and eventually became estranged from one another. (One of Tony's friends, the novelist William Plomer, drew a cruel caricature of her as Lydia Delap in his book *Museum Pieces*, published in 1952.)

In 1910, Mary left 'Salterns' and moved to London to study at Westfield, a college of London University. Her early years in London are obscure; she didn't graduate from Westfield, but little is known about what she did do. Her daughter Camilla believes that she worked for a time in an East End settlement and that she had a 'schoolgirl' affair with another woman.[2]

By the early period of the First World War, however, she'd met the young writer John Rodker, who was a regular contributor to *The Egoist*. By 1915 Mary and Rodker were regular attenders at dinners Pound arranged in Soho restaurants once a week or so, at which, too, H.D., Aldington, Harriet Weaver, May Sinclair, Ford Madox Ford and others were likely to appear. Rodker and Mary Butts married in 1918, by which time she had begun writing. Extracts from her first novel, *Ashe of Rings*, appeared in *The Little Review* in 1919, the same year in which Dorothy Richardson's *Interim* was serialised there.

In the same year, Mary met Cecil Maitland for the first time. He was recovering from a suicide attempt in a hospital where she was doing some volunteer work. He was a young Scotsman of aristocratic origin who had been wrecked by his war experiences. Mary was drawn to him; and then soon in love with him. Shortly after the birth of her daughter Camilla Rodker, she left her husband and baby in order to be with Maitland. Nor did she ever return.

Like the other mothers in our network, H.D. and Mina Loy, Mary was not a conventional mother. Her rejection of motherhood, however, seems to have had more to do with her love for Maitland

and her need to take care of him, than with a need for space to work at her own writing, as was the case for H.D. and Mina Loy. More than space, time or a quiet setting, Mary needed the stimulus of a man to take care of, someone who would inspire her to write. By the time Mary met him, Cecil Maitland – according to all accounts – was quite degenerate; he was an alcoholic, who never either washed or cleaned his nails, who had many love affairs, who was penniless and unable to make any sort of life on his own. But Mary saw other qualities in him. They shared a fascination for magic, for example; and their flat at 43 Belsize Park Gardens was soon adorned with mystic circles and symbols. They met the infamous Aleister Crowley and heard about his island retreat at Cefalu, which intrigued them.

Soon the pair left Hampstead for Paris, though how they managed this financially isn't clear. Mary was possibly living on an allowance from her mother and Cecil may have had some income from his family. In any case, they were chronically poor and often nearly destitute. Camilla, still a baby, was left in England to be brought up by a great-aunt of Mary.[3] Rodker went on with his own life, helping Harriet Weaver to publish *Ulysses* at The Egoist Press and undertaking translations. He seems not to have been vindictive about Mary's desertion and – according to Robert McAlmon – they remained on friendly terms.[4]

Mary and Cecil settled in Paris, sometimes staying at the Hotel Foyot on the Left Bank, later in a flat at 14 rue de Montessuy. They became regulars at Left Bank bars and at Le Boeuf sur le Toit, Jean Cocteau's club. (Mary became a close friend of Cocteau and he illustrated her book *Imaginary Letters* [1928].) Robert McAlmon met them soon after his own arrival in Paris in 1921, by which time Mary's work was known to all *Little Review* readers. McAlmon admired her work, as did Bryher, but they were fascinated too by her personality and lifestyle. They were especially impressed by her ability to take quantities of drugs and yet to seem unscathed, Bryher noting that 'a whole jugful of drugs . . . wouldn't have any effect on her at all.'[5] Although McAlmon was well acquainted with the popular cocaine circuit – particularly in Berlin – he seems to have been less familiar with opium, Mary's favourite drug. In any case, Bryher, McAlmon and H.D. were sufficiently intrigued by Mary and Cecil to make a visit in 1923 to see them on Crowley's island of Cefalu, where he practised black magic rites which often involved slaughtered animals. What precisely happened during this visit isn't known, since none of the party would ever talk about it afterwards.[6]

Back in Paris, Mary continued to amaze and astound her friends. Peggy Guggenheim, for example, once reported that 'Mary took a whole tube of aspirin in one day when her opium gave out.'[7] McAlmon, in an unpublished vignette, records an evening spent drinking with her. After meeting her in her hotel room in Florence and finding her clad in a negligee, he learns that she needs to borrow some cash:

> I do need you I am in a mess, and do need just you to help me. A debt of honour I must pay. I'll give you a post-dated check. I always know you are helpful. You're one of the chaps, a real gentleman, one of us in the greatest way. Mother and brother are being more than ever beastly. I can't tell you what I've been going through lately, and my darling baby needs a little sweet poor clean sunshine, and good sweet wholesome food. Oh, what will become of us all. You . . . you young beautiful American God, you with your health and youth and beauty, you don't realize the depths of Europe. There is only England, and what they have put us through. There's Frank [Cecil], and poor Hubert [Rodker], a dear too if he won't help me support our baby, but what the war years did to us all.[8]

'Neil' (McAlmon) does lend 'Amy' (Mary) some money; and after a few hours drinking at a bar, she makes what was perhaps a typical exit:

> 'Home. No, my dears. No, lamkins, finish your tiddle. I shall get to my hotel. It is but a two minute walk. I wish to think, alone. The impulse of evil. It is strong. It vibrates in the atmosphere tonight.' She tottered slightly before wafting across the room. At the door she turned to smile refulgently back at Neil and Rollo. Then with a resigned but dramatic gesture of renunciation she tossed a kiss from her full blown glistening lips, and murmured, reincaratedly [*sic*] comprehensive, 'Lamkins, if I could save you.' With this she tossed back her flaming hair, stroking those tresses with a pale hand. Her exit was comparable to that of any great actress.
>
> 'Hell, Amy's smoking opium again, isn't she. She'll probably wire Frank to get her some more in Paris,' Neil said.
>
> 'Mad, Neil,' Rollo quavered. 'Mad, just mad, like so many of us.'

'Madder possibly; or perhaps not so mad . . . Hell, she's taken
a small fortune off various people in Paris in the last two months.'
'Frank, you know, Neil. Frank, and Amy's one of the lasses
who likes taking care of her man.'[9]

Indeed, Mary seems to have been much concerned and preoccupied
with 'taking care of her man', both in her living and in her writing.
Her short epistolary novel *Imaginary Letters*[10] explores a woman's
love for a man called Boris who is singularly unattractive; he is vain,
cruel, abusive and a 'fanatical pederast'. The woman tries to take
care of him and to love him. Mary wrote in her journal, shortly
before the book's publication, that she'd always had 'an incompara-
ble pleasure in finding someone psychically sick, and learning about
it, and seeing if there is a way out. This feeling very much mixed up
with sex – bed not necessary, but it makes things work better. That
is, in that relation. I've always wanted to make my lovers well, sense
powers liberated in them . . .'[11]

The Boris of *Imaginary Letters* is certainly 'psychically sick'. And
in some way he starts the imaginary process. The book is a series of
letters that will never be sent, written by a woman in love with Boris
to his mother in Russia. The letters are an attempt to understand
this man. In this case, which closely parallels Mary's actual
situation, the man is beautiful, but 'underhanded, unstable, lost,
homosexual, unavailable'[12] – the kind of 'psychically sick' man
Mary needed to fire her creative imagination. Although she seems
to have failed in her efforts to make such men 'well', she rarely
appears to have been despondent or self-pitying, even when they
refuse, like 'Boris', to make love with her. Instead, her attitude is
one of acceptance, signified – for example – in her choice of
epigraph for *Imaginary Letters*: 'We must not expect all the virtues.
We should even be satisfied if there is something odd enough to be
interesting.'

Throughout such relationships, Mary kept writing. Her stories
and poems appeared in *The Little Review*, *The Transatlantic Review*
and other of the little magazines. She was recognised by other
young writers as someone with exceptional talent, as well as
someone having exceptional vitality. Marianne Moore, writing to
McAlmon in 1922, said 'It encourages me very much that Mary
Butts, Anna Wickham and the Sitwells should admire my work . . .
Mary Butts is quite startling I think in impact and untrammeled
diction . . .'[13]

Her first book of stories, *Speed the Plough*, was accepted by Chapman & Hall in London, after her friend Douglas Goldring persuaded his friend Alec Waugh to show it to his father, who was one of the directors. McAlmon published *Ashe of Rings*, her first novel, in 1925 at the Contact Press and included her work in his *Contact Collection of Contemporary Writers* of the same year. Despite – or because of – dabbling in black magic, smoking opium, drinking to excess and taking care of Cecil and other gay young men, she kept on writing. Her friend Virgil Thomson described her in the mid-twenties:

> Like all well brought up English, she got up in the morning . . . Every day, too, she wrote with pen in large notebooks. She kept herself and her house very clean and roistered only when the day was done. Then she would have tea, toddle out to a cafe, meet friends, go on from there . . . What Mary liked most . . . come six of an evening, was a long pub crawl – going with loved ones from bar to bar, dining somewhere, then going on, tumbling in and out of taxis, fanning youth into a flame. Come midnight she would leave, go home and write.[14]

This intense, frantic even, style of living would not have suited most of the writers in our network. But it worked for Mary Butts. After separating from Cecil Maitland (who went off to live by himself on the French coast), Mary stayed in Paris and tried – though she never quite succeeded – to forget him. She was close to Virgil Thomson for a year, a period he remembers fondly enough: 'We had lovely times together, warmths, clarities and laughter. Then the bickering began; and though our separation was not casual, by the time the year was out we were not meeting.'[15] At the time, Thomson was 30 and Mary 37. Perhaps he wasn't 'psychically sick' enough for her. In any case, by 1930 she'd left Paris and returned to England. Meanwhile Maitland had died; and with his death, even though they were separated, something of Mary's life ended too. She did find, for a while, someone else to 'take care of': a young English artist called Gabriel Aitkin, known for his personal beauty, a homosexual and an alcoholic.[16] They moved together to a small town in Cornwall and Mary continued to write. Her daughter Camilla, now adolescent, came to visit on school vacations and for a time it seemed as if Mary might enjoy a quiet rural life. She published two historical novels in the early thirties and wrote for Bryher's magazine *Life and Letters To-day*. The pair had little money –

Bryher sent periodic help – but that never bothered Mary overmuch. Her rural idyll didn't last long, however. Aitkin, who was – according to some – a mess, soon left her.

Living alone after Aitkin's departure, Mary kept up her enthusiasm and retained her fascination for 'the magic of persons and things, an enchantment, and the loss of it that is no less real than banality'.[17] Her friend Oswell Blakeston visited her in the mid-thirties and recorded: 'She managed. Of course she managed. If there was nothing else to eat, she'd catch snails. She had a special hat with a veil for her snail-catching forays.'[18] And if she couldn't afford to buy anything to drink, there was a local shop that sold 'champagne wine nerve tonic' for tuppence a bottle.[19] She wrote her autobiography *The Crystal Cabinet* (published in 1937), and worked on a further historical novel called *Julian the Apostate* (still unpublished). She did, as Blakeston observed, manage. And yet, in a letter written to her friend Angus Davidson in 1933, she reveals not having ever recovered from the loss of Cecil Maitland:

> You see – since some years ago when the person I loved – & still do – best out of all my life – died – (after a bitter misunderstanding & separation) – I've been alone in a way difficult to define. Anyhow, since I left Paris, over three years ago, I've had no one to talk to as I can talk to you.[20]

Mary died, alone, ten years after Maitland, on 5 March 1937, of a misdiagnosed ruptured appendix. She was 47.

Mina Loy, by contrast, lived to the age of 84, surviving for 40 years the death of her great love. Born Mina Gertrude Lowy in London in 1882, she was the daughter of a second-generation Hungarian Jewish father and an English Protestant mother. Her first avocation was art; and she studied painting in Munich for two years after leaving school at 17. On her return to London in 1901, she continued art classes, including one taught by Augustus John. Firmly established in the centre of young bohemian art circles, she probably frequented the popular student cafés and bars, rather than the sedate ABCs and vegetarian restaurants patronised at the same time by Dorothy Richardson. Darkly, astoundingly beautiful, Mina Loy moved from Victorian England to impressionist Paris, to futurist Florence, to bohemian Greenwich Village and back to expatriate Paris during her long career. Wherever she was, she was noticed. Painter, poet, actress, playwright, feminist, mother, designer, conceptual artist – her range of skills and experience make it difficult to place her too squarely in any one artistic category. Almost consumed by her 'desire to be loved', which she continuously fought against, she developed a strong sense of autonomy, exhibiting in her later life what she called her strongest characteristic, her 'capacity for isolation'.[21]

During Mina's time spent as an art student in London, she became involved with a fellow student called Stephen Haweis. They moved to Paris to paint and were married there in 1903. Instead of taking her husband's name, Mina changed 'Lowy' to 'Loy', struggling with the now-familiar feminist dilemma of trying to choose and define what's in a name. Though she continued to paint, she became pregnant and her first child, Oda, was born in May 1904. By 1905 she was a frequent guest at the pre-Toklas Stein salon, where – in addition to Leo and Gertrude – she met Apollinaire, Picasso and Rousseau. She became a lifelong friend of Gertrude.

Oda died on her first birthday; and the marriage was already faltering by the time the pair moved to Florence later in the same year. Nevertheless, Mina quickly had two further children, Joella in 1907 and Giles in 1908. Haweis, who came from a wealthy and distinguished family, could afford to keep his family in style. They lived in a comfortable villa in Costa San Giorgio and became part of the Anglo-American colony which, by 1910, included Mabel Dodge and, at times, Gertrude Stein and Alice Toklas. During their ten years in Florence, both Mina and Haweis took lovers and developed their separate lives. Mina continued to paint and draw, and began, too, to write, doing her best to marry Art with Life: 'My conceptions of life evolved while . . . stirring baby food on spirit lamps – and my best drawings behind a stove to the accompaniment of a line of children's cloths hanging round it to dry.'[22]

In 1913 and 1914, though she was coping with motherhood, a soured marriage, lovers, and her own artistic aspirations, Mina found time to notice and take part in the emerging Italian Futurist movement, led by Filippo Marinetti[23] and to read Stein's *The Making of Americans* in manuscript. She became, also, at this time, a lifelong convert to Christian Science.[24] By now an intimate of Mabel Dodge, who was her son Giles' godmother, Mina met the imported New Yorkers who flocked to Dodge's Villa Curonia: John Reed, Dodge's current lover; Carl van Vechten; Neith Boyce; Hutchins Hapgood; and others. These contacts would later give

Mina entry into the Greenwich Village avant-garde circuit. Another link was forged when she met the Vail family, wealthy Americans who rented her Florentine villa in 1914. Laurence Vail, the son, was quite a young man then, but within a few years he was married to the heiress Peggy Guggenheim, who became Mina's principal patron in the 1920s.

Mina's first published work appeared in 1914 as a result of her New York contacts, in Alfred Stieglitz's magazine *Camera Work* and in Carl van Vechten's *Trend*. 'Aphorisms on Futurism' and her poems aroused considerable interest in New York bohemian circles; and when a group of poets – disaffected with the editorial policy of Harriet Monroe's *Poetry* magazine – decided to found a new journal, Mina Loy was their rallying-point.[25] The new magazine, *Others*, edited by Alfred Kreymborg, appeared in 1915, with Mina Loy's 'Love Songs to Joannes' prominently displayed. The poems were much talked about in New York avant-guarde circles. The text used intimate material from her own life and were frank to the point of being shocking.

Meanwhile Mina continued sending poems and prose pieces to Mabel Dodge and Carl van Vechten, relying on them to send the work on to appropriate little magazines in New York. She wrote, characteristically, to Mabel Dodge:

> My dearest Moose – glad you gleaned something from the poem – Do put it in *Camera Work*. I don't care a bit about money. I can not tell you anything about my self – without telling you *all* – which is impossible – for I don't know – at present – anyway Life can be interesting even if the old values are gone – & my roots are being tugged out – for experiment – in exquisite & terrific anguish – mais donc si va?[26]

She was indeed experimenting with both her art and her life. Her fifty-one 'Aphorisms on Futurism' attempted to set out the credo she was trying to live and write by:

DIE in the Past

Live in the Future

LOVE the hideous in order to find the sublime core of it.

OPEN your arms to the delapidated; rehabilitate them.

FORGET that you live in houses, that you may live in yourself –

LIFE is only limited by our prejudices. Destroy them, and you cease to be at the mercy of yourself.

CEASE to build up your personality with the ejections of irrelevant minds.

UNSCREW your capability of absorption and grasp the elements of Life – *whole*.[27]

Mina's endeavours to live by such precepts made her life much more than 'interesting':

My beloved Moose,
What is Stephen [Haweis] doing *is* he trying to get an honest job? I am happy but up the spout. Mrs Perkins has gone raving mad *poor* dear – & my antiques are lost or sold for the Lunatic Asylum Bill – & my house is up for sale & glory hallelujah Kingdom come but once an optimist always an Optimist . . . When are you coming over to meet Marinetti his conversation is disgusting – he is so nice . . .[28]

She was, by this time, having an affair with Marinetti, which her daughter, Joella, describes as more intellectual than passionate:

I am in the throes of conversion to Futurism – But I shall never convince myself – there is no hope in any system that 'combats le mal avec le mal' – & that is really Marinetti's philosophy – Though he is one of the most satisfying personalities I ever came in contact with . . . there is every semblance of an explosive atmosphere here – only if you stop for one moment you find there is nothing to explode . . . if you run across Stephen Haweis tell him that I sent him 100 dollars by cablegram to San Francisco . . . I hope he is seriously going to try & work.
My Life is quite changing – one or two of Ste's old female friends dropped *me*! When he went away – what a relief . . . everybody I know at present is trying to forget what a complicated affair life has been mistaken for – we are all busy re-simplifying ourselves – I am 29 – next year I shall be 28 [actually in 1914 Mina was 32].[29]

Before Haweis left, Mina, who suffered all her life from what was then called 'neurasthenia', had some kind of breakdown, writing to Mabel Dodge that she had been 'dreadfully ill – in bed 7 weeks & nervous collapse afterwards'.[30] Writing before Italy entered the war, she described her psychological condition:

I think I am safe in saying that there is not a single personality in Europe barring negatives – that has not undergone metamorphosis during the last six months – when the tension is relaxed shall we revert back to ourselves – or shall we find no way of fitting in anywhere? . . . I want to hear from you. I want to see you & am so afraid of America – I've got the latins in my blood – and the only latin's got me in his spleen –

I don't describe to you my utter defeat in the sex war – you will put it down to feminine pride of which I haven't a jot – I have a fundamental conceit that ascribes lack of appreciation of myself to want of perspicacity in the observer – anyhow Tomasino's [Marinetti's] interest in me only weathered two months of war fever – & we're all betting on whether he's going to [be] doing something huge or bust – lots of his former adherents are fighting him to the death – & he's getting fat & his eyes are brutalized – & politics are a grave – anyhow – Futurism is dead – unless (if he's strong enough – & he's quite inclined to believe it in the face of shrugs & grins alround [*sic*] it [Futurism] survives as a political party – . . . personally I am indebted to M. for twenty years added to my life from mere contact with his exuberant vitality.

My dear – . . . Do tell me what you are making of Feminism? I heard you were interested – have you any idea in what directed [*sic*] the sex must be shoved – psychologically I mean – bread & butter bores me rather – do write Moose – I haven't a wise companion for the moment – entirely dependent on myself for everything – & my mind is half the time immersed in wounds – Red Cross is being feverishly instigated – in a subterraneous fashion – while the papers continue denying that the schools have been commandeered for hospitals! . . . By the way that fragment of Feminist tirade I sent you – I found the destruction of virginity – *so* daring dont you think – had been suggested by some other woman years ago – see Havelock Ellis – I feel rather hopeless of devotion to the woman-cause – slaves will believe that chains are protectors – & so they are – the most effecient [*sic*] for the coward . . .[31]

The 'fragment of Feminist tirade' sent to Mabel Dodge indeed contained several daring ideas:

Leave off looking to men to find out what you are *not*. Seek within yourselves to find out what you *are*. As conditions are at present constituted you have the choice between Parasitism, Prostitution, or Negation.

. . .

The fictitious value of woman as identified with her physical purity is too easy a standby. It renders her lethargic in the acquisition of intrinsic merits of character by which she could obtain a concrete value. Therefore, the first self-enforced law for the female sex, as protection against the manmade bogey of virtue (which is the principal instrument of her subjugation) is the *unconditional* surgical *destruction of virginity* throughout the female population at puberty.

The value of man is assessed entirely according to his use or interest to the community; the value of woman depends entirely on chance – her success or failure in manipulating a man into taking life-long responsibility for her.

The advantages of marriage are too ridiculously ample compared to all other trades, for under modern conditions a woman can accept preposterously luxurious support from a man without returning anything – even offspring – as an offering of thanks for her virginity.

The woman who has not succeeded in striking that advantageous bargain is prohibited from any but the most surreptitious reaction to life-stimuli and is entirely debarred from maternity. Every woman has a right to maternity.

Every woman of superior intelligence should realize her race-responsibility by producing children in adequate proportion to the unfit or degenerate members of her sex.

. . .

Woman must become more responsible for the child than man.

Woman must destroy in herself the desire to be loved.

. . .

Woman must retain her deceptive fragility of appearance, combined with indomitable will, irreducible courage, abundant health, and sound nerves.

Another great illusion that woman must use all her introspection, innate clear-sightedness, and unbiased bravery to destroy is the impurity of sex – for the sake of her self-respect.

In defiance of superstition I assert that *there is nothing impure in sex* except the mental attitude toward it. The eventual acceptance of this fact will constitute an incalculably wider social regeneration than it is possible for our generation to acquire.[32]

Mina Loy struggled with these bold ideas for the next few years. However, by the time her daughter Joella reached adolescence in the late 1920s, some of her radical stances had modified. She did *not* encourage Joella to undergo the "surgical destruction of virginity" or to lose her virginity at all before marriage. Indeed, Joella recalls, her mother was quite Victorian in some ways, ensuring that Joella was chaperoned at Paris parties and that she was brought home promptly at 10.30. Already in September 1914, at the age of 32, Mina was aware of the depth and breadth the struggle with received conventions and pieties entailed:

> I can just hang on to my sanity – by a thread there's not a soul here to *talk* to. If I read my work to anyone they think I'm mad – Giovanni [Papini; a Futurist and her lover after Marinetti] came within an ace of really smashing me for good & all – too much sense of humour I suppose – for here I am longing for a change – Haweis is behaving as I should not have expected even Haweis to behave – Do you remember the American woman who met him at lunch and said – he would turn & bite the hand that fed him? My dear so far life instead of growing easier gets much more difficult – I'm sorry you didn't like my work any more – But never mind – I don't think any one's work or morals should influence one in one's appreciation of *themselves* – do you? My dear the most *satisfactory* thing is the inner tranquillity – has any philosophy succeeded in proving it to be *real* – ? But you can't get it unless you want it more than anything else & I have lost what I had of it – wanting a very cruel grubby – blind man more – still I make gymnastic efforts to recapture it – I succeed for seconds at a time but it's the chaos of the subconscious one gets lost in . . . [33]

She was, according to her daughter, really in love with Papini (who was married and Catholic), but their affair was no less tormented and tempestuous for her than her marriage to Haweis had been. 'I wonder if hatred is the truth & love the lie,' she wrote to the constantly receptive Mabel Dodge; 'Don't ever live to see the day when the man you want sobs out the other one's name in the ultimate embrace. Philosophy is inadequate – '[34]

Despite such emotional battles, Mina kept writing, turning to Futurist satires during 1915–16. She made plans to visit New York. Mabel Dodge offered hospitality, but Mina wrote back, 'at present there is no one who will take my children & the nurse refuses to stay with them if I go away.'[35] Joella and Giles were now aged eight and six. Nevertheless, Mina persisted in her wish to make a living for herself. 'I want to design for a Business,' she wrote to Mabel Dodge; 'I do hope that family arrangements will work themselves out so that I can go to New York later on . . .'[36] Her estranged husband Haweis was by now in New York himself and had just lost another job. In late 1916, she finally managed to leave the children with a nurse and set sail for New York. It was the beginning of a new life.

Now Mina met up with old friends. Apart from Mabel Dodge, there were Carl van Vechten, Neith Boyce and Hutchins Hapgood to talk with. And she was, too, something of an underground celebrity due to her publications in the little magazines. Alfred Kreymborg welcomed her into his circle, which included Walter and Louise Arensberg – financial backers of *Others* – and Man Ray, William Carlos Williams and Marianne Moore. Within a few weeks she was drawn into the Provincetown Players, in December of 1916 playing the lead in Kreymborg's experimental play *Lima Beans*, which the Players put on a double bill with Eugene O'Neill's *Before Breakfast*. *Lima Beans* was a one-act piece with two characters, a husband and a wife. Kreymborg chose William Carlos Williams, who had a crush on Mina,[37] to play the other role; and to everyone's surprise, the play was a wild success, bringing Mina comparative fame, at least within bohemian circles.

She became even better known in February 1917 when a reporter for the *New York Evening Sun* chose her as the representative of the 'modern woman'. Beside her photograph, the article lauded her achievements in the 'modern' world, mentioning her writing of free verse; her painting of lampshades and magazine covers; her acting and stage designs; her costumes; and suggesting that 'This woman is half-way through the door into To-morrow.'[38]

Established in the New York bohemian circle, Mina shone. But then she met Arthur Cravan. Born Fabien Avenarius Lloyd in 1887, Cravan was a nephew of Oscar Wilde's wife Constance Lloyd. He drew crowds around him wherever he went. Known as the 'poet-boxer', he was a 'fugitive, forger, and master of disguise who had eluded military authorities and conscription officers for two years as he roamed through Central and Western Europe'.[39] Physically, he was breathtaking. He'd lived for a while in Paris, becoming intimate with the avant-garde painters and starting a journal called *Maintenant*, a polemical organ consisting solely of his own writing. Here he attacked the modern painters, insulting them all, particularly about their physical shortcomings: 'A bit of advice: take a few pills and purge your mind; do a lot of fucking or go into rigorous training: when you have nineteen inches around the arm, you'll be gifted.'[40]

Cravan loved to provoke and to get attention. He once advertised a lecture, for example, which – for the 'ladies' benefit' – he'd give 'in a jock-strap and put his balls on the table'. Here he would, he promised, end his career by committing suicide in public. He sold reserved seats for this event; and it was packed. But instead of committing suicide, he gave a lecture on Victor Hugo.[41] By the time he arrived in New York in 1917, he had connections with the Arensberg salon; and it was there that he and Mina Loy met.

Mina was waiting for her divorce from Haweis to be finalised. She hadn't become involved with any of the New York crowd and – perhaps in the struggle to be faithful to her feminist principles – she determined not to fall in love again. Cravan changed all that. They had only about six months together, since he had to flee the country in order to avoid the military draft. By September 1917 he was in Canada; by December in Mexico, from where he wrote to Mina, pleading with her to come to him: 'I can't live without you. Tell me that you will come right away and that we will spend the rest of our lives together . . . I want to marry you.'[42] Mina left New York immediately. Her divorce was finalised, and she married Cravan in Mexico City. Her children remained in Florence with their nurse while she and Cravan moved around Mexico, he earning money from boxing matches. When she became pregnant, she sailed on a hospital ship to Buenos Aires where she intended to wait for Cravan. After soliciting some cash somehow, she planned that they would both sail to Italy, collect her children, and then settle in Paris, now that the war was over. Mina arrived in Buenos Aires and waited. But Cravan never appeared; nor was he ever seen again. Mina finally sailed alone to England, where she spent the winter with her mother and where their daughter Fabienne was born on 5 April 1919. In the summer of that year, Mina returned to Florence to her two older children, now aged 14 and 12. She tried to pick up her old life in her villa there, but was obsessed by Cravan. His body was never found and this preyed on her. Desperate, she left Florence in March 1920 to look for him. Leaving all three children behind, she sailed for New York. Renewing her contacts, she became involved again with the Provincetown Players and with the modern poets. William Carlos Williams was starting up a new little

magazine called *Contact* and he introduced her to his friend and
co-editor, Robert McAlmon, who rapidly became fascinated by
her, as he shows in his autobiographical novel *Post-Adolescence*. In
this novel he has Mina ('Gusta Rolph') meeting Djuna Barnes
('Beryl Marks') for the first time; and has, too, Beryl Marks
questioning a further character, called 'Rollie' about the famous
Gusta Rolph:

> 'She is what is commonly known as what is brilliant, isn't she
> Rollie?' Beryl Marks asked sarcastically, opening her handbag to
> take out a lipstick and deliberately apply a straight heavy splash
> of bright rouge across her crooked mouth.
>
> 'People don't grasp her meanings; naturally they think she's
> intellectual. She has a romantic soul underneath sophistication,
> which is painful to herself I suspect', Rollie Walters answered,
> and continued to sit apathetically slunk in his chair, looking
> ahead at nothing with his burnt out grey eyes.
>
> 'Well, for God's sake, all I have to say is I wish she'd show up
> them [*sic*]. I've got to have a bright flash in my life soon.'
>
> 'She's been down on her luck lately, and feeling miserable;
> unhappy about a dead husband, or lover, or some such thing.'
>
> 'Ah that; who in hell is happy anyway; there's too much said
> about that. Does she write anything worth looking at?'[43]

When Gusta does show up, McAlmon has the two women hitting it
off straight away, commiserating with each other about what
they've been through: in Barnes' case, abortions and having to
support her brothers, lovers and a husband; and in Loy's case, three
children, one awful husband and several awful lovers, and a missing
second husband.

Mina acted in a further Playhouse production, Laurence Vail's
What D'You Want, and kept writing poetry. By now she and
Marianne Moore had been grouped together by Pound in a critical
article for *The Little Review* (March 1918) and Mina had become
friendly with its editors Margaret Anderson and Jane Heap. Her
publication in the *Review* was a poem 'Lions' Jaws' in the
September–December 1920 issue, which also carried an instalment
from *Ulysses*. This was the last instalment to appear, since the US
Post Office had seized the issues carrying Joyce and declared them
'obscene literature'. The editors were in the process of being sued
on this count. Mina went with them to court, as she reported to
Mabel Dodge who was now in Taos, New Mexico;

I am sick of New York . . . The Little Review has been arrested for Joyce's Ulysses – the case has been postponed because Quinn [lawyer for the *Review*] was out of town – we looked *too* wholesome in Court – representing filthy literature. I am enclosing an idea for a masque. I think it could be made wonderful.[44]

At about this time, in the autumn of 1920, H.D. and Bryher arrived in New York and were introduced to the Village circle by H.D.'s old friends William Carlos Williams and Marianne Moore. Although none of them has mentioned it specifically, they must have met Mina; and their meeting McAlmon, now a close friend of Mina, would, of course, have important consequences for them all. Within five months Bryher and McAlmon would be married and on their way to Paris, where McAlmon's Contact Press would publish, among other authors, Mina Loy.

But although Mina, too, wanted to be in Paris, she was stuck in New York through lack of funds. She wrote to Mabel Dodge:

Moose – will you help me? I never get time to work because I am so poor. I want to take the Italian woman who used to be my cook & start a little Restaurant in Paris – where I can get Cravan's friends to boom it for me. I could make enough to keep the children myself without this daily anxiety.

I suppose this is a ridiculous thing to ask after all these years – but I was so wondering what to do next. Haweis has been to Florence & taken the Boy & the house away from me & I have suffered so much since the war to keep them going. I want to be free of worry – & work. I have so much accumulated that is bursting for expression – it is getting unbearable. Would you lend me a thousand dollars to be paid back in two years – to help me start a Restaurant. When once I have got it going I shall have some time and peace. I have not been able to get along in the commercial field in New York because I cannot understand their distinctions between one nothingness and another.

I've had a hell of a time off and on – the last few years – & it has fired my imagination – must vent it or break. Do let me know if you will do this for me.[45]

There must have been at least some response to this plea, since shortly afterwards Mina was on her way to Europe. The restaurant in Paris never materialised, however; instead she went on to

Florence to her two remaining children (Haweis had taken Giles, who died two years later). Mina remained in Florence with her two daughters, now aged 15 and 3, for about a year, leaving in 1922 to travel to Vienna and Berlin, where it was cheaper to live. In Berlin she had contacts in the expatriate community which included, among others, McAlmon, Djuna Barnes and Marsden Hartley. Eventually she took up with her old friend Laurence Vail and his wife Peggy Guggenheim, travelling with them to France. By the spring of 1923, she and Fabienne were settled in Paris (Joella was sent to the Elizabeth Duncan dancing school) and the Vails were backing her in a lampshade business.

The business was intended to 'free' Mina to write poetry; but it turned out to be an exciting venture. Mina designed the shades herself; and soon expanded into glass novelties, paper cut-outs and painted flower arrangements. She had a studio in which to work; and Peggy Guggenheim arranged exhibitions and sales on her frequent trips to New York. Most orders came from America. Perhaps Mina's most famous creation was the 'calla lily lamp', a truly beautiful design. For the next six years she flourished, both in the lampshade business and in the writing of poetry. She became one of the Paris 'Bunch' immortalised by McAlmon and numerous other memorists. Sylvia Beach became a friend and admirer:

> We had three raving beauties in 'the Crowd', all in one family, which was not fair. Mina Loy, the poetess, and her daughters, Joella and Faby . . . were so lovely that they were stared at wherever they went . . . if a vote had been taken, Mina would have been elected the most beautiful of the three . . . When you went to Mina's apartment you threaded your way past lamp shades that were everywhere; she made them to support her children. She made all her own clothes, also . . . Her hats were very like her lamp shades . . .[46]

Joella, a teenager during these years, remembers the 'Crowd' very well, recalling that they were 'full of ideas, life and conversation; in Paris because it was a place where they could get their work done and not have families nagging at them all the time.' She saw her mother at that time as 'a goddess – an oracle', though she 'didn't live up to it all the time.'

McAlmon was semi-settled in Paris and just starting his Contact Press. One of the first books he published was Mina Loy's *Lunar Baedecker* [sic] in 1923. This was Mina's only published book until

Lunar Baedeker & Time-tables in 1958, although long sections of her autobiographical poem 'Anglo-Mongrels and the Rose' appeared in *The Little Review* in 1923 and in McAlmon's *Contact Collection of Contemporary Writers* in 1925. During these years, Mina renewed her friendship with Djuna Barnes and, too, her friendship with Gertrude Stein. They all met at Natalie Barney's weekly lesbian salons, with Mina being the 'token heterosexual'.[47] By now it seems that she'd finally succeeded in destroying her desire to be loved, apparently never engaging in further sexual relationships after the disappearance of Cravan. At 41 she *seemed* almost serene, although Joella reflects that she 'never had much tranquillity', no longer the tormented Gusta Rolph of McAlmon's novel, but the mature, beautiful poet in flowing hats, sitting by her calla lily lamps with her two daughters.

Though part of the expatriate community, she remained aloof from it, as well as from Barney's group. Harriet Monroe, visiting Paris in 1923, was captivated by Mina Loy herself as she had never been by her poetry:

A café evening full of color in my memory began with a dinner of four in a little restaurant round the corner from the Boulevard Montparnasse, Robert McAlmon and the David O'Neils (he the St. Louis poet) being the other three. The cafe had been discovered as a rendezvous but a fortnight before, and to it certain Bohemian groups, especially the American groups, had flitted from their other haunts. Ezra Pound came in, and his neighbour R.C. Dunning, a poet whom we published years ago, and Jane Heap with some friends – she hopes to continue *The Little Review* in Paris – and the Lawrence [*sic*] Vails, and Tristan Tzara the original dada-ist, and other Frenchmen whose names are lost in my unserviceable memory. And there was talk and laughter, and a few songs by a new young *prima* or *seconda donna*, and much gayety of spirit. Perhaps a great deal of this gayety and color aforesaid was due to the presence of Mina Loy. I may never have fallen very hard for this lady's poetry, but her personality is quite irresistible. Beauty ever-young which has survived four babies, and charm which will survive a century if she lives that long, are sustained by a gayety that seems the worldly-wise conquest of many despairs – all expressed in a voice which, as someone said of Masefield's is 'rich with all the sorrows of the world.' Yes, poetry is in this lady whether she writes it or not – to those who know her it matters little, probably, that the Contact Press, otherwise Robert McAlmon, has just issued *Lunar Baedeker*, her book of verse.[48]

McAlmon was still one of Mina's great admirers, often joining her in the bars and cafés of Montparnasse:

The Stryx had placed a long table across the street at which various people were collecting. Jane Heap was there with Mina Loy, Clotilde Vail, and Kathleen Cannell . . . Jane Heap and Mina Loy were both talking brilliantly: Mina, her cerebral fantasies, Jane, her breezy, travelling-salesman-of-the-world tosh which was impossible to recall later. But neither of these ladies needed to make sense. Conversation is an art with them . . .[49]

McAlmon reports, too, that Jane and Mina went together to Ezra Pound's opera, based on Villon's poems, in 1924; and that afterwards they all headed for Cocteau's nightclub 'Le Boeuf sur le Toit', a bohemian hangout. Djuna Barnes, too, adds a portrait of the older Mina Loy, as 'Patience Scalpel' in her anonymous *Ladies Almanack*, published by McAlmon in 1928.

During 1927 Mina twice addressed Natalie Barney's gatherings; once she spoke on Gertrude Stein and once she read from her own work. She remained an enthusiastic supporter of Gertrude, having reviewed *The Making of Americans* for the *Transatlantic Review* in 1924, which issue carried also her short poem 'Gertrude Stein':

> Curie
> of the laboratory
> of vocabulary
> she crushed
> the tonnage
> of consciousness
> congealed to phrases
> to extract
> a radium of the word.[50]

By 1928 Mina and Peggy Guggenheim had quarrelled; and Mina's son-in-law, gallery owner Julien Levy was supporting the lampshade business. In this year, too, Mina moved into 9 rue St Romain, the same building where Djuna Barnes and Thelma Wood lived. For the next few years, Djuna and Mina were particularly intimate, helping each other through emotional and practical crises. From New York in 1930, Djuna wrote to Mina:

Mina darling,
  What a perfect angel you are! I did not mean to involve you in
all that work & distress on my damned apt. I meant only that I'd
be glad if you would see that the charges were paid & the
inventory given to the concierge – I can't thank you adequately
for all your trouble. You were a lamb to have it cleaned for me
. . .[51]

In turn, Djuna tried to place Mina's work in New York:

I enclose the letter I got back from the Hound & Horn – So send
them something else – they like your work. I am mailing the two I
have to 'Poetry' – Monroe's you remember – perhaps they will
have some sense.[52]

Djuna, ten years younger than Mina, was coming to the same
conclusions about love that her friend already had; better to destroy
the need rather than be consumed by it, as both nearly had been:
Mina by Cravan and Djuna by Thelma Wood:

I've messed my life up all right – but we all do I presume – by
thinking that life the way it seems in 1920 is going to come to a
logical 1930 – only it never does –
  I don't think I can ever live with *anyone* again – I've gotten
cranky & old-maid like – I don't even like to have an animal
looking at me, & when I lay a thing down I want to find it exactly
where I put it – its as bad as that![53]

Djuna, in her rough way, was very concerned about Mina:

If there is going to be any trouble with France & England – could
you not transfer your ownership of apt. to Jo[ella] – or her
husband? Would this not save your apt? as they are American?
Don't stay there if there is going to be any nasty demonstration
against English – I *don't* want you killed! I often think of the jolly
times we had, do you remember, when there was a fire & I read
aloud & you did cross-word puzzles?[54]

In 1930 Mina gave up the lampshade business and started working
for her son-in-law as the Paris agent for his New York art gallery.
She published hardly anything during the 1930s, although she did
begin to paint again. In 1936 she left Paris for New York, where she
lived first with her daughter Fabienne in Lower Manhattan and then
by herself in the Bowery. At first she had a little contact with her
old friends, but soon none at all, although they frequently wrote to

her asking for news. By 1940 Djuna was also living permanently in New York; but even these two rarely saw one another, though they did speak often on the telephone. Mina published a few poems in the 1940s, but her *Selected Poems* was rejected by Random House.[55] Her chief interest came to be the Bowery bums, about whom she wrote poems and began to assemble 'constructions': montages of street scenes made out of 'found objects' from the streets around her. She scoured back alleys for trash to use in her work and published 'Hot Cross Bum', a long poem, in James Laughlin's *New Directions 12*, 1950.

At the age of 71, Mina finally left New York forever and moved to Colorado, where both her daughters were living. Here she became more and more reclusive, like Djuna in Patchin Place, and like Bryher at Kenwin. She became a colourful town curiosity, visited from time to time by emissaries from the literary world. Jonathan Williams published her second book in 1958, incorporating her first and adding later poems. A few new poems continued to appear in little magazines; and in 1959 a New York gallery exhibited her Bowery 'Constructions'. Mina didn't attend the opening, although a number of her old friends were there, including Djuna, Peggy Guggenheim and Kay Boyle. She remained in Colorado, working on her last creations, her 'experiments in junk'.[56]

Mina Loy had never let go of Cravan; and although she may have succeeded in destroying her need to be loved, she could not destroy her own love. Her last poem was about him:

. . .

My body and my reason
you left to the drought of your dying:
the longing and the lack
of a racked creature
shouting
to an unanswering hiatus
'reunite us!'

till slyly
patience creeps up on passion
and the elation of youth
dwindles out of season.

. . .

Posing the extreme enigma
in my Bewilderness
can your face excelling Adonis
have ceased to be
or ever have had existence?

With you no longer the addresser
there is no addressee
to dally with defunct reality.
Can one who still has being
be inexistent?

I am become
dumb
in answer
to your dead language of amor.

. . .

Withhold your ghostly reference
to the sweet once were we.

Leave me
my final illiteracy
of memory's languor –

my preference
to drift in lenient coma
an older Ophelia
on Lethe.

from 'Letters of the Unliving'[57]

Mina Loy's answer to *The Little Review* questionnaire of 1929 never changed. 'What has been the happiest moment of your life?' she was asked. 'Every moment I spent with Arthur Cravan' was her reply. And to the next question, 'The unhappiest?' she answered, 'The rest of the time'.[58] And for Mina Loy, 'the rest of the time' was 57 years. She died in Aspen, Colorado, in 1966, at the age of 84.

Chapter 9

Loners

Marianne Moore was born in 1887 in Missouri; but when she was very young, her father suffered a nervous breakdown and she went with her mother and brother to live with her grandparents. Subsequently, mother and children moved to Carlisle, Pennsylvania, where Marianne went to school and grew up. She was in H.D.'s class at Bryn Mawr college, both attending as freshmen in 1905; but unlike H.D., she completed her four years successfully, graduating in 1909. This period was the only time in her life when she lived separately from her mother until her mother's death in 1947. Marianne, her mother and her brother developed an intense closeness, calling each other by nicknames such as 'Rat' and 'Mole'. When the brother, Warner, became a minister and moved away from home, both Marianne and her mother wrote to him every day.

After her graduation, Marianne spent a year at a commercial business college, learning typing and shorthand, after which she taught at an American Indian school for four years. During her years at Bryn Mawr she'd worked on the college literary magazine and published some articles and poems in it. In 1915, she wrote to *The Egoist*, where Richard Aldington was assistant editor. The poems he accepted from her were her first published work. In the same year, Harriet Monroe took some poems for *Poetry*.

H.D. then married to Aldington, was an immediate supporter and admirer of Marianne's work and wrote to her asking if she were the same Marianne Moore who had been a classmate at Bryn Mawr. A correspondence developed, in which H.D. remained highly enthusiastic about Marianne's work. Meanwhile, Marianne and her mother decided to move to New York City, in order to live closer to Warner.

Marianne continued to write; and in New York met Alfred Kreymborg, William Carlos Williams and Lola Ridge. Her verse began to draw some attention in the little magazines. Pound wrote to her in 1919, praising her work; and she met Robert McAlmon (whom she and her mother called 'Piggy'), and Marsden Hartley. These and other men in her circle considered her a great intellect,[1] as well as a witty, dry, articulate and retiring woman. But unlike many of them, she seemed never to crave travel or the bohemian life. Her letters to Bryher in the 1920s are full of the reasons why.

Marianne Moore was slender, with 'shining braids' wrapped round her head; and she dressed in an old-fashioned, proper style. From 1921–5 she worked part-time in a branch of the New York Public Library. At a party in 1920 she met Scofield Thayer, who had just taken over *The Dial* magazine; and so began her long association with that journal. In September of the same year, H.D. Bryher and Perdita arrived in New York; and it was Marianne who introduced the two women to McAlmon. Bryher took to Marianne immediately; and decided that she must start travelling. From California, where she and H.D. spent the late autumn, Bryher wrote to Marianne, urging her to travel and urging, too – as she would continue to do – that Marianne accept financial help. But despite Bryher's insistence, she only ever made one trip to the West and one to England, both times accompanied by her mother; and remained reluctant always to accept Bryher's financial gifts.

When Bryher and H.D. returned to New York in February 1921 and Bryher asked McAlmon to marry her, Marianne and her mother greatly disapproved, thinking McAlmon an opportunist. Nevertheless she maintained a lifelong friendship with both Bryher and H.D., even after they published a collection of her poems without her knowledge or permission.[2]

In 1925 Scofield Thayer asked Marianne to take over Alyse Gregory's position as managing editor of *The Dial*. Because her husband, Llewelyn Powys, was ill and had to return to England and Switzerland, Alyse Gregory had to resign. The two women were good friends and corresponded frequently.[3] In 1929 Thayer suffered a nervous breakdown and *The Dial* went out of his control. Marianne and her mother then moved to Brooklyn to be nearer to Warner.

Marianne Moore appears in both McAlmon's *Post-Adolescence*

and Bryher's *Two Selves*. She is presented, too, in the autobiographies of William Carlos Williams, Alfred Kreymborg and Bryher. She knew Mina Loy, Amy Lowell, Djuna Barnes and Margaret Anderson; and later in her life was introduced to Sylvia Beach by Bryher. She became a well-known and respected poet.

Like Marianne Moore, Harriet Monroe never paired off. Nor did she, as a young woman, take the advice offered to her by the established novelist Elizabeth Stoddard, who exclaimed to her when they met at a literary party in the 1880s, 'A literary career! Drop it before you begin – scrub, dig, marry for a living, but for God's sake don't try to write! It's the most thankless, disappointing, utterly devastating pursuit in the world.'[4] In founding *Poetry: A Magazine of Verse* in 1912, Harriet Monroe made a commitment to all writers: one she never relinquished, in spite of years of struggle.

What was she like? Given a place in the annals of American literary history for *Poetry*, she is most often described as a humourless, rigid 'old maid' who baulked at publishing Eliot when Pound first sent her 'Prufrock'; who refused much of the experimental poetry written by Williams, Kreymborg, Mina Loy, Marianne Moore and others. Her personal image is that of a dull, dry 'spinster'. In choosing a life devoted to writing poetry and editing her magazine, rather than one devoted to a man or men, Harriet placed herself at the mercy of such male-voiced speculation.

Born in 1860 in Chicago, Illinois, she was the second child of four who survived to adulthood. Three siblings died in infancy. Her father was a successful trial lawyer until the great Chicago fire of 1871, in which he lost his office, his law library and other property. After the fire, his practice declined, partly owing to 'unfortunate' business connections which his daughter implied had something to do with prostitution and gambling. By the time he died in 1903, he was virtually penniless and was being looked after by his children. Still, Harriet's early life was spent in middle-class comfort in a large house and in a 'good neighbourhood', with servants, nice clothes and good food. As Dorothy Richardson experienced also, Harriet's early security began to crumble with her father's failing career; and collapsed completely with the realisation that her parents' marriage was a disaster. Looking back, she described herself as being in an 'overwrought, nervous condition' between the ages of 13 and 17, which she attributed to 'sex inhibition' arising from the knowledge that her parents' marriage was a failure. It seemed to her that they didn't understand one another at all and were 'united only by the close tie of flesh, and its corollary, the children'.[5]

Clearly her parents' relationship had far-reaching effects on Harriet's notions of sex and marriage in particular, and on intimate relations in general:

> modern psychologists might trace my crisis [adolescent nervous condition] back to sex inhibitions; and indeed, if ever a child or young girl was sex inhibited, that was my fate, shut up as I was in an impenetrable shell of self-consciousness. The subject was secretly whispered around by older girls. Boys became mysterious, inhuman – remote repositories of dread whom I could never meet on simple and natural terms. If involuntary emotional feelers rose to their allure, I crushed them back as shameful, pernicious, and would have died rather than confess them. Thus I always played wrong in the game of sex, and ran away, emotionally, from boy friends; thus through the flowering years I grew up afraid of love.[6]

This reticence about sexual love, shared by her future colleagues Amy Lowell, May Sinclair and Marianne Moore, characterised her adult life.

At 17, presumably recovered from her nervous condition, Harriet was sent to the Visitation Convent in Washington, D.C., where she spent two years among the nuns and the daughters of wealthy and influential Easterners. Here, from 1877 to 1879, Harriet was first encouraged to write poetry and plays. Although she was a Protestant, her exposure to the dedicated nuns inspired her to think of a 'vocation' for herself – not as a nun, but as a 'great poet' or a 'great playwright'. She worked hard at writing and returned to Chicago in 1879 after her graduation. At this time, her father was still trying to keep up appearances and the family still lived in its large house. Harriet, at 19, expected to go on living there in comfort until she married, as she assumed she would. She kept herself busy with her writing, and daydreamed of fame and a grand romantic passion which she felt was sure to appear. But the few young men she met were, from her point of view, hardly worth her while. She didn't want some real, bumbling youth, but a knight. When one young man, perhaps the only one she allowed to be a serious suitor, deserted her at a party to dance the night away with other girls, she 'wrathfully drove him away' out of her life forever.[7] Still, she clung to her romantic dreams about love, insisting, in her autobiography, that this young man 'closed the door on women' and remained a bachelor all his life, owing to her rejection of him. The story is the more poignant given her admission that he was her best chance for a 'good, kind husband'. This unrealistic stance differs from that of Amy Lowell, Gertrude Stein, Marianne Moore and others, who found satisfying ways of fulfilling their desires for love without feeling any regret for not having good, kind husbands.

Harriet never gave up her unlikely ideal of romantic love. Instead of forming intimate connections, she saw herself as deprived:

> It is assumed by certain modern philosophers that sex suppres-sions and inhibitions turn to poison, warping and injuring the character and vitality of the individual sufferer. The medieval Christian . . . felt that such suppression loosed creative energy . . . for the 'higher life' . . . Without accepting either extreme, I should say that unless artificially stimulated by brooding, idleness, or other maladjustments, the normal woman suffers no severe agony, either physical or mental, in accepting a spinster's comparatively narrow lot. Deprived of the love life's supreme fulfilment, she tries to fulfill herself in other ways, and faculties unused become gradually less insistent. As time went on, I became very modest in that important detail, laughed at myself for ever having expected the glorious mutuality of a grand passion . . . Unconsciously I gave up the problem and retired from the great game which I had no talent for . . .[8]

As mere human lovers proved 'elusive and unsatisfactory', she explained, she consoled herself with 'loves of the imagination . . . Shelley . . . Browning . . . Robert L. Stevenson . . .'[9] It was Stevenson she became obsessed by, writing him letters during 1886 and 1887, which he was kind enough to answer. She dreamt of someday meeting him; and eventually did so, during a visit to New York in 1887. The shock of seeing the real man, ill and tubercular, destroyed her illusion. His 'bodily presence' revolted her, making her admit to herself that she didn't like being with 'sick people'. What she didn't, perhaps, realise was that her inability to come to terms with human reality – rather than her status as a 'single woman' – was at the root of the restrictions she felt fate had imposed upon her.

Meanwhile, with her father's fortunes failing further each year, the Monroe family moved from its large house to a much smaller one in a poorer neighbourhood. Then, when Harriet was 27, the family moved to a boarding house. By this time she was aware that she must face earning a living. She looked for work as a journalist; joined a literary women's club where she gave papers; and met Chicago's literati, including the poet Eugene Field. In 1888 she landed a correspondent's job with the Chicago *Tribune* as a result of her friendship with Margaret Sullivan, a well-known editorial writer. Her mother had scraped together enough cash to send Harriet and her younger sister Lucy to New York, where Harriet could write about plays, pictures, music and people for the newspaper. She shared a small apartment with Lucy, and they began to make friends. Harriet began, too, to write blank verse plays, which she circulated in typescript among her new friends. One important connection was Edmund Clarence Stedman, a successful literary anthology editor. Evening gatherings at his home gave Harriet a chance to meet many contemporary writers.

New York perhaps proved too expensive or too overwhelming for Harriet and Lucy. Within a year they moved back to Chicago. The Monroe parents had by now managed to move out of the boarding house into a small house of their own, where the two daughters joined them. Harriet was soon able to take a leave of absence from her *Tribune* job (now as art critic) and join friends on a trip to Europe in 1890. They spent six weeks in London, Paris and parts of Italy.

Harriet returned to Chicago and to her *Tribune* job, only to be fired in 1891 because her sister Lucy was working as art critic for the rival newspaper. Shortly afterwards, Harriet had a minor operation which left her weak and which, she insisted, led to a further 'two years of nervous prostration'.[10]

The attack was more severe than her earlier adolescent crisis. Was it – in spite of her conviction that the single woman suffers 'no severe agony' of mind or body – a symptom of her own perception that her life was a 'narrow lot'? Or was it her way of making sure that she had the time she needed to write what she wanted, without being tied down to a regular, demanding, outside job? She recalled the 'prostration' later:

> At first it was severe; to walk a few yards without collapse was impossible, and the sensations inside my head and limbs were as if little worms were crawling there. One day, as I was trying to read, my eyes suddenly swung out of their orbits and refused to work. Improvement was very gradual and fitful – full of queer sensations that seemed to reveal nature's secret processes . . . On

Harriet Shaw Weaver 1907. *Courtesy of Miss Jane Lidderdale*

Harriet Monroe, c. 1890s.
Department of Special Collections, University of Chicago Library

Marianne Moore in the 1920s, at a New York dock.
The Rosenbach Museum and Library, Philadelphia.

H.D. in Cornwall, c. 1920, taken by Bryher. *Courtesy of Perdita Schaffner*

Bryher in Cornwall, c. 1920, taken by H.D. *Courtesy of Perdita Schaffner*

Bryher and Sylvia Beach at the exhibition *'Des Ecrivains Américains à Paris',* Paris, 1959. *Courtesy of Perdita Schaffner*

ABOVE RIGHT Dorothy Richardson and Alan Odle in the early 1930s. *Courtesy of Sheena Odle*

BELOW RIGHT Dorothy Richardson and Alan Odle, Cornwall Cottage, painted by Adrian Allison. *Courtesy of Sheena Odle*

Mary Butts, 1919. *Courtesy of Mrs Camilla Bagg*

Djuna Barnes and Mina Loy
in France, 1920s.
McKeldin Library,
University of Maryland

Thelma Wood and Djuna Barnes
in Provincetown, Mass., c. 1930.
McKeldin Library,
University of Maryland

the one hand I seemed conscious of whatever went on physically in my own vital organs – the anatomical life of which I had hitherto been blissfully unaware. On the other hand I was taking fierce plunges into infinite heights and depths, or rolling helplessly on a troubled ocean. Meanwhile a glass of champagne or an hour in bright sunlight would make me feel normal for a short time.[11]

For Harriet, this period in her life was a 'tempestuous voyage of discovery'.[12] She accomplished a great deal during 1891–2 while she was in the throes of her 'queer sensations'. First, she obtained the job of writing the 'Dedicatory Ode' for the Chicago World's Fair, to be held in 1892. She worked on it at intervals during her illness and had it ready for the Fair's opening. In 1892, her first book, *Valeria and Other Poems*, was published by subscription and the sponsorship of friends. In the same year she began work on a biography of her late brother-in-law, the architect John Wellborn Root. Her mother died during this year and the rest of the family moved once again, this time to her widowed sister, Dora Root. By the end of the year Harriet had secured work on the Chicago *Times-Herald* (she was to contribute a weekly feature article) and had initiated a lawsuit against the *New York World* newspaper, which had printed her 'Dedicatory Ode' without her permission. (She eventually won the case.) Her 'voyage of discovery' was a fruitful one; and she emerged from her 'prostration' at the age of 32 to a life that she'd now got well under control.

One romantic mystery does surround her personal life. In 1896, a shadowy man did disturb Harriet's calm, though she is elusive – almost coy – about who he was and what exactly took place, saying only that she was 'shaken by a deeply shadowed emotion' and that she wrote several poems about it. They were published under the title 'Love Songs' and all, she explained, refer to this episode:

I

I love my life, but not too well
　To give it to thee like a flower,
So it may pleasure thee to dwell
　Deep in its perfume but an hour.
I love my life, but not too well.

I love my life, but not too well
　To sing it note by note away,

> So to thy soul the song may tell
> The beauty of the desolate day.
> I love my life, but not too well.
>
> I love my life, but not too well
> To cast it like a cloak on thine,
> Against the storms that sound and swell
> Between thy lonely heart and mine.
> I love my heart, but not too well.[13]

However nebulous this relationship was, the man had a powerful effect on Harriet's imagination, as she was proud to confess:

> Underneath the varied texture of my days I was aware of two sources of power. One of these was nature, with its corollary, art . . . The other hidden source of power, the deepest and highest experience of my life, was the rapture and agony of an emotion shared in perfect sympathy and complete in the incompleteness of inevitable separation; a feeling which united for years a man and woman who rarely saw each other, yet whom even death, when at last the blow struck, was powerless to separate utterly – so long as the other lives and remembers. A few lyrics and sonnets may have told the story – if not, it can never be told.[14]

Nothing further is disclosed about this experience. There was a man; they didn't live together; they presumably didn't sleep together; they rarely saw one another; he died before she did; and she wrote several poems about it. Certainly no one who knew the Harriet Monroe of *Poetry* magazine would have guessed the existence of this 'hidden source of power'. Literally, Harriet seems to have lived for love; but it was an idealised and fantastic love, rather than a reckless passion.

Her lifestyle continued without interruption. She lived with her sisters and father, her nieces and nephew, as part of a warm and close family circle. In 1897, the award from her lawsuit finally came through; and Harriet and Lucy embarked on a trip to Europe. Soon after their return, Harriet fell ill with pneumonia and recuperated by travelling out West. This was the first of many forays West; and the one which elicited her love for American Indians. She returned to Chicago to take up freelance journalism, private tutoring and lecturing on poetry. Presumably she contributed to the household finances. Her earnings rose from $573 in 1900 to $1,636 by 1910.

She might just have managed to afford a room – perhaps in a boarding-house attic, as Dorothy Richardson was doing in London at this time – but Harriet Monroe gives no indication of ever wanting to live alone; indeed she describes her family life with great fondness. She enjoyed Sunday-night suppers, with friends visiting afterwards; and the share she had in the upbringing of her nieces and nephew. And staying within the family allowed her to pursue a literary life while earning a very meagre salary. Occasionally the circle changed: her father died in 1903, which may well have been a relief; and the marriage of her sister Lucy in 1904 provided an opportunity for travel that Harriet seized eagerly.

Harriet kept up her freelance journalism until 1909, when she returned to the position of art critic on the Chicago *Tribune* from which she'd been fired 15 years earlier. It paid no regular salary, but brought interesting contacts and friendships. By this time – at the age of 49 – Harriet was becoming more and more convinced of the need to foster the art of poetry in some way. It became her mission, even as she set out to visit Lucy and her diplomat husband in Peking. It was the summer of 1910; and she decided to go via Europe, a decision which would prove crucial to the future of her venture into magazine editing. She was primed to seek out new poets; and in London that summer, she found one: Ezra Pound.

Harriet's meeting with May Sinclair in London that summer, which led to her meeting with Pound, and thence to H.D., Lawrence, Eliot, Marianne Moore, and many others, was a turning point in her life. She returned to Chicago determined to start a new magazine devoted to poetry. From now on, *Poetry* would be her life, soaking up all her time and all her romantic energy. She involved her family in the enterprise from the beginning; though with Lucy in Peking and Dora's death in 1913, she soon had to substitute the magazine for her family, writing that 'I could not pause. The magazine became a consolation and a refuge, absorbing my interest more and more.'[15] The story of *Poetry* is the story of Harriet's vocation, her fight 'for freedom of the creative spirit in the authentic and individual achievement of beauty through the fit expression of its ideas'.[16]

After the first issue in October 1912, Harriet's private life receded more and more. All her contacts involved the magazine in some way. She lived with her niece Polly until 1915, when Polly went to France as a nurse. By this time Harriet was 55 and on her own at last. It was this middle-aged woman whom the literary world came to know; the strait-laced, serious, totally honest woman who ruled the magazine until her death in 1936. Pound made fun of her. Her friend Amy Lowell characterised her as 'as truthful and honest as the Rock of Ages'.[17] But this rock-like edifice of honesty and seriousness was still the incurable romantic whose belief in the perfectibility of love kept her from accepting the imperfections of human nature. 'I insisted that love must be flawless, or I would none of it',[18] she explained. She was never to find flawless love in a person; but her choice of a literary life gave twentieth-century literature one of its most important vehicles: *Poetry: A Magazine of Verse*.

The significance of Harriet Monroe's editorship is acknowledged. So, too, on the other side of the Atlantic, other women exercised editorial skills in the service of their beliefs. Harriet Monroe's devotion was given to art; in England, Harriet Shaw Weaver was motivated initially by social concerns, working for years with the poor and underprivileged and raising funds for causes such as a Women's Hospital in London. Further, she gave away most of her own money to writers and friends she believed in; and edited a magazine and started a press so that work no one else would publish could see the light of day. Harriet Weaver typed Joyce's manuscripts, supported him and his family, and endured isolation and physical hardships in order to help her friend Dora Marsden finish her difficult philosophical writings. In her youth, her leisure time was spent visiting elderly relatives, while in her old age she spent much of it with her nieces and nephews. She was a woman who listened more than she spoke, who gave more than she took, who lived her life according to her principles. On hearing of her death in 1961, Samuel Beckett wrote to Sylvia Beach, 'I . . . shall think of her when I think of goodness.'[19]

Harriet Shaw Weaver was born in 1876 in Frodsham, Cheshire, the sixth of eight children. Her father was a doctor, much concerned with social causes. Both her parents were strict Anglicans and imposed rigid discipline on all their children, including twice-daily attendance at prayers, controlled reading and dress, and bans on dancing and theatregoing. When Harriet's maternal grandfather died in 1892, her mother inherited a large fortune and the family moved to 'Cedar Lawn', an imposing house on the edge of Hampstead Heath. Dr Weaver gave up his practice and concentrated on his many interests: medical missionary societies, the church, medical care for the poor, local government, travel, walking and poetry. Mrs Weaver was a woman of fixed ideas and habits, which didn't change when she received her inheritance. She rose at 6 in the morning to read the Bible before beginning the day; she supervised the children's education; she ran the household; and went to bed after family prayers in the evening. All her children were devoted to her, as she was to them; but she was not sympathetic to new ideas and seems not to have had much of a sense of humour. When she found Harriet, aged about 18, reading *Adam Bede*, she sent her to her room and took the book away. She then called in the vicar and asked him to explain to Harriet why *Adam Bede* was not suitable reading for a young woman. Harriet – who was torn all her life between love and loyalty to her family and her own independent ideas – did not create a scene. But she did continue to read in secret.[20] From this time on, Harriet compartmentalised her life. Her family would never again really know what she was thinking and reading. She was already a firm believer in freedom of speech and thought. When she reached 18, her governess left and her formal education was considered complete. She'd have liked to go to university, but her parents considered it out of the question, since she had no financial need to learn a profession. Instead, she was expected to stay at home, take lessons in cultivated pursuits such as drawing and French, and to help and be a companion to her mother. Harriet concurred. She continued to read a lot, mostly in secret.

In addition to teaching Sunday School, she began – in her early twenties – to undertake social work; first for the 'Children's Country Holiday Fund', for whom she interviewed prospective parents and children, and then – with her cousin Eleanor Davies-Colley – at the Invalid Children's Aid Association, which provided medical treatment and job training for seriously invalided children. Harriet's job here was to visit prospective candidates and write reports of them. When her cousin Elly left the Association to start medical training in 1902, Harriet took over her administrative work and was given an office in the East End. She was a great success and stayed for three years; and then, at the age of 29, she took a decisive independent step.

Disturbed by the poverty and disease with which she'd become well-acquainted, and inspired by one of the officers of the Association, the economist and political philosopher E.J. Urwick, Harriet decided to study at the London School of Sociology and

Social Economics.[21] The course required students to do practical volunteer work, as well as regular classwork; and Harriet went to work for an East End settlement house run by the Society for Organizing Charitable Relief and Repressing Mendicity.[22] Her task on the sub-committee on skilled employment was to help poor girls and young women with promise to achieve apprenticeships or job training. She placed them in such trades as dressmaking, upholstery and millinery, keeping track of each individual case. Through this work and through her studies she became a convinced socialist, though she didn't confront her family – with whom she still lived – with her new ideas.

For the six years between 1905 and 1911 while she was deeply involved in her work at the settlement house, Harriet's home life continued as usual. Her three sisters were also still at home; and there was a comfortable routine of daily life, with family meals, bridge and golf. She and her sister Maude sometimes went on walking tours together; and as her brothers had children, she grew close to these small nieces and nephews. With her parents she travelled to France, Italy and Switzerland. But there were still no plays, no dancing and – for Harriet – no romances. Although she had several (though never many) friends outside the family circle, she apparently never had any suitors. This was probably her own choice, since 'there was never a flicker of a flirtation with anyone'.[23] She appeared to have 'a total lack of interest in the other sex, except as human beings'.[24] From youth to old age, her attitude never changed. She seemed never to have been racked by an unrequited love affair nor ever to have suffered melancholy from being alone. She seems, too, not to have suffered feelings of self-pity or inadequacy from not having any children. She had, however, a great sympathetic capacity to understand all these feelings in her friends.

By her mid-thirties, Harriet's independence of mind began to assert itself. She had long rejected the church and embraced socialism; and although her mother's death in 1909 left her with a substantial inheritance so that she could have moved into a home of her own, she chose to stay at 'Cedar Lawn' and share its running with two of her sisters. However, she did begin to take a more active role in causes she endorsed. She started to read about and to support the suffrage movement; and through her cousin Eleanor, now a surgeon, she became involved in the establishment of a hospital for women. Eleanor and her friend Miss Chadbourn – also a surgeon – began to raise money for a second women's hospital since the one on the Euston Road was seriously overcrowded. Throughout 1911 and 1912, Harriet worked so successfully at fund-raising for this project that the cornerstone of the South London Hospital for Women and Children was laid in the spring of 1913. By then, however, Harriet was involved in another cause.

Although Harriet had subscribed to the WSPU journal *Votes for Women*, she was not entirely in sympathy with their view that the vote would bring an end to women's problems. She had worked for too long in the East End to accept that. Therefore, when she saw a paper called *The Freewoman: A Weekly Feminist Review* on the stands in late 1911, she bought it.[25]

> There comes a cry that woman is an individual, and that because she is an individual she must be set free. It would be nearer the truth to say that if she is an individual she *is* free, and will act like those who are free.[26]

The words of Dora Marsden's editorial spoke directly to Harriet Weaver, as they did to many London women that year. Harriet agreed, too, with the open policy of the paper, which discussed in print such themes as homosexuality, polygamy, usury, unmarried motherhood, divorce law reform. Though Harriet was not directly concerned with all these issues, she heartily approved a forum which would allow them to be discussed. Since the *Adam Bede* incident she'd felt strongly about an individual's right to read and discuss anything, as, in her view, there ought to be no censorship imposed on the mind. Harriet, a quiet, unobtrusive 36-year-old woman, so reserved that she didn't allow her first name to be used outside the family, who never argued or raised her voice in anger, joined the Freewoman Discussion Circle in 1912. She was, therefore, heavily involved in the paper's fortunes when its distributors, W.H. Smith boycotted it in October 1912, thus delivering a mortal blow which quickly resulted in the paper's closure. She was the largest contributor to the fund organised to start the paper up again; and quickly approached Dora Marsden with information about her personal wealth. When Dora suggested meeting, Harriet readily agreed; and at that first meeting in February 1913, the two women found that they liked each other immediately.

Dora Marsden was 31 – five years younger than Harriet – but her crusading spirit was able to fire Harriet's in turn. Harriet would always be a worker behind the scenes, while Dora was out at the front, speaking loudly and confidently, arguing and drawing attention to herself and her cause. Together they began to concentrate on getting *The New Freewoman* started; and their success was largely due to Harriet's organisational skills, financial help and practical mind.

The New Freewoman led to Harriet's involvement with many of the young writers in London. After Pound met Rebecca West, then assistant editor, at a literary party early in the summer of 1913, he began to send contributions to the paper, and to encourage his friends to do the same. H.D. and Aldington were two who did so. Soon afterwards, Rebecca West resigned and Pound became 'literary editor', thus instituting a shift away from Dora Marsden's philosophical essays and towards the new writing he was championing. He brought the paper into contact with Harriet Monroe's *Poetry* in Chicago, with other little magazines in New York, and with Amy Lowell in Boston. Imagist poetry began filling its pages and its focus moved from feminist to avant-garde literary concerns. Harriet, while remaining loyal to Dora, was interested in the new literature and in the writers producing it; in particular, one whom Pound found and urged her to publish. This was James Joyce, whose *Portrait of the Artist as a Young Man* began serialisation in the paper – now called *The Egoist* – early in 1914.

The year 1914 was a watershed for all those who were to live through the war; but it was especially momentous for Harriet Weaver. She became the official editor of *The Egoist* when Dora asked her to take on the job; and she began contributing articles herself under the pseudonym Josephine Wright. At the age of 38, she moved into a flat on her own and began a new life.

Harriet's flat was in Gloucester Place, Marylebone. It was a service flat, so she shared the services of a cook–housekeeper and caretaker with the building's other tenants. Breakfasts and dinners were sent up to her; but at first she was nonplussed by lunches. She had never cooked at home and had no interest in learning. Finally she discovered a health food shop and began to eat fruit, nuts and cheeses, thus avoiding the problem of cooking.[27] The arrangements suited her and she remained in the flat until 1941, when she moved to the country.

Living in the heart of London made it easier for her to run *The Egoist*, whose office was in Oakley Street in Bloomsbury. During the war, too, she began to attend the weekly dinners Pound organised in a Soho restaurant. Regular diners included H.D., described by Iris Barry as 'taller and even more silent than Mrs Pound and looking somehow haunted'; Aldington, who – despite his uniform – 'looked like a farmer'; Mary Butts 'with her long white Rossetti throat and vermilion-red hair'; May Sinclair 'almost always dressed in raspberry pink, with acute dark eyes and a crisp way of speech';[28] and Harriet Weaver:

> the lady sitting up so very straight with her severe hat and nervous air – she might have been a bishop's daughter, perhaps? *That* was the lion-hearted Miss Harriet Weaver who printed Joyce when nobody else would . . . Save under extreme pressure or when business and nothing else made it essential and then only in the lowest tones and with unutterable detachment, she was never known to speak either of herself or anything to do with that very remarkable publishing activity.[29]

Because of her pseudonym, Dora and her other friends began to call Harriet 'Josephine' instead of 'Miss Weaver'. It was a new name to fit her new life. To her family she remained Harriet: devoted, quiet, loving. To her new women literary friends she became 'Josephine', staunch supporter of causes and a clear-thinking and straightforward editor. To everyone else, including her men friends, she was 'Miss Weaver', whom one dared not shock by uttering a crude word or idea. (Years later, when she joined the Communist Party, she added another identity, that of 'Comrade Josephine'.)

From 1914 until his death in 1941, Joyce was a major part of Harriet Weaver's life. She believed in his work and in his genius, as she believed, too, in Dora Marsden's. She supported both of them, financially and emotionally, throughout their lives; and published their books when no one else would. Her devotion to Joyce is well known: how she settled a capital sum on him so that he could receive the income; how she fought for the *Portrait* and published it at The Egoist Press; how she fought for the publication of *Ulysses* in England; how she typed part of the manuscripts and carried on a voluminous correspondence with the writer, becoming involved in all his family problems, from doctors to lodgings to taking care of his daughter Lucia. Nor did this work end with his death, since she took on his literary estate and, until her own death, spent countless hours dealing with all that was thus entailed.[30]

After visiting Dora and Mrs Marsden in the spring of 1920, Harriet began also to concentrate on Dora's work. The Marsdens lived in Glencoin, a remote Northern village, in a row of old miners' cottages called 'Seldom Seen'. Harriet found Dora depressed and suffering from severe headaches, which was hardly surprising, since the bare necessities of daily life were hardly easy to come by. Water had to be drawn from a spring some distance away; firewood had to be gathered; food was scarce; and they lived in nearly total isolation. Harriet realised that her friend's thinking was being affected by this seclusion. Dora wasn't seeing or corresponding with anyone; and was busy evolving an 'electric theory of our experience of substance'.[31] She wanted Harriet to help her with the research she needed to support her theory and asked that Harriet type up her nearly illegible manuscripts.[32] Back in London, Harriet did both the research and the typing. But she baulked when Dora asked her to move permanently to 'Seldom Seen'. She spent more time there, however; and in 1924 enabled the Marsdens to take over two adjoining cottages so they could have more space and comfort. She rented a third cottage for herself and began spending several months at a time there, helping with domestic chores as well as with Dora's book.

Harriet didn't give her entire life to Joyce and Dora Marsden, however, thanks to Bryher and McAlmon. H.D. had introduced Bryher to Harriet in 1920; and the friendship was renewed after Bryher and H.D. returned from New York with McAlmon in tow. Harriet had brought out, at The Egoist Press, a series of 'Poets' Translations', of which H.D. did one; and since H.D. was her assistant for a year, the two women knew each other well. Bryher, with her customary energy, thought The Egoist Press should bring out books by H.D., Marianne Moore and McAlmon; and she put up the funds for Harriet to publish H.D.'s *Hymen* (1921); Marianne Moore's *Poems* (1921); and McAlmon's *Explorations* (1921).

Getting to know 'Miss Weaver' and to like her very much, Bryher and McAlmon took it into their heads that she needed some fun. In the autumn of 1924 they persuaded her to accompany them to Paris. For Harriet, this was extraordinary. She'd never travelled with anyone except family members before; and, in addition, she was always terrified of journeys of any kind. But she wanted to see the Joyces (who'd visited England earlier in the year); and to meet her correspondent Sylvia Beach, with whom she'd shared so many Joyce worries. So she determined to go.

In Paris, she visited 'Shakespeare & Company' and met Sylvia and Adrienne, liking them both immensely. She went to the Joyce household and heard the writer read from his 'Work in Progress'. She was guest of honour at a dinner party arranged by McAlmon, where her fellow guests included H.D., Bryher, Djuna Barnes and Thelma Wood, Pound, and others. Everything went well until Pound, exhibiting the same perverse streak that had led him to taunt Amy Lowell, remarked to Harriet, 'Why, this is the first time I've seen you drunk.'[33] That ended the party; and H.D. walked Harriet back to her hotel, trying to explain away Pound's behaviour. Harriet forgave him; and was probably not as shocked as McAlmon thought. She had, after all, attended many of Pound's dinners in London.

All in all, 'Josephine' enjoyed her trip enormously, writing afterwards to Sylvia Beach:

> I feel so very grateful to you for all your kindness to me during my month in Paris – and to Miss Monnier to whom will you please give my grateful thanks and kindest regards? The visit was a very great pleasure to me and I am so glad to have met you in the flesh after all our correspondence.[34]

To Bryher, who had left Paris with H.D. before she herself left, Harriet wrote:

> I hope the journey was accomplished without mishap and that you were neither of you too dreadfully tired on arrival nor H.D.'s cold any worse . . . The two 'Little Review' editors, with the two small boys in train [Margaret Anderson, Jane Heap, and Jane's nephews] turned up when we were about half way through dinner on Tuesday evening. It amused me to see them together but I should not feel it a terrific loss never to meet either of them again in this world. Yesterday evening, by Robert's arrangement, Mrs Loy came and dined tête-à-tête with me at the Trianon. I like her. At first she was rather restless and disjointed (she doubtless found me heavy and dull) but later she got going and talked till about 9.30.
>
> . . . Thank you very much for the cheque for £7.7.0 for the sets of Egoist for Miss Beach and Miss Heap . . . I am to go to her [Sylvia] this morning at 12 to be photographed and then to have lunch with her . . .
>
> I am so grateful to you and Robert for having pressed me to come to Paris in your party. It has been a very great pleasure and I am so very much obliged to you . . .[35]

Unfortunately the visit was over all too soon. After returning to England, Harriet went almost immediately to Dora's where she not only typed manuscripts, but did chores such as fetching groceries, gathering firewood, and even doing some cooking. Twice a week she made a large stew of meat and vegetables which would be reheated for several days in a row.[36]

The relationship between Harriet and Dora remains unclear, partly because Harriet destroyed nearly all of Dora's letters to her and most of her own to Dora have also not survived. It is clear that Dora depended almost totally on Harriet from the time she retired as editor from The Egoist in 1914. As she became more and more detached from reality, she became more dependent on Harriet. Unlike Joyce, who also made constant demands on Harriet's time and purse, Dora did not have a family to take on some of the burdens of her genius. She did have her long-suffering mother; but Mrs Marsden couldn't begin to share her intellectual endeavours as Harriet could; and she was also getting old. Harriet gave the support Dora required; but refused to move in with her, or to compromise her determination to be 'a person alone'.

Harriet's London life, freshened by her Paris trips and friendships, was very satisfying. In April 1925 she wrote to Sylvia Beach that she wished she could have travelled back with Bryher and McAlmon for a short visit to Paris;[37] and indeed did take a trip by herself, later in the year, spending a lot of time with Sylvia and Adrienne and learning of McAlmon's newest publication, his *Contact Collection of Contemporary Writers* (1925). She didn't know, however, that it would be dedicated to her, writing later to Sylvia: 'I have received also two copies of the *Contact* collection whose third page of printed matter surprised me very much.'[38] It was a token of McAlmon's and Bryher's real admiration, respect and friendship. In London, Harriet was keeping up with Bryher and H.D., reporting to Sylvia;

I saw Bryher for an hour or so on Thursday. The flat is secured but needs much adaptation . . . I have just missed H.D. who is to be in London for two months with mother and daughter in a furnished flat . . . I hope she will remain on till I return late in August or September [from Dora's] . . .[39]

During 1926, Harriet was still seeing a great deal of Bryher and McAlmon, telling Sylvia:

[Robert] presented me with a copy of Miss Gertrude Stein's huge volume [*The Making of Americans*]! – without, however, extracting a promise that I would read it line by line from start to finish! Bryher took me across the street to see H.D.'s little apartment where she seems very happy.[40]

These London days were all too few; although she did tell Sylvia late in 1927 that she'd met Bryher's new husband, Kenneth Macpherson.

Most of Harriet's time was spent, however, with Dora. She was determined to see her friend's book finished, but the task wasn't easy. In 1928 the two women actually quarrelled. Harriet, pushed to the limit, had told Dora that hers wasn't the only work in the world that mattered and that Joyce was producing work at least as good as hers.[41] Dora bitterly resented this divided loyalty. Still, the quarrel didn't last. Harriet, as a sign of her faith in Dora, decided to revive The Egoist Press to publish her book. She wrote to Sylvia:

We are quite happy here now and very busy . . . On Monday I ran most of the two miles to the village to catch the post, accomplishing the journey in a little under 20 minutes! [Harriet was now in her mid-fifties] . . . The rush is on account of negotiations with printers for the protection of Miss Marsden's book. The Egoist Press has been called to life again to be the official publisher . . . It is a wonderful book. I shall send you a copy . . .[42]

At last, in late 1928, Dora's book *The Definition of the Godhead*, was published, financed by Harriet and appearing under The Egoist Press imprint. The dedication read: 'To/The Great Name/Hushed Among Us For So Long/of/Her/Heaven,/The Mighty Mother/of/All'.[43] Dora announced, to follow this book, three more, the first to be *The Mystery of Time*, which Harriet financed and published also. But by now she was beyond any real sympathy with Dora's thinking. Dora became angry about Harriet's lack of intellectual support, though Harriet didn't stop giving financial and emotional help. The world agreed with Harriet, to the extent that Dora's books were ignored, dealing Dora a blow from which she never recovered, though she tried to go on working on the next book in her series. In 1930 and 1931 Harriet spent a lot of time at 'Seldom Seen', but after 1932 went much less often. In 1935 Dora fell and broke her leg. From the Liverpool hospital where she was treated, she was moved directly to a hospital in Dumfries, diagnosed as suffering from severe depression. Harriet continued to support her and to write and visit; but Dora had withdrawn from life. She remained in the hospital until her death in 1960.

Harriet's life was not all duty, however. In the early 1930s she became active in the Marylebone Labour Party and then, later in the decade, she joined the Communist Party and sold *The Daily Worker* on street corners. As was her custom, she remained in the background of the organisation and did the most humble jobs. She contributed funds as well. In 1937 she wrote to Sylvia: 'I have been reading a good deal of 'Left' literature and have been doing what propaganda I could for the People's Front movement, our present British government being such a dangerous one in almost every way . . .'44

In 1941 Harriet left London and moved to a boarding house in Oxford, near a brother and sister-in-law. In that year, too, Joyce died and she became his literary executrix. She joined the Oxford Communist Party and delivered copies of *The Daily Worker*, distributed leaflets and worked at the Party bookstall. She visited both Dora and Lucia Joyce in their respective hospitals. Occasionally she went on walking tours with her friend Edith Walker. She also continued work on a philosophical essay of her own, based on researches she had done years before for Dora: a symposium on 'Time'. In 1955 she had yet another of Dora's books – *The Philosophy of Time* – published. She helped Joyce scholars by correspondence and in person and continued her support of the Joyce family. In 1955, too, she moved for the last time, to her widowed sister-in-law Muriel Weaver, in Saffron Walden. At 80, she was finally consenting to share a household with someone not of her own blood.

Harriet's last contact with Dora was not happy. Dora had remained silent for some years, but she suddenly wrote to Harriet in 1958 that she was at work on her 'magnum opus' and needed a typist. Harriet suggested someone in Liverpool, saying that if she herself were not 83 years old and Dora's writing not so difficult to read, she would offer to do it herself. Dora immediately replied that her manuscript was perfectly legible, assuring her that it was divinely destined that Harriet should do the job:

> Now Deity has enabled you to help me with such spectacular help & in so many ways during an almost *full half century* that it seems

probable that she will help you to complete the full fifty years . . .
You were not on your own. *You were a dedicated being . . .*[45]

The dedicated being wrote back that it was over sixty years since
she'd prayed to any being whom she could regard as divine; and
refused.[46]

Dora never wrote to Harriet again; and died less than a year
later. By that time Harriet was suffering from the after-effects of a
bad fall, which had affected her heart. Shortly after her return to
Saffron Walden from a round of family visits in October 1961, she
died.

Chapter 10

'The stand of the individual against immensities . . .'
– Periodical publishing I

In the early decades of the century, small literary journals and magazines provided a vital outlet for the writing – both experiment and comment – of the network of women we've been surveying. In London, a feminist-based paper called *The Freewoman* was set up by Dora Marsden in 1911. Its evolution into *The New Freewoman* in 1913, under Harriet Shaw Weaver's editorship, and then into *The Egoist* in 1914, profiles a shift in spirit from radical feminist polemic to radical literary debate and experimentation. The pages of the changing paper carried work by H.D., Dorothy Richardson, May Sinclair, Marianne Moore, Amy Lowell, Rebecca West, and other women, as well as by Pound, Joyce and Eliot.

The same contributors appeared also in the small American magazines begun at this time. Harriet Monroe's *Poetry*, started in Chicago in 1912, opened its doors to the 'new' poetry of Pound, Eliot, William Carlos Williams, Marianne Moore and H.D.; while Margaret Anderson's daring *Little Review*, begun in 1914, also in Chicago, went even further, publishing experimental work by Mina Loy, Gertrude Stein, Djuna Barnes, Mary Butts and Kay Boyle, as well as by H.D., Dorothy Richardson and the others. Anderson and her co-editor Jane Heap were prosecuted for publishing Joyce's *Ulysses* in serial form.

In the 1920s, more journals were initiated, including *Transatlantic Review*, *This Quarter*, *transition*, and *Close-up*, among others; and the same network of writers continued to edit and to contribute to them. The interaction – both personal and professional – among the group, and especially between the women, is fascinating; particularly so, given their geographical distance from each other and their mobility between the centres of London, Paris, and the American cities.

That these writers and editors paid close attention to each other's work; that they took each other seriously as writers trying to support themselves by writing; that they took each other seriously as women trying to find consonances between 'art' and 'life'; all these stances are revealed both in their personal correspondence with each other and in their published reviews of each other's work. H.D. reviewed Marianne Moore in *The Egoist*; Marianne Moore reviewed H.D. in *The Dial*; May Sinclair reviewed Dorothy Richardson in both *The Little Review* and *The Egoist*; the list is almost endless. Their personal letters are as revealing in indicating the directions of their interests and influences; Amy Lowell was the first to suggest to Bryher that she read H.D.; Bryher suggested to Marianne Moore that she read Dorothy Richardson; Marianne Moore suggested to H.D. and Bryher that they should read Mary Butts. And correspondences that sprang up because of an initial interest in each other's writing turned, as well, to personal interest in each other's lives and opinions. And besides the poems, articles and short stories appearing in the magazines, numerous books came from them too, both of poetry and of fiction.

The published literary output of this network is, therefore, extensive in volume and variety. But even more extensive is the range of their memoirs. For different viewpoints of themselves and their times there are autobiographies by Harriet Monroe, Margaret Anderson, Sylvia Beach, Bryher, Mary Butts and Kay Boyle, among others slightly more tangential. There are autobiographical novels by H.D., Kay Boyle, Dorothy Richardson and H.D.'s friend Frances Gregg; as well as letters, memoirs and autobiographical novels by many of the men who lived with or near the women: Ezra Pound, Richard Aldington, John Cowper Powys, D.H. Lawrence and the Aldingtons' friend, John Cournos.

Harriet Monroe's *Poetry: A Magazine of Verse* is regarded as marking the turning point in twentieth century American poetry. During her wide reading of current poetry, she compiled a long list of contemporary poets whose work interested her and whom she thought ought to be promoted. In August and early September 1912, she sent a 'poet's circular' to each poet on her list, with proposals for the new magazine. She solicited financial backing from Chicago businessmen and lawyers, together with a plan to gain

100 subscribers at $50 a year for five years. Her circular declared:

> The success of this first American effort to encourage the
> production and appreciation of poetry, as the other arts are
> encouraged, by endowment, now depends on the poets. We offer
> them:
>
> First, a chance to be heard in their own place, without the
> limitations imposed by the popular magazine . . . this magazine
> will appeal to . . . a public primarily interested in poetry as an art
> . . .
>
> Second . . . we hope to print poems of greater length and of
> more intimate and serious character than the other magazines can
> afford to use. All kinds of verse will be considered – narrative,
> dramatic, lyric, – quality alone being the test of acceptance . . .
>
> Third . . . we shall pay contributors. The rate will depend on
> the subscription list . . . If we can raise the rate paid for verse
> until it equals that paid for paintings, etchings, statuary . . . we
> shall feel that we have done something to make it possible for
> poets to practice their art and be heard . . . we ask the poets to
> send us their very best verse . . .[1]

Harriet was a poet herself and shared, therefore, the discourage-
ment of writers whose experimentalism wasn't welcomed by the
editorial policies of the commercial press. She wanted all poets to
have a hearing; and through the influence of Pound, who became
her foreign correspondent, she turned her attention to new verse
forms. *Poetry* carried the *vers libre* debate during the first six years
of its publication.

In the first issue of October 1912, Pound began to explore the
notion of 'Imagism', writing that

> The youngest school here that has the nerve to call itself a school
> is that of the *Imagistes*. To belong to a school does not in the least
> mean that one writes poetry to a theory. One writes poetry when,
> where, because, and as one feels like writing it. A school exists
> when two or three young men agree, more or less, to call certain
> things good; when they prefer such of their verses as have certain
> qualities to such of their verses as do not have them . . .

Although it's true that schools of poetry are more the invention of
literary historians than of practising poets; and that such schools
are, in any case, not restricted to men or to the young; what's
interesting here is Pound's anxiety to impute some measure of

self-consciousness to a group of poets in whose work he can sense similarities of preoccupation. Such a sense is legitimated if the group can in turn accept some kind of collective identity.

In his covering letter to Harriet, which also enclosed a stab at identifying Imagism with H.D.'s poems, Pound makes clear both his personal connection with H.D. and his enthusiasm for this new style:

> I've had luck again, and am sending you some *modern* stuff by an American. I say modern, for it is in the laconic speech of the Imagistes, even if the subject is classic. At least H.D. has lived with these things since childhood, and knew them before she had any book-knowledge of them.
>
> This is the sort of American stuff that I can show here and in Paris without its being ridiculed. Objective – no slither; direct – no excessive use of adjectives, no metaphors that won't permit examination. It's straight talk, straight as the Greek! And it was only by persistence that I got to see it at all.[2]

The implicit themes here are revealing, not the least being the emphasis on H.D.'s American nationality. The tension between Old and New World cultural values, world views, utterance, were marked then as they are now. Pound, enormously enjoying his role as aesthetic broker, lauds the cosmopolitanism of London and Paris, where he 'shows' poems as if they had the glamour of paintings, thus courting the vulnerability of dependence to which the New World was prone. He shared with Harriet, too, the hidden knowledge that his protégée, like all expatriates, may seek the richer (being older) vein of Europe, but will always also be driven by a desire to be 'shown' – and applauded – back home.

Harriet published the poems; and indeed their appearance provoked interest in many and varied quarters. In Boston, Amy Lowell, already a published poet, supported the new venture with $25 and a promise to contribute. Due in Chicago to attend a dinner in honour of her brother (who was President of Harvard University), she met Harriet and they struck up a friendship, Amy being particularly fascinated by the publication of H.D.'s poems.

In the March issue of *Poetry* Harriet carried Pound's 'A Few Don'ts by an Imagiste' and 'Imagisme' by F.S. Flint (but actually by Pound, who perhaps sought, by this device, to suggest that Imagism was a movement rather than a one-man show). Both pieces emphasised, idiosyncratically, that Imagist poets sought to 'write in

accordance with the best tradition, as they found it in the best
writers of all time, – in Sappho, Catullus, Villon'. Their 'few rules'
covered 'direct treatment of the "thing", whether subjective or
objective'; the inclusion of only the most essential words; and, with
respect to rhythm, to 'compose in the sequence of the musical
phrase, not in sequence of a metronome'. The doctrine of the image
held that an image 'presents an intellectual and emotional "complex" in an instant of time'. This complex, Pound declares, gives
rise to a sense of sudden liberation from the limits of time and
space. In the same issue there were poems by Aldington; but
Pound's own new poems, influenced by his Imagist theories, were
held over for the April issue.

Subsequent issues carried work by Frances Gregg, Amy Lowell
and Marianne Moore; and in the twenties came work from Dorothy
Richardson, Bryher and May Sinclair. Harriet Monroe hoped that
poets and poetry could create a great civilisation out of the
exchange between poets and their audience. The magazine's motto
was that 'to have great poets there must be great audiences too', a
line of Whitman's Harriet believed and endorsed, despite Pound's
animosity towards it. 'Once and for all', he wrote to her,
'dammmmm the audience. They eat us. We do not eat them.'[3]

Harriet's tastes were more conservative than Pound's; but Pound
still saw *Poetry* as an opening for work he thought important (not
excluding his own), so he continued to seek space from Harriet. He
tempted her with cosmopolitan success, writing to her that

> there is no earthly reason why *Poetry* shouldn't '*reach* England'.
> 'England' is dead as mutton. *If* Chicago (or the U.S.A. or
> whatever) will slough off its provincialism, if it will feed on all
> fruit, and produce strength fostered on alert digestion – there's no
> reason for Chicago or *Poetry* or whatever not being the
> standard.[4]

Pound insisted that a universal standard, paying no attention to
time or country, was necessary for the health of literature and was
therefore unconcerned whence it came or might be located.

Amy Lowell was another powerful support.

> I wish you could have heard me boom your magazine to all the
> people I met in New York [she wrote to Harriet, early in 1914].
> You cannot think how much I have the welfare of your magazine
> at heart. The more I see of them in New York, editors and their

papers, the more I realize that 'Poetry' has a field all to itself, and one which I believe to be of immense importance.[5]

H.D.'s collection *Sea Garden* was reviewed for *Poetry* in its February 1917 issue by John Gould Fletcher, who wrote:

> The unpractised reader, picking up H.D.'s *Sea Garden* and reading it casually, might suppose it was all about flowers and rocks and waves and Greek myths, when it is really about the soul, or the primal intelligence, or the *nous*, or whatever we choose to call that link that binds us to the unseen and uncreated . . . As I read and re-read this small volume for it is necessary to read it many times, I cease to care whether this is or is not what the academic critics choose to label Poetry, or whether it is or is not Imagism. Whatever it is, the form is as inevitable as the substance . . .

H.D.'s reputation as a visionary, thus begun, remained; and was appropriate enough for the pages of *Poetry*. Harriet wanted new poetry, but she held to traditional literary values, still able – at the height of the Great War – to celebrate the poet as priest and still able to resist polemic in the March 1917 issue:

> Because my favourite painter is not moved to depict cosmic horrors like Verestchagin, shall I bid him burn his brushes and take to brooding in a corner? Because the mad world is at war, shall no one play the piano, or plan a fair house, or dream by a sculptured fountain under the tree? . . . Every artist who helps the world to see truth and beauty – be it merely by a pastel landscape, or a carved kitten, or a song to a butterfly's wing, 'does his bit' towards reminding us of eternal verities, and thereby bringing the world nearer to 'serious maturity'. He is an advance agent of civilization which means wisdom, forbearance, humor, joy in life and magnanimity in death.

The sense of rectitude in such words may seem to border on myopia and complacency, revealing a view of things in which the wise and just take a rightful place among the 'civilised' – whose pursuit is truth and beauty – who may stand aside while the mad and barbarous remnant give themselves over to conflict, confrontation and 'cosmic horrors'. Such a view isn't, of course, unusual; but it's intriguing to speculate about the extent to which Harriet might comfortably court experimentalism in language while sustaining this traditionalist aesthetic; and to wonder, too, whether she realised in the end that experimentalism eventually challenges not only literary conventions but social conventions as well.

Her conservatism didn't escape the sharp, practised and self-interested eyes of the experimentalists. By July 1915, Aldington in London was writing to Amy Lowell:

> As to Poetry – I have written Harriet, suggesting that she write some articles on American poetry for The Egoist, and that I do a short notice on new American periodicals, mentioning the help she gave us. On the other hand, Amy, you know Ezra had to force her to print Hilda and me in the beginning, she always holds our stuff up for months . . . and she has steadily taken Ezra's part against us from the beginning . . .[6]

Half a year later, Amy wrote to H.D.:

> I have written to Harriet to say that I have here any of your poems which she desires. I am not altogether pleased with her attitude just now; there seems to be a great deal of Ezra in it, judging by the last number, although you will see that I did succeed in bullyragging her to put in Flint's things in time for us to use them. I think the best way would be for me to see Harriet when I go out [to a talk in Chicago] and read her these.[7]

By the end of 1918, Harriet's tastes had hardened further, and even Pound's recommendations didn't go unchallenged:

> Your father sent me recently your article *New Poetry: The Un-English*. Of course it's too long for us, unless divided – but anyway it seems to me *Little Review* stuff, and I am returning it to Mr Pound. I can't quite stand for its exaltation of Marianne Moore and Mina Loy to the top of the heap.[8]

Harriet applied her absolutist aesthetics to the task of reviewing, too, taking issue – for example – with Bryher's assessment of Lowell in *Poetry*, November 1918:

> The transcendent art which is seized and carried by the emotion – an impassioned renunciation which triumphs in loss – that I cannot find in this book. The poet may be true to her consumingly restless period, but she does not get a perspective on that period, does not establish its relation with that spacious stillness which we call eternity.

Thus the brochure by W. Bryher, recently published in London, seems to me to rate Miss Lowell too highly in calling her a 'poet of the first order;' though praise from London for any American artist is rare enough for over-generosity to be pardoned. The art which forgets and transcends art is beyond her reach . . .

Here Harriet's need for 'transcendence' battles with her awareness – ambivalent as it must be – about London's cultural dominance. By the time H.D. is herself established as a critic of some note, Harriet again – in the January 1922 issue – takes up the argument against the values of the new style, in this instance with respect to Marianne Moore's radicalism:

Miss Moore's steely and recondite art has long been a rallying-point for the radicals . . . Rumor has hinted that the selection and publication [of *Poems*, Egoist Press, London] were made by certain friends of the author without her knowledge . . .

H.D., surely a critic of authority, calls Miss Moore a poet, and a number of young radicals are eager to pronounce her 'a very great poet' . . . A more moderate admirer, Miss Winifred Bryher [writes] 'The spirit is robust, that of a man with facts and countries to discover and not that of a woman sewing at tapestries . . . Technically it is a triumphant book . . . Her poems are an important addition to American literature of the modern world . . .'

After noting (for the effect of balance) some adverse critics of Moore's work, Harriet goes on to concede that Marianne Moore is indeed a poet, but one who is

too sternly controlled by a stiffly geometrical intellectuality. Miss Moore is in terror of her Pegasus; she knows of what sentimental excesses that unruly steed is capable, and so her ironic mind harnesses down his wings and her iron hand holds a stiff rein. This mood yields prose oftener than poetry . . . If the mood instinctively flouts the muse, what of the method? If the mood may rarely yield more than the hard reluctant beauty of a grotesque, is the method inevitable and right, fitting words musically, magically to the motive, as in all the masterpieces of the art? . . . What I do find in certain poems is a brilliant array of subtly discordant harmonies not unlike those of certain ultra-modern composers, set forth in stanza-forms purely empirical

even when emphasized by rhyme, forms which impose themselves arbitrarily upon word-structure and sentence-structure
instead of accepting happily the limitations of the art's materials,
as all art must.

Harriet's objections to Marianne Moore's tone and style reveal her
values to be fundamentally conventional; sentimentality is to be
eschewed as an incompetence and a vulgarity, but – that aside –
'intellectuality' is not to be prized above music and magic.
Inevitably the rigour in Marianne Moore's relentless pursuit of
meaning and distillation imposes itself on the more usual (and
therefore expected) cadences of utterance, resulting in that singular
abruptness and sense of discourse characteristic of her style. But
Harriet is not seduced. The 'modernism' of this challenge to stanza
and sentence structures she finds arbitrary, as in contemporary
music (at that time revolutionary in its throwing off of the tonal
harmonies which had governed the rules of composition for the
previous three centuries); and it is not difficult to sense that behind
her use of the concept 'arbitrary' is that more basic anxiety in which
the challenge to authority is felt not merely to be arbitrary but
deeply anarchic. The stance is clearly distasteful to Harriet,
although she keeps the basis of her aversion covert, hinting at it
only obliquely in the assertion that artists ought happily to accept
the limitations imposed by their materials. A radical, of course,
would retort that the only limitations worthy of respect are those
issuing from one's own imagination.

Even so, Harriet's thirst for quality traditionally measured can
elicit some sympathy when it is seen upon her own canvas of reality.
To mark *Poetry's* first decade, she wrote, in an editorial comment in
October 1922:

> Of our ten years what will be said – the ten years of the World
> War, of falling and rising nations, of the Russian revolution, of a
> thousand new movements and new hopes? In the face of events
> so tremendous, will the world 'little heed, nor long remember,
> what we say here'; or will it accept our suffering as adequate, and
> repeat over and over, through the crowded ways of the new time,
> the songs which our poets have sung to a changing age?

There are other aesthetes who would never have penned such a
paragraph. Harriet's belief in the transcendence of art, however,
doesn't exclude awareness of the material world in a ferment of

dissolution and change, nor does it avoid a sense of responsibility; will the world find suffering for the sake of a song, adequate? The use of 'suffering' is startling, an instant cue that her theory of poetry and its place is hard won, not complacent.

Next in her comment, Harriet Monroe lists those whose work has appeared in *Poetry* during its first ten years:

> Who are they, these poets of the decade which *Poetry* has counted off from month to month, with never a break, since October, 1912 – since Ezra Pound, with much tumult and shouting, buried the dry bones of the past and sounded the tocsin for a new era? In singles and pairs and cohorts they came trooping: Vachel Lindsay, Robert Frost, Carl Sandburg and Edgar Lee Masters; Wallace Stevens, D.H. Lawrence and T.S. Eliot; Conrad Aiken and Rupert Brooke; Sara Teasdale and Edna St. Vincent Millay; the imagists – H.D. and Amy Lowell, Richard Aldington, John Gould Fletcher; the ironists – Carlos Williams, Alfred Kreymborg, Maxwell Bodenheim, Marianne Moore. Robinson had begun over a decade before, Masefield and Witter Bynner and Arthur Ficke a few years. Ford Madox Hueffer repented Victorian sins and swung new-made into the procession; Tagore translated himself; Waley and others translated the Chinese . . .

The list is impressive; and it extends beyond English speakers to include many foreign poets whose work *Poetry* published in translation. Harriet's comment takes account, too, of the spread of readership across both geographical and educational barriers, referring to readers' letters from China, Port Said, Madrid, Constantinople, Brazil and Tasmania, as well as those from librarians and others living in the remoter corners of the United States. Such testimony is profoundly rewarding for her, not least because of its affirmation of the necessity for American cultural initiative:

> If America is ever to have a rich spiritual life and to express that life in art, this art must come, not from super-civilized coteries, but from the vital strength of the nation . . . If *Poetry* is one of the quickening influences which will make a vital people aware of its imaginative and creative power, then we may feel indeed that our ten years of labor have not been thrown away.

Treading this path had led, inevitably, to a loss of sympathy from those who had originally found the venture exciting and important. Once the magazine was firmly established along the lines Harriet laid down; and given that there were now growing up other periodicals offering publication to more radical spirits; it was safe for former supporters to sneer just a little among themselves. In February 1920, for example, Amy Lowell had written to H.D.:

> Harriet's magazine goes along in its own way . . . It is exceedingly funny to me that a woman could have had a magazine running for six years and never increase its circulation to any amount that counts as a circulation and have no influence on the growth of poetry in any way. It would horrify her if she knew this was the case, but it is, and it is surprising and shows Harriet's glorious ineptness better than anything else could possibly do. Poetry is a power over here. People are avid for it. Poets have no difficulty in getting published. The public is large; the editors eager. And to conduct a poetry magazine which has not counted at all is really a bit singular.[9]

Harriet's aestheticism wasn't blind to other issues; but her rejection of direct involvement was carefully formulated. During the Great War she published editorial articles addressed to the problems of pursuing art in times of war. Artists must, she argued, promote 'that freeing of the mind and lifting of the spirit which perception of beauty brings' since men can be inspired 'by beauty alone'. She wanted artists to be motivated by unity rather than enmity, because only 'a common emotion beyond individual profit or glory' could produce great art equal to that of the past.[10] And she claimed that artists had their contribution to give towards making the world 'safe for democracy', since art was a repository for spirituality;

> For years the poets, the artists, have been dictating terms of peace to the next age. Every painter of his own wood-lot, every poet singing the beauty of working girls instead of queens, or the bravery of common men instead of princes, has been doing his bit to democratize the world . . .
>
> Never was the artist more necessary than now – his freedom of spirit, his self-assertion, his creative fire. When the whole world is in the melting pot, when civilization is to be reminted and no one can tell what stamp its face and reverse will bear . . . then the stand of the individual against immensities, a stand always hazardous, becomes a gesture of incredible power and pride, an attitude of almost impossible heroism . . .

This is the ultimate test of the poet . . . Puny unit of the unconquerable will, he must hold up his little torch between the old and new . . .[11]

In response to readers' demands for more politicised comment and criticism, Harriet's doctrine remained steadfast; and the views she expressed in 1917 she still held decades later.

Each artist, being, like the rest of us, incapable of infinity, feels and expresses that special beauty which is most immediate to his consciousness. He has an inalienable right to his specialty, as good a right as the honey-bee or the bricklayer; and the critic's function is to demand of him, not some other specialty, but sincerity and achievement in the one which has chosen him . . .

The artist, big or little, is in his degree a seer . . . It may be that Verlaine's prison song, or a single drawing of a nude or a tree by Arthur Davies, have more importance in the eternal scheme of beauty, and are more interpretive of their age, than the most shapely revelation of contemporary movements. Movements pass, but beauty endures . . .[12]

Poetry's aims were traditional in the literary sense: 'to give poetry her own place, her own voice'. By contrast, *The Freewoman*, which became – with its successors *The New Freewoman* and *The Egoist* – almost a sister publication in England for the writers we've been considering, had political rather than literary roots. First published in November 1911 and initially co-edited by Dora Marsden and Mary Gawthorpe, it addressed itself directly to 'the woman question' in its first issue:

It is a wholly pertinent matter that the temerious [*sic*] persons who launch *The Freewoman* should be asked, 'who are the Freewomen?' Where are the women of whom and for whom you write who are free? Can they be pointed out, or named by name? There must be, say, ten in the British Isles . . . Bondwomen are distinguished from Freewomen by a spiritual distinction. Bond-women are the women who are not separate spiritual entities – who are not individuals. They are complements merely . . . In the midst of all this there comes a cry that woman is an individual, and that because she is an individual she must be set free. It would be nearer the truth to say that if she is an individual she *is* free, and will act like those who are free.

It will be our business to make clear that the entire wrangle regarding women's freedom rests upon spiritual considerations, and that it must be settled as such. If women are spiritually free, all else must be adjusted to meet this fact, whether physically, in the home, society, economics, or politics.

Although the themes here are presented in rhetorical form, they aren't mere rhetoric. The paper's title itself focuses an anomaly with reference to a citizenship in which the female half of the population is 'bound' – or enslaved – rather than free. In the years just before the Great War, militant campaigning by women demanding the vote was at its height; but suffrage was not yet won. Dora Marsden's address to British freewomen in this opening editorial is, therefore, openly ironic; and she asserts that freedom will only come to women when they are perceived to be – and perceive themselves to be – 'separate spiritual entities', independent and individual. When this kind of freedom is felt and perceived, all other freedoms in social and political spheres will follow inevitably.

Articles in this first issue included 'A German league for the protection of mothers' by Bessie Drysdale; 'Feminism under the republic and the early empire' by Amy Haughton; and 'Contemporary recognition of polygamy' by E.S.P. H[aynes]. The anonymous piece called 'The Spinster. By One.' stated that

> The indictment which the Spinster lays up against Society is that of ingenious cruelty . . . the development of her entire form sets towards a single consummation . . . In babyhood, she begins, with her dolls. Why do not parents of a prospective spinster give her a gun or an engine. If Society is going to have spinsters, it should train spinsters . . . she is ushered into an atmosphere charged with sex-distinctions and sex-insinuations . . . in every conversation, in every social amusement, in every interest in life she finds that the pivot upon which all interest turns is the sex interest.

The recognition and definition of sex-role stereotyping was as evident to this writer as to those feminists of the 1970s who didn't realise that their own complaints had a long – if buried – history. *The Freewoman*'s first issue carried, as well as such articles, many advertisements with a new flavour; one, for example, announced the services of 'Farrow's Bank for Women' at Ludgate Circus.

Subsequent issues of the paper continued to elaborate a radical sexual stance on a wide range of issues. The seventh issue, for instance, carried an article by Harry J. Birnstingl called 'Uranians' which held that

> it is now time that people's eyes were thoroughly opened to the fact that the atoms which go to compose the normal male and the normal female are capable of infinite combinations; and a Uranian is not necessarily a person with sinful tendencies . . . ['Uranian' signified homosexual]

The exploitation of labour was another dominant theme. The same seventh issue carried an article called 'Biscuits' by K.D. Scott, who alleged that the biscuit producers Huntley and Palmer were ill-treating their employees. One among many responses was a letter from the psychoanalyst Barbara Low, published in the thirteenth issue, in which the author declares, 'I have already forsworn Huntley and Palmer's goods . . . I wish all your readers would do likewise.'

By the thirteenth issue, too, interest and controversy among the readership had become so aroused that *The Freewoman* carried a boxed advertisement suggesting the formation of 'Freewoman Clubs'; informal gatherings of women and men for discussions about the issues raised by the journal. In addition, the correspondence columns of the paper were swelling issue by issue, taking up responses to such subjects as 'The Chastity of Continence?'; 'The Excitation of Sex Discussions'; and the ubiquitous Uranians.

By 4 March 1912 Dora had become sole editor, owing to Mary Gawthorpe's ill-health. Among other themes, Dora explored the notion of wages for motherhood. *The Freewoman's* stance in its 14 March issue was that women should 'work and earn money'; and would-be mothers are counselled: 'Cover the cost of your motherhood just as you would arrange for the cost of your holiday.' This view was provoked by H.G. Wells' suggestion that the state ought to support motherhood as a trade. The point was debated back and forth during subsequent issues.

The nineteenth issue announced the formation of 'A Discussion Circle' to meet at the International Suffrage Shop in the Strand. Barbara Low was one name on the organising committee. Between 80 and 90 people attended the first meeting on 18 April. For the second meeting on 8 May, the venue was changed to the Eustace Miles Restaurant at Charing Cross; and the subject for discussion – 'Freewomen and Evolution' – was to be opened by Dora Marsden.

By the time of the meeting planned for 22 May, the numbers wanting to attend were already so large that the restaurant had to be abandoned in favour of Chandos Hall, Maiden Lane. Reports of these and subsequent meetings were prepared by Barbara Low and published in the paper, together with announcements of forthcoming meetings. The 'Programme of Sessions' for 19 June until 12 October 1912 covered the following topics: 'Sex Oppression and the Way Out', led by Mr Guy Aldred; 'Some Problems of Eugenics' led by Mrs Havelock Ellis; 'The Problems of Celibacy', led by Mrs Gallichan; 'Prostitution' (no leader seems to have been brave enough to be publicly announced for this one!); and other subjects ranging between domestic drudgery and the divorce laws.

The paper's 31st issue, 20 June 1912, carried a leading editorial headed, 'The Immorality of the Marriage Contract', which stated, among other points: 'Marriage is the formal repudiation of freedom, a repudiation which a very complete code of penal law protects against subsequent recantation.'

In its issue for 15 August 1912, the paper – now into its second year – carried a piece by D[orothy] M[iller] Richardson called 'The Disabilities of Women', which addresses diet, one of Richardson's lifelong preoccupations: 'The Feminist movement has been accompanied at every stage of its progress by an undertow of commentary from the medical profession.' Richardson goes on to reject medical orthodoxies and to promote the idea that most diseases are 'by-products of alimentary digestive errors, and must be treated by the nutritional function' in relation to 'feminine ailments'. She suggests that 'the finest results in this direction have so far been attained by the fruitarians – i.e., those who base their dietary on raw fruits and salads.' Uncannily resonant with 1970s feminism, the piece recommends to women that changes in diet will result in much greater health improvement than will recourse to other remedies;

> The fact that infectious diseases and chronic infections such as tuberculosis and cancer, that influenzas, catarrhs, viscosities, all the migraines and 'nerves' pains and penalties of the physical life of women are due to the imprisonment of the eager spirit of life in bodies clogged and weakened by malnutrition, the fact that they give way before rational diet is, in the opinion of the writer, worth a very great deal to the Feminist movement, and should effectually arm even those who are at present pathological against orthodoxy's list of 'inherent disabilities'.

The flourishing periodical was, however, only two issues away from disaster, despite its growing circulation and the immense popularity of the discussion circle. Unhappily, the bankruptcy of the publishers, Stephen Swift and Co., led to a crisis for the paper, which Harriet Weaver later recounted:

> In the year 1911 a feminist weekly publication, *The Freewoman*, was started by Miss Dora Marsden who had previously worked for the Women's Social and Political Union, a militant suffrage organization. After running for a year or so under Miss Marsden's editorship *The Freewoman*'s career was cut short through the bankruptcy of the publishers . . .[13]

Nor was that the only crisis to be faced. In August 1912 the distributors, W.H. Smith and Sons, boycotted the paper, objecting to its overtly radical subject matter and stance. W.H. Smith and Sons were then – as they still are – the chief newspaper distributors in the land; and, in addition, they owned large numbers of bookshops and stalls at or near railway stations – shops and stalls which were important retail outlets – so a W.H. Smith boycott was clearly a mortal blow for any struggling periodical.

The issue of 5 September 1912 carried a 'Notice to Readers' which explained:

> During the last few days the difficulties which have beset *The Freewoman* from its start, which are inseparable from the life of a free organ, have been increased in a highly hampering degree by the boycott of Messrs. W.H. Smith and Sons, newsagents. These gentlemen have notified their intention to take *The Freewoman* off their stalls, for reasons which they give as follows:
>
> 'To Stephen Swift and Co.
>
> Dear Sir, – In reply to your letter of yesterday, we have come to the conclusion that the nature of certain articles which have been appearing lately in *The Freewoman* are such as to render the paper unsuitable to be exposed on the bookstalls for general sale. We have decided that in future we cannot do more than supply it when it is specially ordered. – Yours faithfully,
>
> August 28th, 1912   *W.H. Smith and Sons.*

The 'Notice' goes on to say that – more than animosity 'roused on the subject of sex-discussion' – enmity has been 'aroused on the question of capitalism'. The connection is made clear:

The opposition in the capitalist Press only broke out when we began to make it clear that the way out of the sex-problem was through the door of the economic problem. Failing to find the opportunity to fight *The Freewoman* in the courts on some hatched-up case of puritanism, the attack proceeds by the hole-and-corner method of breaking down our circulation. A better method could not have been found for the purposes of its ill-wishers. The paper *must* show some signs of living by its circulation, for it *cannot* live by its advertisements. We put the case, then, to our readers. The fate of the paper *is entirely in their hands*. We write it, print it, publish it, and push it. It remains for them to get it . . .

Readers are asked to drop their orders with W.H. Smith and to order from the publishers direct, sending as large a subscription as they can manage.

The main debates conducted through the pages of the paper and through the discussion circle up to this point reveal the wide interest and support for a feminism that wasn't constricted by the narrow aims of securing votes for women. *The Freewoman* targeted its questioning at the relationship between women's sex-role functions and their social oppression by men, so that motherhood, domestic enslavement, virginity, chastity, prostitution, marriage and divorce all became subjects open to exploration and criticism. Attitudes to sexual morality, reproduction, child-care, wages for housework, the family, and related subjects, all fuelled (and were kept fired by Dora Marsden) the attacks on stereotypical womanhood – including the stereotypes which campaigners for the vote didn't question – which radicals saw as the only route capable of leading to change.

The Freewoman was not, however, straightforwardly Marxist, though its editorial stance endeavoured to find parallels between women's sexual and economic subordination:

both Marsden and her paper can be seen in the context of the contemporary revolutionary movement, partly as a result of their growing criticisms of parliamentary democracy and capitalism . . . What was particularly striking about *The Freewoman* approach was its attempt, not always successful, to link the economic inequalities resulting from capitalism to the oppression of women. Allied to a growing sympathy with syndicalism, the debate within *The Freewoman* again contrasted sharply with the attitudes of suffragists who, after all, wanted to enter the political structure, not change it.[14]

Appealed to for support in the paper's crisis, readers responded as best they could, given that they hardly commanded the resources of a mass circulation base. Inevitably, in spite of an intense and widespread support and interest, the W.H. Smith boycott led to shifts and changes in editorial policy, one of which was to ask readers for financial contributions, since the original backer had now ceased to support the enterprise. Readers were asked, too, to send in their names if they wanted the paper to be relaunched. Harriet Weaver was one such reader; and, being wealthy, she sent with her name the significant contribution of £200. As a result, she began corresponding with Dora and, after meeting and liking each other, they decided to start 'The Thousand Club', an organisation with the stated goal of raising £1,000 in Britain to fund the relaunch of the paper. A similar drive had already started in the United States. Harriet Weaver became the Club's treasurer; and office space was offered by the Blavatsky Institute at Oakley House in Bloomsbury Street.

The flier for 'The Thousand Club' set out the new editorial policy:

> it will endeavour to lay bare the individualist basis of all that is most significant in modern movements including feminism. It will continue *The Freewoman*'s policy of ignoring in its discussions all existing tabus in the realms of morality and religion. It will regard itself free to lay open any question to debate . . .[15]

Harriet Weaver took her job as treasurer seriously, keeping careful notes and accounts of all subscribers. By the end of May 1913 there were already 180 names. The first issue of the relaunched paper, now called *The New Freewoman* and backed with a capital of just £1,000, appeared on 16 June 1913. Its subscribers already included Amy Lowell, Dorothy Shakespear, Brigit Patmore, May Sinclair, H.D. and D.M. Richardson.

Money kept coming in from the appeal and Harriet Weaver made up any necessary differences. During all this time Rebecca West, who had known Dora through common work in the suffrage movement, had involved herself in *The Freewoman*'s struggles, both as contributor and fund-raiser; and she continued to work for the new paper. In the summer of 1913, when she was in her early twenties, she met Pound at one of Violet Hunt's literary parties in Kensington and it was this meeting which led to Pound's involvement with *The New Freewoman*, as Harriet later recalled:

in the summer of that year approaches were made to Miss
Marsden by Mr Ezra Pound to whom Miss Rebecca West
(assistant editor for a few months, after which she resigned) had
shown the new paper. Mr Pound suggested broadening of the
basis by the inclusion of a literary side to which he himself would
be prepared to contribute regular articles and in which he would
secure the collaboration of other young poets and writers. Miss
Marsden agreed to this proposal . . .[16]

Dora remained editor, assisted first by Rebecca West and then by
Richard Aldington. The subtle shift from feminism to individualism
is apparent in the new paper's opening editorial for the issue of 1
June 1913:

There is only one thing the down-trodden with retained dignity
can do, and that is to Get Up . . . The efforts to dodge the
responsibility of self-defence, self-appropriation, to assume the
mastership in their own person, is the unmistakeable mark of the
lean.

Dora, in her 'Views and Comments', makes clear that she is against
all 'Causes', including the suffrage cause. She rails against Mrs
Pankhurst for changing her stance from demanding the vote to
giving her life to the Cause. Dora's view is that only the shackled
can free themselves:

Shackles must be burst off; if they are cut away from outside, they
will immediately reform, as those whose cause is 'our poor sister'
and 'poor brothers' will find. The prostitution and poverty
problems will be solved when the prostitute refuses to be
prostituted and the poor refuse to be poor.

Dora's greatest success was in selling subscriptions before and just
after the relaunch. *The New Freewoman*'s largest circulation was
achieved in its first six months: some 400 copies of each issue,
two-thirds being sold by subscription. After this beginning, however, the paper suffered a long decline, bottoming out in November
1916, by which time it had changed its title to *The Egoist*. The
long-term subscriptions then ran out, leaving a circulation core of
some 200, which remained constant throughout the remainder of its
run.[17]

In its successful first six months, *The New Freewoman* carried
articles on free love by Theodore Schroedor and on the women's

movement by Barbara Low; reviews by Rebecca West; a regular column by American anarchist Benjamin R. Tucker; and a long series of articles on 'The eclipse of woman'. Until the August issue it carried neither poetry nor literary articles, but in August Pound was informally appointed literary editor. In that issue Pound's *Contemporania* poems and an article called 'Imagisme' by Rebecca West appeared, just five months after Imagist verse – sent by Pound – began to appear in Harriet Monroe's *Poetry*. From this point on, *The New Freewoman* published poems by H.D., Amy Lowell, F.S. Flint, William Carlos Williams, Ford Madox Ford and Frances Gregg. The rest of the paper carried Dora's 'individualist' editorials, as well as radical articles on social issues of special significance for women.

As with *Poetry*, Pound had seen an opening for the publication of new writing and had taken it. He wrote to Harriet Monroe:

> I'm sending you our left wing, *The Freewoman* [*sic*]. I've taken charge of the literature dept. It will be convenient for things whereof one wants the Eng. copyright held. I pay a dmd. low rate, but it might be worth while as a supplement to some of your darlings . . . Will tell *The Freewoman* [*sic*] to exchange. They will.[18]

After Rebecca West's invitation to Pound to join the paper, he more or less wrote his own brief. He wrote to Dora that he expected to 'fill a page per number, for, say, six months', though he was willing to consider going on after that. His plans were

> 1st of each month. verse, selected by me. Including my own stuff and other work which I should be able, probably, to pay for and thus to spare the authors the disgrace of printing creative stuff without being paid. 15th of each month. prose article. critique presumably of current books, especially poetry. here, and possibly in france.[19]

In each issue after 1 September 1913, *The New Freewoman* carried a quarter-page advertisement for *Poetry* magazine. Harriet Monroe in Chicago, and Dora Marsden with Harriet Weaver in London, were now publishing women writers who were becoming familiar with each other's work. H.D., for example, read a poem of Marianne Moore's in *Poetry* and was prompted to write to her, from which correspondence a lifelong friendship developed.

The March 1913 issue of *Poetry* had provoked Amy Lowell to

plan a visit to London to find out more about the new poetry and its
Imagist school. Harriet Monroe gave her a letter of introduction to
Pound. When they met, Pound agreed to take one of her poems for
the group of Imagists he was publishing in *The New Freewoman*.

The two journals evolved and continued, inspiring and publishing
both experimental and radical writing. Women editors and women
writers focused and fuelled the drive to challenge literary convention. Pound's role in this network was to catalyse the writing with a
theoretical prose in which he constructed an aesthetic from
assumptions he perceived to be implicit in the new poetic style.
Where he perceived talent, he pursued and encouraged it and was,
in addition, canny enough to know how to manipulate the
appropriate publishing vehicles, so that women's work was not only
fostered, but also printed.

By the issue of 15 December 1913, Dora had changed her paper's
title to *The Egoist*:

> In adopting the neutral title *The Egoist* and thereby obliterating
> the 'woman' character from the journal, we do not feel that we
> are abandoning anything there would be wisdom in retaining.
> The emphasis laid on women and their ways and works was, as
> was pointed out in the early days of the first Freewoman, more in
> the nature of retort than of argument. 'Feminism' was the natural
> reply to 'Hominism', and the intent of both these was more to
> tighten the strings of the controversy than to reveal anything vital
> in the minds of the controversialists . . .
>
> The time has arrived when mentally-honest women feel that
> they have no use for the springing-board of large promises of
> powers redeemable in a distant future. Just as they feel they can
> be as 'free' now as they have the power to be, they know that
> their works can give evidence now of whatever quality they are
> capable of giving to them. To attempt to be 'freer' than their own
> power warrants means that curious thing – 'protected freedom,'
> and their ability, allowed credit because it is women's, is a
> 'protected' ability. 'Freedom,' and ability 'recognised' by permis-
> sion, are privileges which they find can serve no useful purpose.

This stated shift from feminism to humanist individualism reflects
less, perhaps, than Dora claimed, on social change than on her own
philosophical pursuits and on the weariness felt by any editor of a
marginal publication whose message fails to appeal to the imagina-

tion of large numbers. The shift went happily, however, in line with the preoccupations and beliefs of the journal's literary contributors. *The Egoist: An Individualist Review* was edited by Dora Marsden between January and June 1914 and then until 1919 by Harriet Weaver. Its assistant editors were, consecutively, Richard Aldington, H.D. and T.S. Eliot. Editorially its Imagist tone was maintained and it carried – in addition to Dora's philosophical pieces – poetry, literary reviews, some fiction, and articles about social issues. *The Egoist* carried the same advertisement for *Poetry* magazine as had its predecessor; and from September 1914 it carried, too, an advertisement for the new magazine called *The Little Review* in which Joyce's *A Portrait of the Artist as a Young Man* was being serialised.

Contributors to *The Egoist* included H.D., Amy Lowell, May Sinclair and Dorothy Richardson, all of whom offered reviews, in addition to their own poetry and fiction. The paper carried, too, discussions of foreign literatures and philosophies, as well as Dora's column 'Views and Comments' which, in the 2 February 1914 issue, attacked – among other issues – Christabel Pankhurst's recommendations on 'Chastity for Men' as the answer to the scourge of venereal disease.

Dora argued that

It is the failure to appreciate the fact about life that it is only its positive aspect that matters, which causes such radically different attitudes towards life. All the negative things, fear, hopeless misery, all forms of the thing called 'disease' are specific forms of weak vitality. It is more important to heighten vitality than to combat disease . . . and there is more danger to 'health' to be awaited from the misery of renunciation and the dull heats of virginity than from the ills of syphilis and gonorrhoea . . . the prostitute is the twin-trader of the legally-protected 'pure' woman. Where there are excise officials there are smugglers. Let therefore the womanly women abandon the 'privileges' which enable them to make a corner in a commodity the demand for which they sedulously stimulate, and the pirate brigs which ply on the outskirts of the trade will become purposeless . . .

Dora held no brief for marriage and 'purity', her theory and analysis issuing from a view of the ego, or self, as a consciousness which would be – in a healthy condition – self-directing; a view similar to that held by feminists in our own time, who celebrate 'autonomy'. The difference lies in the context for such a view. Dora's was a spiritual one, thus leading to an analysis where all individuals somehow end up equal in the quest for enlightenment; whereas feminists now who pursue autonomy owe their position to a political analysis in which phenomena like prostitution and rape are given global causes (and remedies) beyond the resources of any individual to manipulate. Individualist analysis, therefore, of the kind Dora Marsden offers, fits amicably alongside the anti-conventional poems of H.D. and Amy Lowell, for example, since they, too – in tone, mood and image – disclaim to represent or to speak with familiarity to a known congregation as do the feminist poets of our own time. In the same issue as Dora's dismissal of Christabel Pankhurst, for instance, appears H.D.'s 'Hermes of the Ways':

I

The hard sand breaks,
And the grains of it
Are clear as wine.

Far off over the leagues of it,
The wind,
Playing on the wide shore,
Piles little ridges,
And the great waves
Break over it.

But more than the many-foamed ways
Of the sea,
I know him
Of the triple path-ways,
Hermes,
Who awaiteth.

Dubious,
Facing three ways,
Welcoming wayfarers,
He whom the sea-orchard
Shelters from the west,
From the east
Weathers sea-wind;
Fronts the great dunes.

Wind rushes
Over the dunes,
And the coarse, salt-crusted grass
Answers.

Heu,
It whips round my ankles!

II

Small is
This white stream,
Flowing below ground
From the poplar-shaded hill,
But the water is sweet.

Apples on the small trees
Are hard,
Too small,
Too late ripened
By a desperate sun
That struggles through sea-mist.

The boughs of the trees
Are twisted
By many bafflings;
Twisted are
The small-leafed boughs.

But the shadow of them
Is not the shadow of the mast head
Nor of the torn sails.

Hermes, Hermes,
The great sea foamed,
Gnashed its teeth about me;
But you have waited,
Where sea-grass tangles with
Shore-grass.

No reader of this poem needs even the slightest classical education
in order to enter the richness, the desolation, the longing of these
images. There is the intensely personal voice of authentic lyric; but
the 'you' to whom the voice speaks remains unspecific and

undifferentiated. The image itself, the meeting of sea and land, the movement of wave and wind and the contrasting immateriality of the silent Hermes – this imaging of an imagination in the act of perception – takes its place among those other 'timeless moments' central to the literature of modernism: the 'epiphany' shown by Joyce in his *Portrait of the Artist as a Young Man* to be his instant of self-discovery as an artist; and the 'moment in the rose garden' celebrated by Eliot as the instant of spiritual insight in his *Four Quartets*, being two of the most famous instances. The development of the image in H.D.'s poem follows the logic of association rather than the logic of discourse: it is not necessary to know – but it is wonderful to know – that the wind and the grass rush and whip.

Some months later, in a review-article called 'Modern Poetry and the Imagists' (1 June 1914), Aldington chose 'Hermes of the Ways' as an example of Imagism *par excellence*, saying that it

> is as good a specimen of Imagism as can be found. Hard, direct treatment, absolutely personal rhythm, few and expressive adjectives, no inversions, and a keen emotion presented objectively. I don't think you come to like that kind of poetry until you have read a good deal of other poetry first, but when you do come to like it there is a greater emotional pleasure than in any other sort of writing.

Early in 1914 Dora was considering resigning as editor and Pound's manipulative genius was once more aroused. Why not have the paper edited by a poet (and a woman of means, into the bargain)? Its metamorphosis into a literary periodical would then be assured. He wrote to Amy Lowell:

> Do you want to edit The Egoist? Present editrix writes me this A.M. that she is willing to quit. (This is in confidence.) Of course there is a string to it. The paper made enough in the first six months to pay for the next three. It is assured up to June . . . I think it would have paid better to pay an occasional 'selling' contributor than to trust too much to voluntary work . . .
>
> If the idea amuses you, you should make arrangements for American distribution before you come over.
>
> At present the paper is printed at Southport. An editress and editorial secretary are paid, also useless office rent in London. Richard [Aldington] could perfectly well do all that for another ten dollars a month. I don't know how many subscriptions your name is good for in Boston . . .

If you want that sort of lark you could at least have a run for your money . . .

If the thing were run seriously, I would, I think, get almost anyone to write for half-rate for a while at least.[20]

Pound emphasised two points in his strategy: first, contributors ought to be paid; and secondly, fortnightly information for the provincial reader was necessary, in his view, for successful circulation. A month later, he wrote again:

Re The Egoist. Of course you won't get it for nothing unless Miss Marsden can keep her corner or some corner to let loose in. She has her own clientele who look for her.

About the policy and mistakes, you realize that nothing is paid for (save the verse sometimes); Aldington and Miss Marsden and a couple of clerks get a guinea a week. If people are writing for nothing they only do so on condition that they write as they dammmmm please. Also one can't afford time to write carefully.[21]

H.D. was also writing to Amy:

R[ichard] has done his best for that blooming old Egoist – though I know how disappointed you & Fletcher will be to see Miss M. on the first page. I assure you we both fought hard enough – But Miss Weaver runs the paper for Dora Marsden – swears by her – and R. is after all only sub-editor![22]

Aldington and H.D. – together and in turn – tried to bring the paper's editorial stance into line with their own views, but met with resistance. For the paper to yield what the Imagists wanted from it, Dora Marsden would have to go.

Chapter 11

'Life for Art's sake . . .'
– Periodical publishing II

Amy Lowell, who was unimpressed by Dora Marsden, didn't yield to Pound's persuasive efforts or to his implicit flattery. In any case she was involved with *The Little Review*. In December 1914, Aldington took up the correspondence, thanking Amy for forwarding some of his work to *The Little Review* and adding, 'will you always remember that the Egoist is open to any of your friends who want to air their opinions . . .'[1]

It proved not so easy, none the less, to gain control of the paper. Aldington fell out of favour, informing Amy that

> Hilda is taking over the Egoist [i.e. taking over from Aldington]. I seem to be a little 'out' with Miss Weaver just now. Whether it is due to Ezra or to Miss Marsden I can't say, but there it is . . . Miss Marsden seems to have a great 'down' on you – anyhow she is a beastly woman, I dislike her very much.[2]

Amy maintained her distance and H.D. got on with managing the literary contributions. By September of the following year, for example, she wrote to Marianne Moore:

> Miss Weaver, I think I wrote you, liked your article very much. So please do the comparison of Poe, Byron & Bacon. I do wish that the magazine could pay for contributions! It is very generous of you to send us your work.[3]

From issue to issue the pages of *The Egoist* carried, with supreme vigour, the alternating tones of passionate rage, earnest entreaty and scornful wit around three predominant issues: suffrage, art and the war. Pound, writing under the pseudonym Bastien von Helmholtz (a deliberately provocative Germanism, given the prevailing jingoism of the time against the hated Hun), married Dora's lofty condemnation of the wrong-headedness of the suffragettes' campaign with his own witty arrogance in the pursuit of what has since been called élitism.

Dora's more tempered prose is addressed to rationalising her judgement that the campaign for the vote rests on wrong-headed assumptions. In the issue for 1 October 1914, she writes about the suffragettes' aims in the context of a war which has brought an abrupt end to the debate about women's rights. In this carefully worded piece – one among many – she makes explicit her condemnation of marriage and suggests that campaigning for rights is doomed to fail because it avoids tackling the fundamental error by which women permit themselves to become men's property in marriage:

> Confused observation is the only explanation of the trend which has been set to the 'Woman's Movement' during the century and more which constitute its first stage, and to which the war has now affixed the term. For instance, only confusion could account for women's umbrage at being 'property', while at the same time they insist on retaining and augmenting those protective advantages they are possessed of, just because they *are* property . . . Thus women, being property, have no rights beyond 'courtesy' permitted ones; but their owners have responsibilities towards them, which at their minimum they must fulfil because of the demands of their fellow-owners, and at their maximum in order to gratify vanity in the pride of possession, and to increase that attraction between women and their owners, which is at the root-cause of men's assumption of responsibility . . .
>
> Whether the 'revolting' women will ever move on to the point of acquiring the elements of self-defensive and aggressive force depends on the extent to which the ardour of ambition can survive the depressing effects of the present too realistic presentation of their actual position.

The piece goes on to argue that those few women who understand that setting themselves 'straight for individual power' – thus, by implication, refusing marriage – will understand that achieving power depends on rejecting passivity. It is clear from Dora Marsden's writing elsewhere that she never advocated celibacy as a corollary to rejecting marriage, though her support for free love is stern rather than sentimental, since her emphasis is always on the 'freedom' component of any concept.

In the issue of 15 June 1914 Dora had announced her retirement as editor of the paper and explained that in the future her function would be that of contributing editor. The editorship passed to Harriet Weaver, though it wasn't until the first issue of 1916 that Harriet wrote her first 'Views and Comments' column. Here she followed a previous piece of Dora's about journalism and literary theories; and claimed for *The Egoist* a non-journalistic disinterestedness which set it apart from any other paper or periodical:

> the 'Views and Comments' of November 1 . . . distinguished journalism from literature in that the prime purpose of the former lay in the effort to impose a doctrine . . . However rough and ready the distinction may be, it is an advantage to be able to remember that the writer of genuine literature is no theory-lover, not primarily the defender of an opinion for its own sake but caring only to get understanding of his kind, let it be ugly or pleasing . . .
>   . . . if we claim any distinction for *The Egoist* it is because it has . . . failed to evince the journalistic instinct. It has skirted all movements and caught on to none. That is its distinction and one which we aspire to retain.

Inquiring 'what men *are*', rather than concluding 'what they *should be*', the piece suggests, is – both for Harriet Weaver and for *The Egoist* – a characterising trait of the literary-minded. It isn't difficult to see that this anti-moralistic stance would fit well together with a hostility towards ideology. Harriet Weaver's base-line is that proper observation will 'regard nothing in human nature as foreign to it'; though the irony perhaps escapes her that ideologies and belief-systems are as much excrescences of 'human nature' as any other social phenomena.

From this point on, *The Egoist* became clearly a literary periodical. The shift to straightforward humanism was established in its editorial idiom, in its use of the male pronoun as a universal, and in its endorsement of anti-polemicism. The authoritative character of the writer's stance as a torch-bearer for 'civilization' and 'art' was consistently made explicit.

In addition to *Poetry* and *The Freewoman/Egoist*, there were other publishing outlets important for the work of the writers we've been considering. *The Little Review*, which appeared between March 1914 and May 1929 was set up in Chicago by Margaret Anderson with funds made available by a friend of hers called Dewitt C. Wing. Wing wasn't particularly wealthy – he worked as a staff writer on an agricultural journal – but he believed in Margaret's conception of the *Review* and agreed to put aside each month enough cash to pay the printing bill and the office rent. Once publication began, he also contributed book reviews.

Editorial announcements for the new periodical proclaimed it to be a magazine that 'believes in Life for Art's sake' and said:

> Its ambitious aim is to produce criticism of books, music, art, drama, and life that shall be fresh, constructive, and intelligent from the artist's point of view . . . Since *The Little Review* . . . is neither directly nor indirectly connected in any way with any organization, society, company, cult or movement . . . it shall enjoy that untrammelled liberty which is the life of Art.[4]

Much later, recalling her convictions in founding the *Review*, Margaret Anderson asserted that 'people who make Art are more interesting than those who don't', since they have 'a special illumination about life' which is the 'subject-matter of all inspired conversation'.[5] Despite such aestheticism, *The Little Review*'s early issues concentrated on social and philosophical issues. Between 1914 and 1917 it carried articles on Nietzsche, Bergson, anarchism, feminism and psychoanalysis. The issue for May 1914 created a scandal about an article written by Margaret Anderson about Emma Goldman, in which private property was denounced. Publishing this piece lost Dewitt Wing's financial support and from then on the magazine had to make its own way.

Between 1917 and 1921 the *Review* passed through its Pound period. As with Harriet Monroe's *Poetry*, Pound became the *Review*'s foreign correspondent and predictably published a great amount of material by and about Imagists, as well as work by Marianne Moore, Mary Butts, Mina Loy, Djuna Barnes, Gertrude Stein and William Carlos Williams. Its carrying of Joyce's *Ulysses* provoked a New York obscenity trial in 1920 as a result of which Margaret and her co-editor Jane Heap were found guilty and fined $100. Dorothy Richardson's *Interim* – a chapter-volume of her long *Pilgrimage* sequence – was also serialised at this time.

In 1922 the editors took the *Review* to Paris, and met those of their contributors who lived and wrote there. Margaret eventually lost interest in the enterprise and turned the magazine over to Jane, who took it back to New York where she began to focus more on visual arts than on literature, covering developments in cubism and dadaism. In 1929 Margaret Anderson worked on the final issue, which included answers to questionnaires she'd sent out to all contributors.

The Little Review's financial stability was always under threat. The magazine never paid contributors, but even so – after losing Wing's backing – Margaret was constrained to mount a subscription campaign and took part-time reviewing work herself to help cover costs. Amy Lowell offered financial support in exchange for the position of poetry editor, but Margaret – sensing potential editorial conflict – declined. As the *Review* became steadily more anarchistic, subscriptions fell off, but Margaret refused to submit her views to a consensus judgment. In 1916, Margaret and Jane put out an issue from California. It consisted mostly of blank pages, with a statement that since no real art was being offered and *The Little Review* would never publish anything second-rate, it would therefore publish nothing at all.

Pound's first editorial as foreign correspondent, in the May 1917 issue, stated

> In so far as is possible, I should like *The Little Review* to aid and abet *The Egoist* in its work. I do not think it can be too often pointed out that during the last four years *The Egoist* has published serially . . . the only translations of Remy de Gourmont's *Chevaux de Diomedes* . . . Mr Joyce's masterpiece *A Portrait of the Artist as a Young Man*, and is now publishing Mr Lewis's novel *Tarr* . . . but *The Egoist* has not stopped there; they have in a most spirited form carried out the publication in book form of the *Portrait of the Artist*, and are in the act of publishing Mr Eliot's poems . . .

Privately he was even more explicit about his promotional goals, writing to Margaret Anderson that

> *The Little Review* is perhaps temperamentally closer to what I want done????? . . . I want an 'official organ' (vile phrase). I mean I want a place where I and T.S. Eliot can appear once a month . . . and where Joyce can appear when he likes, and where Wyndham Lewis can appear if he comes back from the war.

Definitely a place for our regular appearance and where our friends and readers (what few of 'em there are), can look with assurance of finding us . . . I must have a steady place for my best stuff (apart from original poetry, which must go to *Poetry* unless my guarantor is to double his offer . . .).[6]

Pound was patronised by John Quinn, who gave him a monthly sum to pay contributors to *The Little Review*. Although Pound believed that payment for contributions was an essential strategy for ensuring circulation success, he did not regard payment as unproblematic. He wrote to Quinn:

I hope you aren't going to be offended by my remarks on artists and patrons in the editorial I sent direct to Miss Anderson. I was wroth with the editorial in *Poetry* on the same topic. H. Monroe seems to think that if her Chicago widows and spinsters will only shell out she can turn her gang of free-versers into geniuses all of a onceness. Hence my remarks on the inability of patrons to create artists . . .[7]

At almost the same time he wrote to Margaret Anderson:

Quinn is not a rich man in the American sense of the word. He has what he makes month by month, and most of it goes to the arts . . . Quinn wanted me to take £120 a year for myself in connection with *The Egoist* a year or so ago. The point is that if I accept more than I *need* I at once become a sponger, and I at once lose my integrity. By doing the job for the absolute minimum I remain respectable and when I see something I want I can ask for it . . .

My whole position and the whole backing up of my statement that the artist is 'almost' independent goes with doing the thing as nearly as possible without 'money'.[8]

But Margaret's enthusiasm for what Pound had to offer wasn't shared by everyone. Amy Lowell wrote to H.D.:

How does it happen that you have resigned the assistant editorship of 'The Egoist'? Ezra's coming back on the paper fills me with horror, and he seems to have got in with Margaret Anderson. Her little sheet is entirely full of him.[9]

Apart from pique that Anderson preferred Pound's involvement to her own offer of literary editorship, it's clear that Amy's tastes did not conform to his. She wrote to Margaret:

I enclose my check for $150.00, as I agreed to do, but there is a string attached to it: I want you to get out one number, as I told you in Chicago, which will not advocate violence. Also, I want you to get out one number in which your real principles appear more perfectly than they sometimes do.

You remember our conversation on the difference between love and lust, when I was in Chicago; and you remember how well we agreed on the subject? Now, you see, love on the purely mental side is apt to be as dry and brittle as a withered leaf; but love on the purely physical side is as unpleasant as raw beef steak. It is the combination of the two which is perfection.

Now your contributors, in their fear of not speaking out plainly enough and representing facts as they are, always err on one side . . . the love in most of the stories you publish being merely a question of brute animal appetite. This is doing your own point of view as much injustice as if you were to write the goody-goody stories of the ordinary magazines.

Is it not possible to find authors with a sufficiently all-round sense of the views of life to portray the combination which makes human life what it is, in which neither manifestation is obscured to bring out the other? I would give anything to see it in some number, but why not this one? I have tried to do it myself in my own work, but a poet can do so little. Story-telling is so much more direct.[10]

Correspondence between H.D. and Amy reveals some of the depth of antagonism Pound's involvement with the *Review* aroused. H.D. wrote:

Miss Anderson writes us very charmingly – and we may send some poems later to the Little Review. Just now I don't feel much like contributing. Aren't E.P.'s antics amusing? From a distance, yes, but one wants to keep out of the purlieus.[11]

Amy is more forthright: 'Margaret Anderson has gone over body and soul to Ezra; and I have told her that while she is running him so hard, I will not put anything into her magazine.'[12] H.D. responded:

I did go to a party of E.P. and satallites [*sic*]. He seems untouched by all the realities that are torturing us all. I don't know exactly how he got hold of the 'Little Review'. He was very scornful of it in the early days. However that is nothing. Only I did like the little rag at times. Miss Margaret wanted R. and me to contribute regularly but me thinks, for the present, we will keep entirely out.[13]

Amy replied that she found H.D.'s 'method of being on perfectly good terms with them all' was 'a good one'; and that although she didn't bear Pound 'a grudge', she didn't want, either, 'to be mixed up with him publicly' since he had – in her view – 'queered himself all over the shop'.[14]

Pound, in turn, felt antagonistic. He wrote to Margaret:

If London and particularly Mayfair, is going to take up the magazine, we must be more careful than ever *not* to have in too much Amy, and suburbs.

Re Amy: I don't want to hedge too much. I don't think we need bar her from the magazine, but she can't write for the mondaine London clientele. At least I can't see Lady Randolph Churchill (or May Sinclair, for example) reading her with any spirit of reverence. These people can take it just as strong as Lewis can pitch. Your own tone suits 'em OK. (*Not* that you'd care a damn if it didn't but you may as well know it.)[15]

A month or so later, he was more trenchant:

Re Amy. I *don't* want her. But if she can be made to liquidate, to excoriate, to cash in, on a magazine, *especially* in a section over which I have no control, and for which I am not responsible, *then* would I be right glad to see her milked of her money, mashed into moonshine, at mercy of monitors. Especially as appearance in U.S. section does *not* commit me to any approval of her work.

Of course *if* (which is unlikely) she ever wanted to return to the true church and live like an honest woman, something might be arranged. *But* . . .[16]

Amy didn't, however, give up her own notions in order to return to Pound's true church; nor did Margaret renege on her commitment to Pound's judgment. Ardent or obstinate, she stuck to her own vision of quality and her own convictions of self-dependence. She'd written, for example, for *The Little Review*'s first anniversary, in the February 1915 issue:

as 'sanity' increases in the world *The Little Review* will strive more and more to be splendidly insane: as editors and lecturers continue to compromise in order to get their public, as book-makers continue to print rot in order to make fortunes, as writers continue to follow the market instead of *doing their work*, as the public continues to demand vileness and vulgarity and lies, as the intellectuals continue to miss the root of the trouble, *The Little Review* will continue to rebel, to tell the truth as we see it, to work for its ideal rather than for a policy . . .

There are other people who argue that we might be hugely successful by being better: that we might borrow a lot of money (they always say this so casually), pay high for contributions, become acutely sophisticated, fill a wide-felt need, etc. Now the first thing we shall do, as soon as we are able to pay our printer's bills without paroxysms of terror, is to pay for contributions; it is disgusting that writers who do real work don't make enough out of it to live on at least.

It was more purist than politic to reproach such a range of groups, not omitting the public, from whom her readership had to come. But it's precisely the force of this commination which kept her steadfast to her vision of fanning into flame in America that self-conscious cultural superiority which she and her peers sensed to be characteristic of European values. Part of the purism – traditionally and obviously – was the capacity not to be bought and therefore constrained by the holders of purse-strings. Though writers should be paid (so they could go on doing their 'real work'), the means whereby that work reached the public should remain uncompromised. The irony in this contradistinction was, of course, unconscious, but reveals a faith that real artists who do real work are constitutionally not vulnerable to the same seductions.

Given such convictions, it's hardly surprising that the *Review*'s stability was always precarious. In its infancy it had possibly 2,000 subscribers, who paid – at first – $2.50 per year; and later, $1.25. During its New York period until 1922 the production of the magazine cost some $10,000 per year. The editors sometimes even went without food in order to ensure publication. They eventually opened a bookshop in their office to raise more cash. In 1920 they appealed for $5,000, hoping to persuade 1,000 people to contribute $5 each; but the appeal was unsuccessful. In 1921 they went quarterly, thus reducing some of the costs.[17]

Apart from perpetual money worries, there was that more explicit – and equally perpetual – anxiety about American provincialism and its dependent need either to be better than the

Europeans or, failing that, at least to be as good. Pound, reviewing an anthology called *Others*[18] in the March 1918 issue, wrote:

> This [anthology] gives I think the first adequate presentation of Mina Loy and Marianne Moore who have, without exaggerated 'nationalism', without waving of banners and general phrases about Columbia gem of the ocean, succeeded in, or fallen into, producing something distinctly American in quality, not merely distinguishable as Americans [*sic*] by reason of current national faults.
>
> Their work is neither simple, sensuous nor passionate, but as we are no longer governed by the *North American Review* we need not condemn poems merely because they do not fit some stock phrase of rhetorical criticism.

The preoccupation that there should be something 'distinctly American' in contemporary literature is not mere petty nationalism. It was clear to Pound and his peers – as it has been for the generations of writers since – that sharing a language is not the same thing as sharing a culture; and that the representing and expressing of the newer society becomes particularly problematic when it must take place within language traditions born at other times and in another place. Even more urgent, for a woman writer, is the dilemma of being, at one and the same time, both an inheritor of her own society and an outsider from it.

One of the most interesting pieces published in *The Little Review* is a lengthy article called 'The novels of Dorothy Richardson' by May Sinclair. At the time – April 1918 – Dorothy Richardson had published the first three chapter-volumes of her *Pilgrimage* sequence: *Pointed Roofs*, *Backwater* and *Honeycomb*. The style sent May Sinclair back to some fundamental problems of criticism and its duty to taste:

> I have been asked to write – for this magazine which makes no compromise with the public taste – a criticism of the novels of Dorothy Richardson. The editors of *The Little Review* are committed to Dorothy Richardson by their declared intentions: for her works make no sort of compromise with the public taste. If they are not announced with the same proud challenge it is because the pride of the editors of *The Little Review* is no mate for the pride of Miss Richardson which ignores the very existence of the public and its taste.

I do not know whether this article is or is not going to be a criticism, for so soon as I begin to think what I shall say I find myself criticising criticism, wondering what is the matter with it and what, if anything, can be done to make it better, to make it alive. Only a live criticism can deal appropriately with a live art . . . I mean that it is absurd to go on talking about realism and idealism, or objective and subjective art, as if the philosophies were sticking where they stood in the eighties.

In those days the distinction between idealism and realism, between subjective and objective was important and precise. And so long as the ideas they stand for had importance and precision those words were lamps to the feet and lanterns to the path of the critic . . .

The piece continues with an account of J.D. Beresford's introduction to *Pointed Roofs*, in which he describes his initial confusion about whether the book's style was subjective or objective; and how he decided finally that the novelist who wants to be close to reality must simply 'plunge in':

Mr Beresford also says that Miss Richardson is the first novelist who has plunged in. She has plunged so neatly and quietly that even admirers of her performance might remain unaware of what it is precisely that she has done. She has disappeared while they are still waiting for the splash . . .

Perhaps, May Sinclair suggests, Dorothy Richardson is not actually the first to have 'plunged in' – she mentions the Goncourts and Marguerite Audoux – nor has Richardson plunged deeper than Joyce in his *Portrait*. What she has done, however, is achieve such a perfection of her method in the removal of her authorial omniscience that 'she would probably deny that she has written with any deliberate method at all'. And the originality of the style leads, inevitably, to the problematic nature of the form of the work:

And I find it impossible to reduce to intelligible terms this satisfaction that I feel. To me these three novels show an art and method and form carried to punctilious perfection. Yet I have heard other novelists say that they have no art and no method and no form, and that it is this formlessness that annoys them. They say that they have no beginning and no middle and no end, and that to have form a novel must have an end and a beginning and a middle . . . In this series there is no drama, no situation, no set scene. Nothing happens. It is just life going on and on. It is Miriam Henderson's stream of consciousness going on and on. And in neither is there any grossly discernible beginning or middle or end.

In identifying herself with this life which is Miriam's stream of consciousness Miss Richardson produces her effect of being the first, of getting closer to reality than any of our novelists who are trying so desperately to get close . . .

Pilgrimage has never been popular; and May Sinclair's remarkable ability to discern and describe the essential features of Dorothy Richardson's work seems even more acute now than it must have done then, when after more than half a century the book still waits for its just due and wider readership.

May Sinclair's piece was by no means unique, nevertheless. *The Little Review* carried a large number of articles both by and about the women writers we've been considering, each of which testifies to careful and scrupulous reading. There are (and this is just a sample list) Amy Lowell's 'Letter from London'; Margaret Anderson's review of Amy Lowell's *Sword Blades*; Harriet Monroe's *You and I* reviewed; Richard Aldington on H.D., Amy Lowell and J.G. Fletcher on *Some Imagist Poets*; F.S. Flint on Amy Lowell; J.G. Fletcher on H.D.; *Some Imagist Poets* reviewed; a piece called 'The Vers Libre Contest'; Pound's review of Marianne Moore; various reviews of Dorothy Richardson by John Rodker, William Carlos Williams and Robert McAlmon (in addition to May Sinclair's piece); Mina Loy on John Rodker; Mary Butts on *The Poets' Translation Series*; and Gertrude Stein on Jane Heap.[19] In its final issue, for spring 1929, *The Little Review* carried answers to questionnaires, many of which were answered by these writers and are revealing about the preoccupations they held in common.

In May Sinclair's piece, as in many of the other *Review* articles, we see as clearly as anywhere how the 'individualist' stance informing female modernism differed from the straightforward humanist aestheticism which preceded it. 'Art for Art's sake' – or even 'Art for Life's sake' – rapidly becomes absolutist, procuring a concept of art as an entity with identifying traits and corresponding rules to govern them and theories to explicate them. Abstractions multiply and consequential discourses become increasingly philosophical, until even the artistic products themselves, under the influence of such views, become refined to a degree where compatibility with the notion of 'Art' (or 'Poetry') is immensely more important than a resemblance to 'Life'. Nowhere is the attitude more obvious than in the aesthete's repugnance towards politics, about which artists and their acolytes remain often illiterate or contemptuous. And aestheticism, with its built-in tendency towards abstraction, is more easily appropriated to the classic modes – poetry, sculpture, music, for example – than to the more recent and untidy modes, such as the novel. It's easier for Pound to construct the theory of Imagism from H.D.'s poems, for instance, than for May Sinclair to deal with Dorothy Richardson's prose; partly because the lyric has an ancient and discrete form and the novel does not. It seems hardly accidental that the quest for psychological realism should take place in the novelistic mode and that a new use of prose diction should be necessary to such an undertaking. The novelistic convention requiring a beginning, a middle and an end, could be upturned as soon as the story to be told became a story of inner life rather than of external events.

The modernists' obsession with reality (as counterposed to the aestheticists' obsession with truth) leads implicitly and necessarily to preoccupations with the material, the social and the transient – with all the jumble of human experience at its most ordinary – rather than with metaphysics and ultimate realities. The aesthetic position properly denigrates the crassness of activities such as politics because such things are irrelevant to the pursuit of the sublime. For modernists the problem is more ambiguous, since the pursuit of reality always ends in some confrontation or other between the individual and the group. The modernists, like most artists and literati of any time or philosophy, eschewed politics on the macrocosmic scale; they didn't form or follow parties or seek bureaucratic power. They did, however, acknowledge the political features of art (which they called 'civilisation' or 'culture'): the need for the artistic body corporate; the need for dissemination; and the dependence of excellence on those who control standards (such as publishing networks). Furthermore, they sensed – tenuously, but more than had most who'd gone before them – that there are connections between challenging literary conventions and challenging social ones. William Carlos Williams comments, for instance, about Dorothy Richardson and James Joyce, in the September 1919 issue:

Of course they are not writing of the war, nor is their work influenced thereby but I cannot help that. Their form lives! It is not a bed. It is not to put one to sleep. It lives in its today.

They plunge naked into the flaming cauldron of today. Insofar as their form goes the war exists in it, carries its own meaning. It is a different war, it is not like other wars, it is modern, it exists, it is not a thing to spitlick . . .

It was left to later generations, and to feminists and Marxists especially, to explore the subtleties of connection between literary forms and social forms; but the seeds were already sown both in the works of modernists and in their reactions to each other's writing.

Poetry, *The Egoist* and *The Little Review* – all edited by women – were of major importance over a long period for most of the writers we've been considering. But there were, too, more ephemeral periodicals which also carried new work. Writing is mysterious and problematic; and acting out one's passions is potentially all-consuming of time and energy. Support and encouragement from friends and peers is essential for most writers if they're to carry on; and reassurance from the network is necessary to unconventional people if they are to avoid isolation and neurosis. But necessary as such support systems are, they're not enough. Writers need a public, however small; they crave publication, the chance for their work to be read by strangers. And if the major publishing outlets don't take up their work and promote it, they must find alternatives. So it happens that periodical publishing – however small, specialist, erratic or partisan – is where writers turn if they're young or experimentalist, and if they're seeking an audience for non-populist forms; lyric poetry, short fiction, essays, plays, literary sketches and polemical pieces. Fees may be small or non-existent, but the chance of an audience is compelling and overriding.

Among ephemeral periodicals in the early part of the century was *Bruno's Weekly*, one of Guido Bruno's many publications. This, together with his other magazines, devoted space to discussions of bohemianism in general and life in New York's Greenwich Village in particular, as well as comment about European art and literature. He used the same material more than once in his various organs and had among his contributors Marianne Moore and Ford Madox Ford. Bruno issued, too, a series of 'Chapbooks' in which he published work by Djuna Barnes and H.D., among others.

The Glebe, appearing regularly between 1913 and 1914, was

edited by Alfred Kreymborg, an impoverished New York writer who wanted to establish a magazine which would publish experimental writing. He met Man Ray, then working in a New York print shop; and Ray persuaded his employer to donate an old press to the venture. Pound heard about the magazine and sent manuscripts from London, mainly work by H.D., Aldington, Amy Lowell, Flint and, of course, himself. In the meantime, the printing press was damaged during delivery and couldn't be used; so Kreymborg persuaded Albert and Charles Boni, owners of the Washington Square Bookshop in Greenwich Village, to put up the finances needed for publication. The work sent by Pound was published as the special *Imagiste* number in February 1914 (the magazine's fifth issue) and was later reissued in book form by the Bonis as *Des Imagistes*. Before long, the Bonis wanted more European work published; but Kreymborg wanted the emphasis to be on the home-grown product. Under pressure of this disagreement, Kreymborg resigned.

He went on to found *Others: A Magazine of the New Verse*, which ran until July 1919. Co-edited with W. Saphir between 1917 and 1918 from New Jersey, it began as a vehicle and encouragement for those whose poetry hadn't yet appeared – or had only appeared infrequently – in *Poetry*. *Others* carried more experimental contributions than Harriet Monroe's magazine, including poems by Marianne Moore, Mina Loy, H.D., Amy Lowell, T.S. Eliot, Aldington and Pound. It was a monthly, designed to remind readers that 'there were others' writing verse. Mina Loy's *Love Songs*, published in the first issue (July 1915), were among those poems arousing mockery and resentment from the literary public:

> Spawn of fantasies
> Sitting the unappraisable
> Pig Cupid   his rosy snout
> Rooting erotic garbage . . .

Its financial backing came from Walter Arensberg whom Kreymborg had met at a New York party. The two men had no thought of making money; but were ambitious to publish the avant-garde. About 300 copies of each issue were printed on average, though at times the print run reached 1,000.

Although contributors received no fees, Kreymborg and his wife constantly met and entertained them at their house. However, by the end of the first year of publication, Arensberg and Kreymborg were at loggerheads and the magazine fell into financial difficulties. Kreymborg had been working part-time as a letter-writer for a New York financier, but that didn't make enough money to subsidise a magazine. At this point, Alfred Knopf offered to publish a yearly *Others* anthology; and John Marshall, from 'The Little Bookshop around the Corner', offered to finance the magazine. Still, this injection of capital didn't last long and soon *Others* began to appear sporadically rather than monthly. In its last two years it carried a number of experimental plays, including some by Djuna Barnes. Kreymborg was less involved in these issues, so much of the editing work and entertaining was taken over by his friend Lola Ridge.

Kreymborg went on to start yet another magazine, this time called *Broom*, a venture given a caustic welcome by Harriet Monroe in the 'Our Contemporaries' column of *Poetry*, for the June 1921 issue:

'*The Dial* for May opens its page of *Comment* by quoting this remark of W.C. Blum: Williams' first suggestion was that someone give Alfred Kreymborg one hundred thousand dollars. And the editor goes on to inform us of a windfall of money: What do you know? Somebody's gone and done it! Alfred Kreymborg and Harold Loeb announce an International Magazine of the Arts, to be printed in Italy and sold all round the block.'

Some people are born lucky! Nobody ever offered *Poetry* an hundred thousand . . . And *Poetry* has been a conspicuous target for such windfalls these ten years – nearly – Whereas Mr Kreymborg carried *Others* scarcely more than a year. The new international is to be called *The Broom*. May it sweep clean without raising too much dust.

The Dial, in its volumes 68 to 86, appearing between 1920 and 1929, pursued an avant-garde editorial policy which placed it among the small literary journals of this period. It moved from Chicago to New York in 1918, when Harold Stearns became editor and brought in as principal backer his Harvard classmate Scofield Thayer. In his turn, Thayer brought in as a partner Dr James Sibley Watson. Between 1925 and 1929 Marianne Moore co-edited the magazine.

During the decade of the twenties, *The Dial* published translations from German, French and Russian fiction and verse; philosophical essays by George Santayana and Bertrand Russell; and fiction and poetry by Djuna Barnes, Marianne Moore, Amy Lowell, Ezra Pound, William Carlos Williams, D.H. Lawrence,

Richard Aldington, Mina Loy and May Sinclair. Its editorial stance, stated in the first issue, came down clearly on the side of standards rather than of commercial expedience:

> If a magazine isn't to be simply a waste of good white paper, it ought to print, with some regularity, either such work as would otherwise have to wait years for publication, or such as would not be acceptable elsewhere.

And Marianne Moore, recalling the magazine's character during this period, surmised:

> I think we thought individuality was the great thing. We were not conforming to anything. We certainly didn't have a policy, except I remember hearing the word 'intensity' very often. A thing must have an 'intensity'. That seemed to be the criterion . . . It was a matter of taking a liking to things. Things that were in accordance with your taste. I think that was it. And we didn't care how unhomogeneous they might seem.[20]

Contact, published irregularly between December 1920 and June 1923, resulted from William Carlos Williams' desire to have his own magazine. Edited by Williams and Robert McAlmon, its first editorial stated 'faith in the existence of native artists who are capable of having, comprehending, and recording extraordinary experience'. It carried critical work by Williams, McAlmon and Marianne Moore, as well as poetry by Mina Loy, John Rodker, Kay Boyle and, of course, Williams.

The birth of the *Transatlantic Review* was the outcome of a series of coincidences, the most significant being the meeting in Paris of Ford Madox Ford and Pound, already old friends. Ford was in Paris during Christmas 1922 and visited Pound, who was living there at that time. Ford returned the following spring, having decided to give up living in England. At about this time his brother offered him the backing of a group of financiers to support a new review journal. Ford was well known because of his editorship of the *English Review* during 1908–9. Ford relayed the offer to Pound and news of it spread through the Paris literary network. But the backers, after meeting Ford and Pound, found Pound shocking; and, in addition, they didn't want Joyce published in the new magazine. The proposed deal inevitably fell through.

Pound then approached John Quinn; and with some success. Quinn had advanced him funds in 1913–14 and again some years later, when Pound wanted to pay contributors to *The Egoist* and *The Little Review*. Quinn agreed to put up 49 per cent of the capital needed for a review journal; and Ford agreed to put up the remaining 51 per cent.

Ford sold his English house and used money from his lover, Stella Bowen, to make up his share. He met Bill Bird, whose Three Mountains Press was, by this time, in association with McAlmon's Contact Publishing Company. Bird let Ford have an office in his building in Paris and Pound found editorial helpers. In late 1923, Ford started appealing for funds and sent out a prospectus, defining the journal's aims to be, first, a widening of the field in which younger writers could find publication and, secondly, an introduction into international politics of a more genial note than had previously prevailed. The brief continued:

> The aim of the Review is to help in bringing about a state of things in which it will be considered that there are no English, no French – for the matter of that, no Russian, Italian, Asiatic or Teutonic – Literatures: there will only be Literature, as today there are Music and the Plastic Arts each having Schools, Russian, Persian, 16th century German, as the case may be . . .
>
> The politics will be those of its editor who has no party leanings save toward those of a Tory kind so fantastically old fashioned . . . or in such Communism as may prevail a thousand years hence . . . [21]

With the prospectus, Ford sent out a preliminary number, most of the material of which appeared in *The Transatlantic Review*'s first issue. Initially, the magazine's title was not capitalised, which caused some shock, anger and amusement; but this phenomenon had little to do with political policy and much to do with space limitations, Bill Bird later claimed. *The Transatlantic Review* was to be published in Paris, New York and London, with different wrappers made in each of the three capitals. Duckworth was Ford's English publisher; Thomas Seltzer his American one. Both agreed to distribute the magazine. In Paris, bookshops – including 'Shakespeare & Company' – agreed to sell it. Each issue was planned to be book-length, at some 100 pages; and contributors were to be paid, initially at a rate of 30 francs per page.

Ford began to give parties for contributors every Thursday afternoon, both at the office and in his apartment. Early in 1924 he met Hemingway, who became his sub-editor. The first issue finally appeared in January 1924; and was favourably reviewed in *Mercure de France* and *The Spectator*. There were probably 5,000 copies of each issue printed and equally divided between the three cities. However, the magazine failed to make money; and in summer 1924 Ford went to New York to try to raise further funds from Quinn. The mission failed. Quinn was seriously ill and died before putting up any cash.

On returning to Paris Ford found, through Hemingway, another backer, Krebs Friend, who had a wealthy wife. They put up funds, but wanted editorial control in return. Nor did they want to pay contributors, other than 'writers in distress'.[22] In addition, Ford and Hemingway fell out. Ford suspended publication in 1925.

Although *The Transatlantic Review* enjoyed only a short run, its list of contributors reads like a précis of modernism: H.D., Gertrude Stein, Mary Butts, Djuna Barnes, Dorothy Richardson, Bryher and Mina Loy, among the women; and Joyce, Pound, McAlmon, Conrad, Williams and e.e. cummings among the men. The editorial design covered 'Verse', 'Prose', 'Musical Supplement', 'Serials', 'Communications' (letters to the editor and short pieces), 'Chroniques' (short editorial pieces) and 'Notes and Reviews'. Advertisements included booksellers; Duckworth's and Seltzer's publishers' lists; American newspapers in Paris; hotels; and American Express. Work by French writers appeared without English translation.

This Quarter, appearing quarterly between spring 1925 and winter 1932, was financed by Ethel Moorhead, a Scotswoman who had been active in the suffrage movement and who came from a wealthy family. She met and fell in love with the young Ernest Walsh, a penniless Cuban-American some twenty years younger than she. Together they set up the magazine, writing for contributions to Pound, McAlmon, Gertrude Stein, Kay Boyle, Joyce, and others. Walsh had known Harriet Monroe in Chicago; and some of his verse had been published in *Poetry*. His views and style, however, were more radical and he wanted to start his own journal to disseminate them. Ethel Moorhead and Ernest Walsh visited as many of their chosen writers as they could, taking the resulting manuscripts to the south of France to work on. Through correspondence with Kay Boyle, Walsh learned she was ill with suspected TB, though she was then only 22 years old and not long married. Walsh suggested she come south, which she did, only to fall in love with him, thus creating havoc between him and Ethel Moorhead.

Ironically, it happened that Kay Boyle was not suffering from TB, but Walsh was. Kay Boyle stayed and helped the other two with the next issue of the magazine. The two editors – not surprisingly – argued; and Ethel Moorhead eventually declared that she'd edit the magazine herself. At about this time, summer 1926, Walsh grew suddenly very ill and died in October after only two issues of the magazine. Ethel Moorhead carried on for a while but in 1927 gave control to Edward Titus in Paris, who changed its direction entirely.

The first issue of *This Quarter* was dedicated to Pound and carried articles about his work. Its editorial, written by Walsh, declared:

This Quarter exists primarily to publish the artist's work while it is still fresh . . . This Quarter recognizes that if publication is to help the artist it must publish his work at intervals of not less than three months and publish each work under no greater delay than the editing and printing demand.

This Quarter insists that the vital need of an artist is to be published and read during his creative life and that periodicals delaying publication over long periods possibly protect the editorial reputation of the periodical but in no way may claim to assist the artist.

Our critical approach to the art of this age is revolutionary in that we discard the usual tools of criticism and valuation and are concerned first and last with discovering identity in work.

We have received cheques towards the sum of two thousand dollars or five hundred pounds to be given to the contributors publishing the best work in the first four numbers of This Quarter.

Each issue was very large, consisting of over 200 pages, divided between prose, verse, reviews, editorials, 'miscellany', and an art supplement. Under Walsh's co-editorship, contributors included Gertrude Stein, Kay Boyle, H.D., Hemingway, Bryher, Djuna Barnes, Joyce, McAlmon, Williams and Pound.

Close-up, running monthly, then quarterly, between July 1927 and December 1933, advertised itself as 'An International Magazine Devoted to Film Art'. It was financed – and its business details organised – by Bryher, who also assisted Kenneth Macpherson's editing. She recalled its origins:

We lived at Territet [Switzerland] and one day as we were

walking beside the lake and Kenneth compared the ripples drifting across the water with an effect that should be tried on the screen, I remembered my Paris training of the early twenties and said, 'If you are so interested, why don't you start a magazine?'

So *Close-up* was born on a capital of sixty pounds. We expected it to last three issues and had five hundred copies printed. It was an immediate success and when we ended after the collapse of the silent film, six years later, we had five thousand readers . . . To our utter amazement, the first issue of *Close-up* sold out within a month and it was enthusiastically reviewed. There was one film that we felt expressed our generation. It was *Die Freudlose Gasse* (*Joyless Street*) directed by G.W. Pabst and starring Greta Garbo for the second time in her career.[23]

The magazine sold in London at Bumpus' bookshop and was also available by subscription. Macpherson's first 'As Is' editorial, in the July 1927 issue, announced:

> The first two numbers of Close-Up will deal with the film problem as a whole. After that we propose in each issue to deal with special conditions in Europe and the States with numbers on the Negro attitude and problem and on the Far East in their relations to the cinema.

And in the second issue:

> People are still apt to sneer when you talk of films being art . . . It has been a film industry, film *industry*. And quite right up to a point . . . But we are going to talk film *art* at them until the right balance is established.

The second issue's list of contributors included Macpherson and Bryher for essays, film reviews, interviews and columns; H.D. for Film Criticism and essays; Dorothy Richardson for a regular column called 'Continuous Performance' which set out to examine the aesthetics of the cinema; Barbara Low for articles about film in education; Hanns Sachs (Bryher's analyst) for pieces on psychoanalysis and film; and correspondents from Hollywood, Paris and New York. There were also some contributions having nothing to do with film: poems by H.D. and Marianne Moore; stories by Gertrude Stein; and other occasional pieces. Some articles in French (not translated into English) appeared in each issue; as did many stills from current films.

Dorothy Richardson was not only a contributor but also an enthusiastic supporter. Writing to Bryher at the time of the first issue she declared:

> I think we were the first that ever burst into Bumpus's for Close Ups that lay in a pile very visible just inside the door. Began reading in the street & were so thrilled that we fell into the nearest tea-shop & sat down. I read, running breathless in the wake of the contributors, sometimes crawling after them on my knees . . . The Lord be with you all. A great day.[24]

And again:

> Many thanks for cheque for C[ontinuous] P[erformance] which I am glad to know is not the deadly thing I thought it . . . I am enchanted by your whole enterprise. We tell everyone we meet & will get a number of copies & broadcast them in suitable quarters . . . You know Lawrence *loathes* films? *Foams* about them. I'm sure he'd foam for you. Villa Mirenda, Scandicci, Florence. And Barbara Low is sound on Educ: & the cinema . . . Let us know if you think of anything we can do to help launch your infant . . .[25]

transition, beginning in the same year as *Close-up*, ran until spring 1938. A monthly edited from Paris by Eugene Jolas and Elliot Paul, it became an important American expatriate 'little magazine'. Jolas' main interest was Joyce; and the magazine published much by and about him. For Jolas, the ultimate expression of the artist lay in a union of the subconscious with the supernatural. Contributors included Gertrude Stein, Kay Boyle, William Carlos Williams, Bryher, H.D., McAlmon, Hemingway, Emily Holmes Coleman, Kreymborg, Djuna Barnes, Rodker and Laurence Vail, as well as Joyce. The magazine did well, not only because of the range of its contributors, but because it reached a wide readership. The combination of successful elements was well designed. The magazine was edited from Paris, which was – much more than London – the centre of the irrationalist intellectual current; it was distributed from New York's Gotham Book Mart, at that time a hub of avant-garde radicalism; it was satirised in such quarters as *Life* magazine; and it had a massive circulation. All this favoured a successful dissemination of European preoccupations among the American intelligentsia.

Within the parameters of these periodicals: their locations, their editors, their backers and resources, it becomes significant that many of the writers we've been considering were expatriates. Unlike the quintessentially English traits common to the Bloomsbury set, this network shared no common cultural allegiance. The interdependence for the English upper middle classes of traditional values in education, social courtesies (and snobberies), literary achievements, and so on, make clear to any English man or woman that a Strachey or a Bell schooled at Cambridge would not discuss aesthetics in the same vein as Dorothy Richardson or H.D., Djuna Barnes or Mina Loy, D.H. Lawrence or James Joyce, whose views would be perceived as possibly brilliant, but certainly barbarous. It isn't unimportant that the men hailed as great writers of modern English – Eliot, Joyce, Yeats, Pound, Conrad – were none of them English.

Virginia Woolf, being English, certainly had the correct class background to be 'literary'; but she belonged to the wrong gender. She tried more assiduously and with more success than most modern Englishwomen to find a central place in the literary tradition of her nation; but even she wrote of the woman writer's exile in her polemical *A Room of One's Own*. The expatriates – H.D., Katherine Mansfield, Gertrude Stein and other women writers – had to cope not only with the same psychological exile, but also with actual displacement from their roots. And that situation is even more complex for an English speaker who is not English; for whom allegiance to her language and to the social roots of the language remain separable. For an American, or any other non-English speaker of English, the attractions of what is perceived as dynamic, radical, forward-looking, will predominate over an adherence to an 'Englishness' which is at best acquired, and at its worst misplaced and distorted. A network of writers flexible enough, heterogeneous enough, to include expatriates, is more likely than an English counterpart to respond with positive enthusiasm to non-English literary currents. Where Paris is foreign territory to an English man or woman, it is hardly less foreign to an American than is London; and for the American reader back home, whether new American writing derives from London literary life or from bohemian Paris is of very little significance.

Chapter 12

'The public is a stupid beast . . .'
Book publishing I

Getting into print for the first time is achieved, as often as not, via periodical publications; but hardly any writer's thirst for audience and critical appraisal is slaked by such appearances. Writers want to be published in book form: poets in anthologies and collections; polemicists at the length and in the scope allowed by a book; novelists, obviously, and even writers of short fiction want their work collected between the boards of a book. Books aren't merely bigger and longer; they're also more permanent, more discrete than the ephemeral-seeming journal (which libraries may not acquire, or, having acquired, may not be able to keep). Above all, books – on the whole – aren't shared space; the writer, having successfully engaged the attention of a publisher, may now hope equally to engage the all-powerful attention of newspaper literary editors. The two-way traffic between literary periodicals and book publishing was much more common earlier in the century than it is now; so that appearances in the 'little magazines' might well lead on to appearances in book form. Indeed, many of the magazines we've considered carried 'Work in Progress' sections where novels, in particular, were serialised.

Anthologies serve, clearly, as a half-way house, both for poets and for short fiction writers. *Des Imagistes, An Anthology* first appeared as the fifth issue of *The Globe*. Pound had orchestrated all the contributors by writing to them; and had added Amy Lowell, whom he'd met the previous summer in London. He wrote to her in September 1913, asking her to contribute; but J.G. Fletcher, one of the American expatriate Imagists, had by this time become disillusioned with Pound and warned Amy not to agree, on the grounds that the collection would only serve Pound's and Aldington's own ends and not those of other contributors. Amy did agree, however, along with all the others Pound asked. The Boni brothers issued *Des Imagistes* in book form in April 1914, with 480 advance orders in hand. The book was reviewed everywhere; established poets and academics reacted caustically, whereas other readers were both enthusiastic and confused. Harold Monro arranged publication in London; the unbound sheets were sent over and issued with the Poetry Bookshop imprint. By contrast with its American reception, the book aroused little response in London, and some disenchanted buyers even sent their copies back.

By this time a break between Pound and the others was inevitable. In September, Amy wrote to Harriet Monroe:

> You ask about the quarrel between Ezra and the rest of us. It is not a quarrel now, it is a schism . . . In thinking over what I could do to help the poets less fortunate than myself, and also to help myself in somewhat the same manner that a review would do, it seemed to me that to republish the 'Imagiste Anthology' with the same group of people, year after year, for a period of five years, would enable us, by constant iteration, to make some impression upon the public . . . I mentioned this first to the Aldingtons because I saw them first after I conceived the idea.[1]

Amy, like many of the others in Pound's collection of new writers, had begun to suspect that his judgment wasn't infallible and his motives not always unimpeachable. Pound, in turn, consistent as ever in his autocratic temperament and values, was furious to be challenged by a protégée. Amy wanted Imagist collections to have a democratised editorial base. She explained to Harriet Monroe:

> I suggest that the last little book [*Des Imagistes*] was too monotonous and too undemocratic in that certain poets were allowed much more space than others; and I suggested that in the 'New Anthology' we should allow approximately the same space to each poet, and that we should get a publisher of reputable standing, and I offered, in case we could not get any publisher to take the risk of the volume itself, to pay for its publication.[2]

Amy told Harriet that H.D., Aldington, and the others she'd approached were enthusiastic about her proposals, but Pound, of course, was annoyed:

He accused me of trying to make myself editor instead of him, and finally tried a little blackmail by telling me that he would only join us on condition that I would obligate myself to give $200 a year to some indigent poet . . . I absolutely refused to be intimidated into buying anything, or to buy his poems at the expense of my self-respect.

Pound was not to be thwarted by someone he didn't regard as his peer; and, in any case, was unlikely to accept Amy's statement that she wouldn't have suggested the anthology if she'd known he wouldn't like the idea, since it was intended to benefit him quite as much as the other contributors:

He was perfectly furious for some time, and sent for the Aldingtons, and told them they must choose between him and me, which was awful for them . . . They behaved with the utmost honour in the matter. They told Ezra it was not a question of me at all, but a question of the principle, that they felt it only fair to let the poets choose their own contributions and to give each poet an equal space. He then tried to bribe them, by asking them to get up an Anthology with him, and leave me out. This they absolutely refused to do.

We had many consultations on the subject, in which Flint, Lawrence, and Ford Madox Hueffer joined us, and we all agreed that Ezra could not expect to run us all his own way forever, and that if he chose to separate himself from us, we would be obliged, although most regretfully, to let him.

Amy goes on to say that the new anthology has been set up and that, to save Pound's feelings as much as possible, they've written a preface which states that Pound has withdrawn for artistic reasons. (The preface was later changed, nonetheless; and Pound's name was omitted.) She shows herself well aware, too, that her view of him could hardly concur with his self-image:

Ezra has always thought of life as a grand game of bluff. He never has learned the wisdom of Lincoln's famous adage about 'not being able to fool all the people all the time.' Advertising is all very well, but one must have some goods to deliver, and the goods must be up to the advertising of them. Now that Ezra has ceased to be a youthful phenomenon he must take his place in the steady march by which young men of talent gain to a real reputation, and he finds himself falling back at every step, and this naturally makes him exceedingly bitter . . .

Pound's view, of course, was that Amy – and the others – should do his bidding, not only with respect to literary judgments, but also in the matter of financial backing:

> Do you remember, Ezra was very anxious to run the *Mercure de France*? He came to me at once as soon as I got to London, and it transpired that he expected to become editor of said 'Review' with a salary. I was to guarantee all the money, and put in what I pleased, and he was to run the magazine his way. We talked over the cost of expenses, and we both thought that $5000 a year was the least that such a magazine could be run on.

However, Amy didn't, she'd explained to Pound, have $5,000 a year that she could afford to put up; but he didn't believe her:

> Like many people of no income, Ezra does not know the difference between thousands and millions, and thinks that any one who knows where to look for next week's dinners, is a millionaire, and therefore lost his temper with me completely, although he never told me why, and he accused me of being unwilling to give any money towards art.

Amy wasn't intimidated. She proceeded to organise contributions from H.D., Aldington, Fletcher, Lawrence and Flint – to which she added her own – and to arrange publication of this collection, to be called *Some Imagist Poets* – with Houghton Mifflin. She lectured, for the first time, on the new poetry at a meeting of the Poetry Society of America in New York in March 1915, just before this anthology was published.

Of the 750 copies printed, 481 were sold in advance; and the book met with more success and more controversy than anyone had foreseen. The special Imagist issue of *The Egoist* for 1 May 1915 carried poems by H.D., Amy Lowell, Marianne Moore, May Sinclair, Fletcher, Flint, Lawrence and Aldington (who'd arranged for the others to contribute). The issue was planned to come out and to be distributed in America at the same time as *Some Imagist Poets*, but – due to shipping delays – it was late. Ferris Greenslet and Amy Lowell had arranged to distribute 150 copies of *The Egoist* in American bookshops; but they were disappointed with it and decided not to do so, partly because Harold Monro's article on

Imagism in the issue was unfavourable, but partly – also – because they found Lawrence's poem 'indecent'.[3]

Conrad Aiken's hostile article, 'The Place of Imagism', in the issue of *The New Republic* for 22 May 1922, gave *Some Imagist Poets* a great deal of publicity; and suddenly it seemed that *vers libre* had finally taken root in America. More reviews followed, including a favourable piece by W.S. Braithwaite in *The New Republic*; and an 'anonymously disgusted' piece in the London *Times*. Two Russian magazines, *Apollon* and *Strelitz*, carried approving articles about Imagism.

Amy Lowell then organised two further anthologies, both called *Some Imagist Poets*, for 1916 and 1917 respectively. She personally kept track of sales and royalties, periodically undertaking to send each contributor's due. Sometimes she sent more, as to H.D. and Aldington for the 1915 collection:

> We have sold 428 books, and the total amount of sales amounts to $219.08, of which one-sixth is $36.51; therefore I owe you and Richard $73.02. I added just a little to it to make it a round sum, as I thought that probably you were still stuck . . . Please do not think anything about it, and do not dream of paying it back . . .[4]

Encouraged by Amy's handling of the first two collections, H.D. had written to her in October 1915, enclosing poems with an eye to further publication:

> I am sending you some grubby type-writen [*sic*] copies of all that I have done since the last Imagist Anthology. The 'Huntress' appeared in Guido Bruno's paper – 'Mid-Day' in the Egoist. The others have appeared nowhere. If you think it a good thing, perhaps you would offer one or two of them to Harriet or the other Poetry magazine in Boston, or anywhere else . . . But let me know, as Margaret Anderson asks me for a poem and I feel so in sympathy with her work that I will give her one of these I send you, if you don't think it best to try them elsewhere.[5]

Amy replied:

> Your second set of poems was certainly better than the first . . . Personally, the one I like best is 'Midday'. I love that one. They are all beautiful. Your things always are, and give me the very greatest pleasure. As to my being able to get them into any magazines, that is more doubtful. Most of the magazines here do

not understand them – that is the frank truth; and except for
Harriet and 'The Little Review' and things of that sort, it is
almost impossible to place them . . . although I will see what I
can do . . .[6]

H.D. persisted:

I have sent the 'Shrine' direct to Miss Monroe. I have told her
that you had the other poems, and if you haden't [sic] already
placed them, would send to her. I really diden't [sic] want you to
take any special trouble with placing the poems. Thank you so
much for the bother. If pear-tree comes back, please chuck it in
the fire. I have written a much better version. Also destroy 'Late
Spring'. I think them very rotten . . . I do hope the new lot
pleased you – the three long sea-poems . . .[7]

Amy, perhaps half from enthusiasm but also half from a desire not
to become a permanent literary agent, suggested a book:

Now, Hilda, don't you think it would be a good idea if a book of
yours came out in print? Have you got enough things to go in a
book? I will do my best to force Ferris Greenslet to take it if you
have.[8]

Ferris Greenslet worked as an editor at Houghton Mifflin in
Boston, but was also sometimes in London. Having effected an
introduction, Amy awaited progress, soon hearing from H.D. that
she and Aldington were to have tea with him. H.D.'s collection,
called *Sea Garden*, was published by Houghton Mifflin in America
in 1916 and by Amy's London publisher, Constable, in Britain in
the same year.

The book was greeted with small, lukewarm reviews in the
London *Times* and the *Times Literary Supplement* (who assumed
the poet to be a man writing anonymously). Within the smaller,
more selective readership of the literary network, praise was more
usual. Privately, Amy Lowell was fulsome:

You know I am lecturing about you at the Brooklyn Institute of
Arts and Sciences . . . I have read your book with the feeling of
greatest envy and admiration. No one of us is so perfect in
technique as you; and the beauty of your work never ceases to
satisfy me. I only hope that these lectures and the book may be a
means of making more people understand you than do now. The
public is a stupid beast.[9]

Apart from lecturing, Lowell devoted a chapter to H.D. in her volume *Tendencies in Modern American Poetry* (1917). This was the book she sent to Bryher, with information that *Sea Garden* was available from Constable and that many copies of the Imagist collection were stocked at The Poetry Book Shop. Bryher responded: 'I have got 'Sea Garden' and I know I shall enjoy every poem in it, and yet from the few I have read they enhance by contrast the value of your own poetry . . .'[10]

H.D.'s first published novel, *Palimpsest*, written between 1922 and 1925, was published in Paris in 1926 by McAlmon's Contact Publishing Company. The book comprises three interrelated stories, the title-piece symbolising a parchment or tablet that has been written on or inscribed two or three times, the previous text or texts having been imperfectly erased and remaining, therefore, still visible. The stories take place, respectively, in the Roman Empire, and in London and Egypt soon after the Great War. Each tells H.D.'s life story, or parts of it, in poetic-prose style.

The book was an outsider, defying both established criteria and popular tastes and asserting its own aestheticism. McAlmon was enthusiastic about it and wrote a companion piece about it called 'Forewarned as regards H.D.'s prose' (which wasn't, however, published until the 1968 reprint), in which he immediately perceived the individualist values of the style:

> H.D. has written, not in a tradition, not striving to be English, or American; she has written as an individual with an individual's rights. That is best in a generation where America is Art-climbing, and when the older countries – more particularly England – react with cautiousness towards criterions come from a sense of what is best because of what has been tried and is fairly safe through not having dismally failed.[11]

Louise Morgan, a literary journalist who was friendly with McAlmon and H.D. (and later Dorothy Richardson), wrote in a review for *Outlook* (London):

> [H.D. is] interested in writing not as a method of national self-glorification, or as a social pose, or as a paying profession, or as a means to any end whatsoever outside itself. It is writers like H.D., who are above the vulgarities of affection or the stupidities of propaganda, writers whose immediacy of thought and feeling burn to ashes all intervening falseness, that have always been the hope of life as well as of literature.[12]

Alyse Gregory, married to Llewelyn Powys and editor of *The Dial*, was also approving, though less devoted, seeing some of the drawbacks to a total commitment to individualism:

> it is surprising to discover a poet with so slight a respect for the right use and economy of words that she can repeat, over and over and over, the same ones, such as stark, singular, pollen-dusted, and hyacinthine, in places where a more detained attention would have shown them to be easily substituted for fresher ones . . . one feels that although H.D. has emotional power and authentic inspiration, her passion, when it does lapse, becomes by turns turgid, arid, or irritatingly mannered.[13]

McAlmon sold 700 sets of sheets to H.D.'s American poetry publishers, Houghton Mifflin: an unprecedented event for a Contact publication. The book elicited a large number of American reviews, also unusual for a Contact edition; McAlmon normally had difficulties with distribution, owing to the view of both American and British customs officials that anything printed in Paris must be obscene, so books were very often seized at the border.

HERmione, written in 1927 and posthumously published in 1981, is the third of four autobiographical novels, two of which, by early 1987, remained unpublished: 'Paint It Today', written in 1921; and 'Asphodel', written in 1921–2. The fourth, *Bid Me to Live*, was published in 1960 a year before H.D.'s death in 1961.

Written in associational, poetic-prose style, *HERmione* covers the story of H.D.'s involvement with Frances Gregg during their time together in Philadelphia in 1910, as well as being a picture of her family life at that time and her misery in the face of Pound's departure for Europe. *Bid Me to Live*, first titled *Madrigal*, was begun in Switzerland in the summer of 1939. H.D. left the unfinished manuscript behind when she went to spend the years of the Second World War in London. She began work on it again when she returned to Switzerland in 1948:

> I had been writing or trying to write this story since 1921. I wrote in various styles, simply or elaborately, stream-of-consciousness or straight narrative. I re-wrote this story under various titles, in London and in Switzerland. But after I had corrected and typed out Madrigal, last winter, I was able conscientiously to destroy the earlier versions. I had expected at first sight of the torn and weathered MS, to destroy Madrigal. The last sections were

carelessly assembled, so I finished the story after the 'Greek' prelude when Julia writes to Rico. On re-reading the typed MS, I realized that at last, the War I story had 'written itself'.[14]

The 'earlier versions' are those earlier novels, 'Paint It Today', 'Asphodel' and *HERmione*. In the end, she didn't destroy them, although she wrote the word 'Destroy' on at least one of the copies later deposited in the Beinecke Library at Yale. *Bid Me to Live*, in any case, covers different ground: the H.D.–Aldington–Lawrence drama which took place during the First World War years in London.

Following the chronology of H.D.'s life, the next autobiographical fiction is the third story of *Palimpsest*, which takes the H.D. character 'Mary Fairwood' on a journey to Egypt in 1923, a journey H.D. actually made with her mother and Bryher. (Autobiographical elements in the other two stories include the H.D.–Aldington relationship and the Brigit Patmore episode.) Three further autobiographical fictions were privately printed by Bryher in very small editions: *The Usual Star* (1934); *Kora and Ka* (1934); and *Nights* (1935). All carry the imprint 'Pool Editions' and the words '100 copies only'. These three volumes continue to relate aspects of H.D.'s life into the 1920s, covering her relationships with Bryher, with Kenneth Macpherson and again with Frances Gregg. They were scarcely circulated, if at all, during her lifetime and seem to have attracted no reviews. By contrast, *Bid Me to Live* was widely reviewed, owing principally to the interest in its portrayal of D.H. Lawrence and unjustified claims that Lawrence was the centrepiece of H.D.'s life.

H.D. fits the romantic image of a poet; she was no great socialiser, preferring her inner landscapes to the hustles of public literary life. On the other hand, she wasn't monomaniacal and indeed read the work of other poets with zest and attention. She particularly admired Marianne Moore's work immediately she came across it; but Marianne Moore was truly a closet poet, eschewing not only the public gaze, but even publication itself. H.D., driven by her tremendous enthusiasm for Marianne's work, initiated a correspondence which eventually led – among other things – to book publication under Bryher's patronage. The story of this publication perfectly illustrates the mixing of friendship and professional support typical of the relations between women writers. H.D. began her approach to Marianne in a letter.

I remember you at Bryn Mawr May Fete, in a green dress. I imagine that this you, which sends poetry to the 'Egoist' is the same . . . lady: I am 'H.D.' also Mrs R. Aldington, and R. has spoken often of your work! We both think you have acheived [*sic*] a remarkable technical ability! . . . I wonder if you ever feel like coming here for a time! I assure you, my husband and I would be delighted to have you near us! . . . We are – what is known in America as 'poor' – but there are others like us! . . . Perhaps next summer you could come? You could stay near us! Write me and tell me what you are doing . . .[15]

Marianne didn't visit; but she kept up the correspondence. A year later, H.D. was not only enthusiastic and encouraging about Marianne's work, but intent on promoting it:

Miss Weaver, I think I wrote you, liked your article very much . . . I do wish that [*The Egoist*] could pay for contributions! It is very generous of you to send us your work.

Miss May Sinclair is very anxious to see more of your work – so if Mr Cournos can not yet place the book, I will give it to her keeping for a time. She has a certain amount of influence & thinks your poems are very fine. But we will wait as Mr Cournos is still hoping to place it for you. I am quite confident that we will find some intelligent publisher in time . . . R.A. [Aldington] by the way wants to do another article on you![16]

Nothing came of these attempts. But by the following summer, H.D. was still persisting:

I am sending your new poems . . . to my friend D.H. Lawrence . . . He has curious gifts of intuition and I wonder what he will say of your work. You are very rare . . .

You are already perfect. You *are* perfect. You are static, mettalurgic [*sic*]. You are something finished. When and how will you begin again? . . . Send me all you do, Marianne.[17]

Nor was H.D. the only prompt. Pound, too, was pushing Marianne towards book publication:

Now, to be more amiable, have you a book of verse in print? And, if not, can I get one into print for you? . . . For what it is worth, my ten or more years of practice, failure, success, etc. in arranging tables of contents, is à votre service. Or at any rate unless you have a definite scheme for a sequence, I would warn you of the very great importance of the actual order of poems in a booklet . . . *Does* your stuff 'appear' in America?[18]

Marianne was unenthusiastic, however, and responded:

Any verse that I have written, has been an arrangement of stanzas, each stanza being an exact duplicate of every other stanza . . . I do not appear. Originally, my work was refused by the Atlantic Monthly and other magazines and recently I have not offered it. My first work to appear outside of college was a poem, which one of three, I do not recall – published by the Egoist in 1915 and shortly afterward, four or five poems of mine were published by Poetry, a fact which pleased me at the time, but one's feeling changes and not long ago when Miss Monroe invited me to contribute, I was not willing to. Alfred Kreymborg has been hospitable and does not now shut the door to me and Miss Anderson has been most kind in sending me copies of a number of The Little Review in which some lines of mine have appeared with which I am wholly dissatisfied . . . I grow less and less desirous of being published . . . My work jerks and rears and I cannot get up enthusiasm for embalming what I myself, accept conditionally . . .[19]

Pound had other irons in the fire; but H.D. kept trying. After five years of corresponding, the two poets were finally able to meet when H.D. made a visit home. She wrote to Marianne:

I have thought of you and been on the look-out for your remarkable poetry in magazines. Why do we not see more of it? . . . But yours is a strange mind! . . . Does anyone really appreciate your value as I do?

I am crossing on the 'Adriatic' on September first. Are you likely to be in New York after the eighth? . . . I am coming with a friend, W. Ellerman who (as W. Bryher) has just written a very fine prose 'adventure' . . . called 'Development'. I am also bringing Frances Perdita, my little girl & her nurse.

I feel that I should have made people realize you more. But I have had such a struggle just living through the war . . .[20]

The three women indeed met, Bryher writing afterwards to Marianne: 'I have been reading your poems with great interest. I hope you will soon have them published together in volume form . . .'[21] Marianne's response was measured:

It was a pleasure to have your letter and your interest in my poems does me a great deal of good. Moreover, it is so easy to comment favorably on work in passing, and leave the matter at that, that I am doubly grateful to you for wishing that something could be done about having the poems published in a volume. I should not care to have published by itself, what I have done so far, but I should like, I think, as I said to H.D. if I were to have a book of prose published, to have my poems published as an appendix . . .[22]

Despite Marianne's express wish that she 'would not care' for her poems to be published by themselves, H.D. and Bryher decided unilaterally that her poems should appear in book form and secretly set up the project with Harriet Weaver's Egoist Press.

Harriet had started The Egoist Press in order to publish Joyce's *Portrait of the Artist*, which *The Egoist* had serialised. She wanted to use her own funds to publish Joyce; but was willing to bring out subsidised books by other authors. Through H.D., she and Bryher met, probably in 1920; and after H.D. and Bryher returned from America in 1921, Bryher asked Harriet to publish Marianne's poems as a book, offering to pay the costs. Harriet agreed. Some 500 copies were printed, of which 110 were distributed free, 268 remaindered and 98 sold. The Egoist Press receipts show £42 received, of which £9 were royalties and £31 'other costs', giving the Press a profit of £2. The £31 'costs' were given to Harriet by Bryher to subsidise the publication.[23]

The poems are uneven, many of them mere posturing; but they already bear the stamp of Marianne Moore's mature style: the sharp, epigrammatic insistence, the air of knowing, the sombre ironies:

Poetry

I too, dislike it: there are things that are important beyond
all this fiddle
Reading it, however, with a perfect contempt for it, one
discovers that there
is in
it after all, a place for the genuine.

Is Your Town Nineveh?

Why so desolate?

And why multiply
  in phantasmagoria about fishes,
    what disgusts you? Could
      not all personal upheaval in
        the name of freedom, be tabood?

  Is it Nineveh
    and are you Jonah
      in the sweltering east wind of your wishes?
      I, myself have stood
        there by the aquarium, looking
          at the Statue of Liberty.

Some other titles in the collection are, 'To a Steam Roller'; 'Feed
Me, Also River God'; 'You Are Like the Realistic Product of an
Idealistic Search for Gold at the Foot of the Rainbow'; 'Dock Rats';
and 'My Apish Cousins'.

Critical reception was mixed. Harriet Monroe, writing in *Poetry*,
called the volume a 'provocative little pamphlet' and questioned
whether the pieces were poems at all. Still, she continued, H.D. –
'surely a critic of authority' – regarded Marianne Moore as a poet;
and Bryher, contributing from England to *Poetry*'s 'Symposium',
has called the book 'triumphant'. Then, after listing other supporters and dissenters, she adds, provocatively (and disingenuously):
'Rumor has hinted that the selection and publication were made by
certain friends of the author without her knowledge.'[24] No one, of
course, could be more provoked by the *fait accompli* than the poet
herself. Guessing who was responsible, she wrote to H.D., 'I know
it was you who made Miss Weaver think of bringing out poems for
me';[25] but H.D., full of enthusiasm, responded, 'I am waiting
breathlessly to know what you think of the distinguished little
volume, newly set up by the Egoist Press.'[26] She hadn't long to wait.
Marianne wrote to Bryher:

> I received a copy of my poems this morning with your letter and a
> letter from Miss Weaver. Now that I am a pterodactyl [Bryher's
> pet name for her], it is perhaps well that you even with your
> hardened gaze, cannot see what it is to be a pterodactyl with no
> rock in which to hide. In 'Variations of Plants and Animals under
> Domestication,' Darwin speaks of a variety of pigeon that is born
> naked without any down whatever. I feel like that Darwinian
> gosling. You say I am stubborn. I agree and if you knew how

much more than stubborn I am, you would plume yourself more than you do, on having put a thing through, over my head. I had considered the matter from every point and was sure of my decision – that to publish anything now would not be to my literary advantage: I wouldn't have the poems appear now if I could help it and would not have some of them ever appear and would make certain changes . . .

She was, nevertheless, gracious about everyone else's work for the book, and continued:

I am very much touched by the beauty of all the printing details. I like the paper, type, title-label, the fact that the printing was done at the Pelican Press, there is not a single misprint and nothing could exceed my appreciation of the unstinted care and other outlay bestowed on the book. But what shall I say of your activities as press-agent? Poor Mr Child, browbeaten into an attempt to launch a review . . .

I should like to be very decent to Miss Weaver but so far have ordered only ten copies. I don't know what to do with these and don't know what to do next.[27]

Late in her life, in an interview with Donald Hall, Marianne Moore recalled – without resentment – her reaction to H.D.'s and Bryher's kidnapping of her poems:

To issue my slight product – conspicuously tentative – seemed to me premature. I disliked the term 'poetry' for any but Chaucer's or Shakespeare's or Dante's. I no longer feel my original instinctive hostility to the word, since it's a convenient, almost unavoidable term for the thing – although hardly for me:– my observations, experiments in rhythm, or exercises in composition . . . For the chivalry of the undertaking – issuing my verse for me in 1921, certainly in format choicer than in content – I am intensely grateful.[28]

Bryher was a benefactor to many, including the impoverished Dorothy Richardson.

Unlike H.D. and Marianne Moore, Dorothy Richardson was unquestionably a prose-writer. The material she drew on for her massive thirteen-volumed sequence *Pilgrimage*, was, like H.D.'s prose, autobiographical – her relationships with H.G. Wells, Benjamin Grad and Veronica Leslie-Jones. After leaving her salaried job in a dental practice in 1908, she scratched a living from freelance journalism and translation; but her stories, sketches, articles, essays, reviews and other pieces – scattered through an array of periodical publications – remain (early 1987) uncollected. Although Wells and others had urged her to write a novel, she'd resisted, objecting to the falseness and artifice of novelistic conventions. Finally, however, prompted by J.D. Beresford – then a well-known novelist with whom she was friendly – she agreed to accept the loan of his cottage in Cornwall between autumn 1912 and spring 1913 in order to see if she could write a novel as faithful to reality as she thought novels should be. The result was *Pointed Roofs*. The manuscript was read by Edward Garnett and accepted by Duckworth, who published a small edition early in 1915 with an introduction by Beresford. Knopf took the sheets and issued it in New York the following year.

The subject matter – the experiences and perceptions of a young mistress in a girls' school in Hanover – wasn't one to endear a general public locked in mortal combat with the dreaded Hun. But the style, even more than the subject, drew intense responses from reviewers, who treated it either as mad, self-indulgent and 'neurasthenic', or as wonderfully original and radically creative. This was modernism in its extended prose form and it took the literary establishment completely by surprise.

The Sunday *Observer* called it 'a fine new novel' and praised its clarity; the *Saturday Review*, on the other hand (to which Dorothy Richardson regularly contributed 'middles'), printed a scathing notice by a hostile reviewer who found the presentation pathological and the material little more than 'foolish or fevered fantasies'. Nevertheless, it soon became accepted that Dorothy's name was linked with those of Joyce and Proust in any discussion of stream-of-consciousness technique (much though she loathed the term).

The next two volumes – *Backwater* and *Honeycomb* – followed quickly, in 1916 and 1917 respectively. In April 1918 May Sinclair wrote for *The Egoist* what became the most influential review of Dorothy's work and one which focuses many of the issues raised by prose modernism. A longer version appeared in *The Little Review* for the same month; and the material was also used as an introduction to Knopf's new edition of *Pointed Roofs* in 1919. May Sinclair used William James' phrase stream-of-consciousness to signify the author's technique of writing only from the vantage-point of the first-person narrator; and of passing from description to association to memory to speculation and back again, without explanation or justification.

Bryher, too, found Dorothy's work immensely stimulating, recalling late in life the reaction of her 20-year-old self:

> In 1916 I read a review of Dorothy Richardson's *Backwater*. It was said to be critical of education so I immediately bought a copy. I defied all rules and read on until I had finished it. For the first time as I said excitedly to my schoolfellows, 'Somebody is writing about us.' . . . We had faced the same reproaches . . . and shared the same fury that social conventions were considered more important than intelligence. Perhaps great art is always the flower of some deeply felt rebellion. Then there was the excitement of her style, it was the first time that I realized that modern prose could be as exciting as poetry and as for continuous association, it was stereoscopic, a precursor of the cinema, moving from the window to a face, from a thought back to the room, all in one moment just as it happened in life.[29]

Amy Lowell wrote to Bryher in 1918:

> Do you know the three books by Dorothy Richardson . . . They are what might be called an 'Imagist novel', and I think they are remarkable. I do not know who Miss Richardson is, or anything about her, but she is an Englishwoman, and these books are most interesting.[30]

Bryher waited, however, until 1923 – by which date the next three volumes in the sequence had appeared – before approaching the writer. In the meantime, the later volumes had attracted a large number of reviews (though not sales) and the fourth volume – *Interim* – had run in serial form in *The Little Review* alongside *Ulysses*. Bryher's letters to Richardson have not survived; but in her memoir *The Heart to Artemis*, Bryher recalled writing, 'When I want to remember England, I think of your books.'[31] This initial letter, carefully composed 'as if it were the first chapter of a novel', resulted in an invitation to tea and thus began a friendship that lasted for thirty years.

Despite the enthusiastic dedication of Bryher and other supporters, *Pilgrimage* suffered a sad publication history. Duckworth published the first ten volumes in separate editions between 1915 and 1931; J.M. Dent and The Cresset Press published *Clear*

Horizon in 1935; *Dimple Hill*, never published separately, was included in the Collected Edition published by Dent in 1938; and the unfinished *March Moonlight* was added to the subsequent Collected Edition, published by Dent in 1967. Dorothy was never satisfied with the Duckworth editions, as she explained to S.S. Koteliansky, who was sympathetic:

> And here, for you, is *Pilgrimage*, which has, so to speak, never been published. Ten chapter-volumes have found their way into print, into an execrable lay-out & disfigured by hosts of undiscovered printer's errors & a punctuation that is the result of corrections, intermittent, by an orthodox 'reader', & corrections of those corrections, also intermittent, by the author . . .[32]

She wanted a 'real edition by a real publisher'; and set out for Koteliansky – some months afterwards – her terms for an authoritative text:

> really my *Pilgrimage* business is very simple: The rights are available for any reputable publisher who will:
> 1) pay Duckworth, (a) £57.19.3, which is the amount of my mortgage still not paid off (b) £242 –, for stock, plates & moulds.
> 2) issue a definitive, corrected edition, unlimited, of *Pilgrimage* in four volumes, beginning either at once or almost immediately after the publication of the new volume, now half written.
> 3) pay £30 advance royalties on the new volume.[33]

Dent agreed, finally, to publish the Collected Edition, which remains the most authoritative source for the sequence, since – except in three instances – the manuscript versions have not survived. In February 1949, desperate to help a relative in America, Dorothy wrote to a friend explaining her attempts to sell the manuscript of *Pointed Roofs*: 'I am trying, through Knopf, to discover a possible purchaser of the only *Pilgrimage* ms I ever kept: that of *Pointed Roofs*.'[34]

With respect to foreign translations, Dorothy Richardson was equally unlucky. She believed that neither of her publishers had taken intelligent initiatives in creating a European readership for *Pilgrimage*:

> Duckworth, by repeatedly asking too much, missed chance after chance of French & German translations – foolish to expect anything from trans. beyond publicity – so there is only a strange

little *Pointed Roofs* in Japanese, all preface & footnotes & Glossary, very pretty to look at.[35]

Pointed Roofs – always the most popular of the sequence – was finally published in French, in 1965, after Dorothy's death. A proposed Spanish translation was rejected by the Spanish censors; and a German translation was never suggested, despite the relevance of *Pilgrimage* to similar preoccupations in the German literary scene.

Nevertheless, despite poverty, the hostility of the literary establishment, low sales figures and relative obscurity, Dorothy remained undaunted, pursuing her massive, self-appointed task of presenting female realism throughout the latter half of her long life. Nor was she ambivalent about the central social cause of her embattlement:

> Art demands what, to women, current civilization won't give. There is for a Dostoyevsky writing against time on the corner of a crowded kitchen table a greater possibility of detachment than for a woman artist no matter how placed. Neither motherhood nor the more continuously exacting and indefinitely expansive responsibilities of even the simplest housekeeping can so effectively hamper her as the human demand, besieging her wherever she is, for an inclusive awareness, from which men, for good or ill, are exempt.[36]

More than twenty years later, she held to the same view, explaining to her sister-in-law Rose Odle:

> most Englishmen dislike women . . . The English pub is alone in being, primarily, a row of boys of all ages at a bar, showing off. That of course is a bit harsh & insufficient. Volumes would be required to investigate & reveal the underlying factors. Vast numbers of Englishmen are so to say spiritually homosexual. Our history, our time of being innocently piratical, then enormously, at the cost of the natives in our vast possessions, wealthy & 'prosperous' so that our culture died, giving place to civilization (!), is partly responsible. For it made millions of women unemployed, vacuous, buyers of commercialised commodities, philistine utterly . . . [men's] picture of 'the Absolute' is male entirely, as is that of the Churches, who all moan & groan & obsequiously supplicate an incense-loving divinity. Mary Baker Eddy's picture is essentially feminine. Is that not why the

Christian Science churches grow & spread & are hated, unexamined, by all clerics?[37]

Nor, in her old age, did she change her mind, writing to the poet Henry Savage:

> I am not 'literary' Henry. Never was. Never shall be. The books that for you, perhaps for most men, come first, are for me secondary. Partly perhaps because they are the work of men, have the limitations, as well as the qualities of the masculine outlook. Men are practitioners, dealing with things (including 'ideas') rather than with people . . . knowing almost nothing of women save in relation to themselves.[38]

Amy Lowell, treated with even greater disdain by the literary critical fraternity than Dorothy Richardson has been, was never impoverished; although, as we've already seen, she suffered in her early years from low self-esteem and from loneliness. Like Dorothy Richardson, she didn't start writing seriously until she was well into adulthood. Although she had a collection of poems privately printed early in the century, she didn't have an independent book publication until Houghton Mifflin's *A Dome of Many-Coloured Glass*. Published in 1912, this collection comprised poems written during the previous decade, several of which had appeared in *The Atlantic Monthly*; their appearance there had caught Harriet Monroe's eye and had prompted her to write to Amy when she was starting up *Poetry* magazine.

The book resulted from an approach Amy made to Houghton Mifflin – the most respected literary publishing house in Boston at the time – at the suggestion of Josephine Peabody, an acquaintance and well-known writer. The manuscript was accepted and was edited by Ferris Greenslet, whom she later introduced to H.D. and Aldington. (Indeed, Houghton Mifflin later became H.D.'s American publishers.) *A Dome of Many-Coloured Glass* was, however, a publishing failure, selling only 80 copies in its first year. In spite of this, a second edition was prepared and published in 1915. Reviews were lukewarm. The *Minneapolis Journal* said, 'The volume is, on the whole, slightly over the average, and the average is very low. Never do we feel that behind the lines lurks a dynamic personality.'[39] Louis Untermeyer, in the *Chicago Evening Post*, wrote, 'to be brief, in spite of its lifeless classicism, [the book] can never rouse one's anger. But to be briefer still, it cannot rouse one at all.'[40]

Amy's second book, however, was a different story. *Sword Blades and Poppy Seed*, published by Houghton Mifflin in 1914, contained a number of poems which had already appeared in *The Egoist* and *Poetry*; and which were, in any case, written after the impact on Amy of H.D.'s poems and of Imagist theory. During her visit to London she'd arranged for Macmillan to publish *Sword Blades*; they agreed to take 100 copies to be issued with the Macmillan imprint but the proceeds of which would go to Amy, except for a 10 per cent commission.

With this book, Amy's career really began. Like Dorothy Richardson, she'd already turned forty. Her association with H.D., Pound and Imagism had focused her style; and the schism with Pound prompted her to push on with her own work and to promote that of others. *Sword Blades* elicited many reviews: from Aldington in *The Egoist*, Harriet Monroe in *Poetry*, Margaret Anderson in *The Little Review*, and others in *Harpers*, *New York Times*, and Boston papers, as well as in *The Dial* and other smaller magazines. 500 of the 1,500 copies printed in America sold before Christmas 1914. But in England, only four copies had sold by spring 1915.[41] In September 1917, Bryher wrote another of her initiating letters, in response particularly to Amy's *Six French Poets*. Bryher found Amy's commentary unusually stimulating; and having, with great trouble, procured the poetry, she found she liked that too:

'Six French Poets' is the primary reason for this letter . . . one Sunday in 1916 I read a review in the 'Observer' of [it]. I can never express to you, the joy it was to me, in my utter isolation, to feel such a book had been written . . . I sent a copy of your book at once to the school where I had been . . . To me, 'Six French Poets' was like having a friend . . . It was not until this year I began reading your poems, in fact, I had the greatest difficulty to get them. I have read 'Sword Blades and Poppy Seeds' and 'Men, Women and Ghosts', both books, many times.[42]

Amy responded. It was a 'great pleasure' to know that her books 'had found a response so far away'. She sent Bryher a copy of her *Tendencies in Modern American Poetry*. Encouraged by Amy's response – and encouraged by Clement Shorter, a friend of her parents – Bryher wrote *Amy Lowell: A Critical Appreciation*, which was issued by Eyre & Spottiswoode in 1918, possibly with a financial subsidy from her father. She sent the 48–page study to

Amy, who wrote back:

> The pamphlet arrived. What shall I say? I do not know; I am
> taken off my feet. That my poems should have met with so much
> response is a happiness I hardly expected on this side of the grave
> . . . It means a great deal to me to have this pamphlet appear in
> England . . . 'The Sphere' has come with Mr Shorter's pleasant
> article. I am sure I owe his interest in me entirely to you, since he
> says that he knows you, and again I am grateful . . .[43]

Two months later, Amy wrote to H.D.:

> I wonder if you have come across a little pamphlet on me written
> by an unknown admirer, Miss Winifred Bryher. I know nothing
> whatever about the girl; perhaps you do. She is a great admirer of
> yours, and writes extremely good poetry. But this pamphlet is the
> first of her published works, I believe. I judge that she has been
> very much protected and cared for by Mr Clement R. Shorter,
> the editor of 'The Sphere', and other gentlemen of good standing,
> since her pamphlet has been sent not only to all the English
> newspapers, but to all the American periodicals as well . . .
> Seriously, the girl has insight and a good deal of critical faculty,
> but she expresses herself with such extreme admiration that I am
> afraid that perhaps her very words cause their own reaction . . . I
> feel quite sure that the Ezra crowd will get hold of it and make
> awful fun of it in 'The Egoist'.[44]

These fears were unfounded, however. Some two years later, the
two women met, when Bryher and H.D. visited America; but Amy
and Bryher were never to make the same close friendship which the
same possibility of meeting had generated for Bryher and Marianne
Moore.

Amy wrote a preface for Bryher's first novel, *Development*,
published in London in 1920 by Constable; and in New York, in the
same year, by Macmillan. Based on her experiences as a schoolgirl
at Queenwood, the book was written with great difficulty 'at the
rate of about a phrase a day, written almost with blood'.[45] She'd
sent drafts of work in progress to Amy and others, seeking reaction
and encouragement; and was aware, too, that she needed to explain
her pseudonym. In addition to having fallen in love with the Scilly
Isles, she felt overshadowed by her rich and powerful father, writing
to Amy, 'I am very proud of all my father has done for shipping but
it is very hard to find that if any of my work gets praised or even

printed people ascribe it to his influence and openly tell me my love of literature is a passing whim.'[46]

H.D., too, read and re-read Bryher's drafts, making suggestions and encouraging her friends Brigit Patmore and Havelock Ellis to read them too. Bryher later wrote that she owed to Clement Shorter the book's publication by Constable. Sales went well, but success was not without pain:

> I knew that my family would dislike the volume, not because they were against my writing as some have said but because I was attacking what would now be called the Establishment. I wanted, anyhow, to kick my way up the ladder alone. I therefore chose the name Bryher . . . Educational reform was the topic of the moment, *Development* started a controversy in the *Daily Mail*, no other book of mine has been as successful and a second printing was needed within a few weeks. 'Old girls' from Queenwood protested bitterly, Miss Chudleigh was furious, Shorter stood by me. My parents were shocked and upset. 'How could you write such a dreadful book?' they asked.
> 'I am sorry if it worries you but it was my duty to protest.'
> 'But you cannot go against everyone else.'
> 'Why not?'
> 'Because it will set you apart from others to lead a lonely existence.'[47]

Bryher's early drive to protest – dissimilar to many of the writers we've been considering – took this straightforward social form, not least, perhaps, because of the privileged background she'd enjoyed. But there were more hidden determinants leading to her rejection of convention, despite her affection for her parents. She'd met, and been entranced by, H.D.; and despite marriages, male friends and lovers, psychoanalysis and separations, the two women were to form a lesbian partnership ended only by H.D.'s death. Educational reform aside, an unconventional sexuality already sets any woman 'apart from others'. Bryher recalled:

> My instinct about writing had been correct. I knew that *Development* was not a book of which Mallarmé would have approved but I really objected to the human wastage of school. My family bowed to the inevitable. I had committed the unpardonable Victorian sin and made myself 'conspicuous.' (I enjoyed this very much.) I was allowed to join H.D. in a small

apartment that she had rented in Kensington, not far from where the Pounds and Mrs Shakespeare were living and where I tried, without success, to write my second book.[48]

Development was reviewed on both sides of the Atlantic: *The Athenaeum*, London *Bookman*, *Nation*, *The Spectator*, and the *Times Literary Supplement* carried favourable notices; and the *Boston Evening Transcript*, *New York Evening Post* and *New York Times* found the book worthy of attention. Marianne Moore reviewed it for *The Dial* of 21 May 1921:

> I have your *Development* at last and hardly know what to say of the pleasure that it has given me . . .
> I am anxious to have you see the May number [of *The Dial*] (though I am not sure you will be pleased with it) for I have a review in it of *Development* . . .[49]

Her caution was not unwarranted, since her piece is less supportive of Bryher's incipient feminism than the author might have wished:

> One might easily expect to find conclusions arrived at by the small heroine, immature; and possibly in her protest against woman's *role* as a wearer of skirts – in her envying a boy his freedom and his clothes – her view is somewhat curtailed. One's dress is more a matter of one's choice than appears; if there be any advantage, it is on the side of woman; woman is more nearly at liberty to assume man's dress than man is able to avail himself of the opportunities for self expression afforded by the variations in colour and fabric which a woman may use.

The anonymous *Nation* reviewer contextualises the style as 'imagistic', calling the piece 'The Making of a Vers-Libriste':

> This brief and beautifully written book is the first instalment of an artist's autobiography. It gives us access to a literary psychology which, in this special form, is both new and important.
> [Nancy, the novel's principal] finds her medium of expression by way of a curious and widespread misconception. She reads the great French vers-libristes and proceeds to write like H.D. and Miss Amy Lowell. 'Rhyme had already begun to grate harshly on an ear that daily grew more sensitive to curve of rhythm and subtlety of phrase.' What has that to do with the stormy but elaborate harmonies of Verhaeren or the suave, round melodies of Regnier? Both poets are among the most heavily rhymed in the

world . . . Their verse was called free in France because they did not confine themselves to the traditional stanzaic forms and did not always alternate masculine and feminine rhyme . . . Perhaps in 'Adventure', the promised continuation of *Development*, Nancy will meet the passions of life and find rhythm and thus pass from imagism to poetry.[50]

Dorothy Richardson found the book 'a tremendous prelude' and determined to 'voyage it through again'.[51] And McAlmon, later married to Bryher, saw in it the basis for enjoying much in common with its author.[52] Having generously praised others, Bryher, too, was now a published novelist.

Chapter 13

'There is a climax in sensibility' –
Book publishing II

Gertrude Stein owed the eventual publication of her magnum opus *The Making of Americans* to McAlmon's Contact Press and therefore, indirectly, to Bryher. Its tortuous publication history[1] serves as a stern reminder of the resistance and hostility to modernism endured by authors; and of the power of censorship exercised by the publishing industry at any time when its conventions are threatened by experimentalism of a particularly powerful (and lengthy) variety.

This epic novel, discontinuously written between 1903 and 1911, was begun as a history of Gertrude's own family; but rapidly developed into a history of everyone known to the family; and then finally extended to embrace simply everyone.

In 1911 Gertrude wrote to the English publisher Grant Richards about possible publication of her 'long book'. He looked at the manuscript, but rejected it. Next she approached Mrs Westmore Willcox, an American staff writer at *The North American Review*, to help her place the book. The manuscript at this stage was some 325,000 words long. Mrs Willcox suggested sending it to Benjamin Huebsch, a New York publisher. After he turned it down, Mrs Willcox wrote to Gertrude explaining that in her view the book's length made it too expensive for any American publisher to undertake. Nevertheless, Gertrude asked her to send the manuscript to a former classmate, Mabel Weeks, then teaching at Barnard. Miss Weeks, in turn, sent it to May Knoblauch, who had helped Gertrude arrange for the publication of her *Three Lives*. Mrs Knoblauch did her best to place it with Mitchell Kennerley in New

York. Receiving no response from Kennerley, Gertrude asked Mabel Dodge, then living in New York, to check up on what – if anything – was happening to the book. Kennerley refused either to talk to Mabel Dodge, or to yield up the manuscript. Eventually, under threat of legal action, Kennerley returned the manuscript to Mrs Knoblauch, who sent it back to Gertrude in Paris. All these efforts took up some three years; and by the time Gertrude received back the much-travelled manuscript, the Great War had begun. She put the book away.

It was not until 1922 that the possibility of publication arose. Gertrude's friend, Carl van Vechten, prompted her to try again. She sent the manuscript to him in New York and he gave it to Knopf, his own publisher. Knopf, like Kennerley, sent no word. In 1924 Hemingway visited Gertrude and asked to see her one other copy of the manuscript. Immediately he persuaded Ford Madox Ford to publish part of it in *The Transatlantic Review*, the first instalment appearing in the April issue of 1924. This brought an enquiry from the firm of Liveright, who rejected it in the end, and from Jonathan Cape, who learned of its existence through McAlmon. *The Transatlantic Review* continued to print instalments, but Hemingway had trouble persuading Ford to pay Gertrude for the work, since the magazine was in financial difficulty.

Meanwhile, in London, Jane Heap was trying to encourage T.S. Eliot at the *Criterion* to take the book, while McAlmon in Paris was considering whether he could somehow publish it. McAlmon had met Gertrude in 1923 through Mina Loy, who'd known her since before the war. In any case, McAlmon's *Contact Collection of Contemporary Writers* (1925) already carried one of her pieces. He agreed to plan publication of the book either as one large volume or as two smaller ones; but pointed out that they would have to begin by getting subscriptions to cover costs. About 500 copies would be printed.

Gertrude wanted a contract. After some hesitation, McAlmon sent one, which Gertrude criticised in detail, insisting that the book remain her property. McAlmon eventually agreed to her requests; and finished sheets, proof-read entirely by Gertrude, were sent out by Darantière, the printers, at the end of October 1925, and received by Bill Bird (who, in association with McAlmon, ran 3 Mountains Press) early in November. Five de luxe copies to be bound in leather were sent to the binder and ten copies of the ordinary, paper-bound edition were delivered to Gertrude. The book was 925 pages long.

By this time – perhaps predictably – Gertrude and McAlmon were no longer friends. Even after he'd decided to publish the book, Gertrude and Jane Heap had continued to look for someone else to publish or distribute it in America. Jane tried Huebsch again; and the Dial Press. Albert and Charles Boni were interested; Jane had contacted them and was trying to sell sheets to them at one dollar a copy, without asking McAlmon. When he found out, McAlmon told Jane he'd have to receive three dollars per volume for the sheets in order to recover his investment, though he agreed to discuss the matter with the Boni representative in England. Boni then agreed to buy up McAlmon's edition, take the sheets to America, bind them there and sell them. It was August 1925; and at this point McAlmon had only received orders for about 15 copies and he agreed to the plan. Still, when it came to the crunch, the Bonis backed down, even though Gertrude had agreed to the deal.

In the interim, Jane had proposed a new plan. She herself would buy up the sheets. Gertrude asked McAlmon to agree to this, but he refused, considering the offer of $1,000 too low and asking why 'the syndicate' (meaning Jane Heap) hadn't dealt with him directly. Jane, ever resourceful, had at the same time been busy trying to work out another deal with Stanley Nott, who asked Darantière to send 400 sets of sheets to his shipper in Paris, claiming that McAlmon had agreed. On checking with McAlmon, he discovered that 200 sets had been agreed, but not 400. McAlmon fired off an angry letter to Gertrude saying – among other things – that the book was now complete and she could have ten author's copies. Nott in the end acquired no sheets, but the Bonis finally bought 100 sets.[2]

McAlmon remained angry with Gertrude, writing to her six months after publication to say that she had done nothing to help sell the book, that he had achieved reviews in *The Dial* and *The Irish Statesman*, and that he had a large number of books left. He instructed her: 'If you wish the books retained, you may bid for them. Otherwise, by Sept. – one year after publication – I shall simply rid myself of them en-masse, by the pulping proposition.'[3] By the end of December 1926, 1 de luxe, 28 leather and 74 paper-bound copies had been sold and paid for. Gertrude never bought the remaining copies; nor did McAlmon pulp them. He recorded that something under 200 copies were distributed to bookshops and only about 5 per cent of those were paid for. What became of the remainder of the edition, neither McAlmon nor Bill

Bird later recalled; but it's clear that very few copies actually reached the hands of readers.

McAlmon concluded – somewhat caustically – his own version of these events:

> Incidentally *The Making of Americans* is a beautiful bit of printing and make-up and binding, and Miss Stein complimented M. Darantière for the job. M. Darantière did do a very fine job, but the publisher chose the paper, the print, the binding, and designed the jacket and make-up of the book. Nevertheless, Miss Stein has qualities which command admiration; she has vitality and a deep belief in the healthiness of life, too great a belief for these rocky days.[4]

Despite such poor sales, after publication the book's reputation grew steadily. In 1929, about 60 pages were translated into French and printed in Paris. An abridged version was published by Harcourt, Brace in 1934 after the success of Gertrude's best-known work, *The Autobiography of Alice B. Toklas*. Still, the wretched publishing history of *The Making of Americans* – by any stretch of the imagination a *tour de force* in its combined experimental style and massive canvas – must have been a great blow.

Orthodox critics, as might be expected, condemned the style. Many writers, however, were admiring and percipient. Marianne Moore, writing in *The Dial*, compared the book with Bunyan's *Pilgrim's Progress*, finding that – just as 'Christian is English yet universal' – the family's progress is both distinctively American and yet comprehends 'a psychology which is universal'.[5] Mina Loy, in two extended pieces for the *Transatlantic Review*, felt the design and vitality in the complex interplay of reversions and elaborations was characteristic of the style:

> Gertrude Stein obtains the 'belle matière' of her unsheathing of the fundamental with a most dexterous discretion in the placement and replacement of her phrases, of inversion of the same phrase sequences that are as closely matched in level, as the fractional tones in primitive music . . .[6]

This 'process of reiteration' typical of the earlier writing leads into a second, 'impressionistic' phase, where the writer 'telescopes time and space and the subjective and objective in a way that obviates interval and interposition', giving 'an interpenetration of dimensions analogous to Cubism'. Mina Loy – like most writers in their reading and criticism of writing they admire – responds to Gertrude Stein's prose from the core of her own motivation, finding that 'It is the variety of her mental processes that gives such fresh significance to her words, as if she had got them out of bed early in the morning and washed them in the sun.' But she suggests, too, that the style springs from the culture's 'bankruptcy of mysticism':

Modernism is a prophet crying in the wilderness of stabilized culture that humanity is wasting it's [*sic*] aesthetic time . . . The flux of life is pouring it's aesthetic aspect into your eyes, your ears – and you ignore it because you are looking for you [*sic*] canons of beauty in some sort of frame or glass case of tradition. Modernism says Why not each one of us, scholar or bricklayer pleasurably realize all that is impressing itself upon our subconscious . . . Modernism has democratised the subject matter . . . of art . . . and Gertrude Stein has given us the Word, in and for itself.

Would not life be lovelier if you were constantly overjoyed by the sublimely pure concavity of your wash bowls? The tubular dynamics of your cigarette?

In reading Gertrude Stein one is assaulted by a dual army of associated ideas, her associations and your own . . .

Apart from all analysis, the natural, the debonaire [*sic*] way to appreciate Gertrude Stein, is as one would saunter along a country way side on a fine day and pluck, for it's beauty, an occasional flower.[7]

The massive scope of Gertrude Stein's work makes it foolish to attempt to take one passage and imagine it to be representative. But we can, at least, sample the flavour of her extraordinary *Making of Americans*:

Sometime there will be a history of all of them. Sometime there will be written a long book, a history of all of them of the two kinds of them. Some time it will be clear to some one the whole history of every kind of men and women, the two kinds of them, the kinds in each kind of them, the mixture of all of them. Sometime then will be written a long book, a history of every kind of men and women and all the kind of being in them.

Now this is a history of one of them. As I was saying Mrs Hersland had three seamstresses working for her when she was living in Gossols in her middle living when she was strongest in her feeling of being herself inside her in her living.[8]

This speculative narrative movement, with its curious echoes of Old Testament tale-telling, its plays of repetition and juxtaposition, and its intimate address, characterises the voice of this prose epic. Like Dorothy Richardson's *Pilgrimage*, *The Making of Americans* remains one of the great unread prose works of the century. Gertrude Stein's wit and inventiveness (and obscurantisms, too) are better known from her short occasional pieces. *Capital, Capitals*, for example, appeared in the first issue of *This Quarter* in 1924. It begins:

> Capitally be.
> Capitally see.
> It would appear that capital is adapted to this and that. Capitals are capitals here.
> Capital very good.
> Capital Place where those go when they go.
> Capital. He has capital.
> We have often been interested in the use of the word capital. A state has a capital a country has a capital. An island has a capital. A main land has a capital. And a portion of France has four capitals and each one of them is necessarily on a river or on a mountain. We were mistaken about one of them.

Such associational abilities, linked with the skill to combine moral observation with abstracted linguistic patterns, generate in the reader a very particular attention and sense of satisfaction. This is a writer with an unusual confidence in – and consciousness about – what she is saying. The piece ends explicitly with that point:

> I know why I say what I do say. I say it because I feel a great deal of pleasure of satisfaction of repetition of indication of separation of direction of preparation of declaration of stability of precaution of accentuation and of attraction. And why do you spare little silver mats. Little silver mats are very useful and silver is very pretty as to colour.[9]

Mina Loy, who was friendly with Gertrude in Paris, as well as being a professional admirer of her work, was – of course – busy with her own writing during this period. Her first published book, *Lunar Baedecker* [sic], was brought out by Contact Editions in 1923. The poems in this collection had been written over a number of years and many had appeared in the little magazines. After her second husband, Arthur Cravan, had disappeared in 1918, she'd moved from New York to Paris; and had therefore met Sylvia Beach, Joyce and Pound, and renewed her friendships with Djuna Barnes, McAlmon and Gertrude Stein.

Lunar Baedecker was one of the first books McAlmon published. He printed 300 copies of which some were sent out for review and some sold, mainly through Sylvia Beach's 'Shakespeare & Company' bookshop. Edwin Muir, reviewing all the Contact books for 1923 in *New Age*, called Mina's book 'the surprise of the bunch', commenting that although it was 'very unequal' it was nevertheless 'arresting'. Yvor Winters wrote possibly the only American review in *The Dial*, also finding the poems startling:

> If she has not actually conquered the clumsiness which one can scarcely help feeling in her writings, she has, from time to time, overcome it; and these occasional advantages have resulted in momentous poems . . . She moves like one walking through granite instead of air, and when she achieves a moment of beauty it strikes one cold.[10]

Her 'Feminist Manifesto', of which she'd sent a draft to Mabel Dodge, she wrote and revised during 1914 and 1915, though it remained unpublished until the 1982 *Last Lunar Baedeker*. Its radicalism for the time was extraordinary, pinpointing the enmity between women and men; and exhorting women to discard their illusions. 'Are you prepared for the *wrench*?' she demands that they ask. No half-measures will do; there must be 'Absolute Demolition' of the lies of tradition, rather than the trusting of any legislation, crusades or reforms.

The argument proceeds by asserting that women are not the equals of men, simply because men should not be used as any yardstick of anything in a feminist debate (a point Dorothy Richardson also made countless times, both in her letters and in her fiction). Women must look within themselves to discover what they're like. Under the conditions prevailing, women could choose between 'Parasitism, Prostitution, or Negation'. Men and women are enemies, with their only point of convergence 'the sexual embrace'. To find freedom, women must first destroy the notion of 'virtue' by employing 'the *unconditional* surgical *destruction of virginity*' at puberty.

Mina Loy rails against marriage in much the way Dora Marsden does, though her language is both briefer and more shocking.

Marriage confers on women 'ridiculously ample' advantages in exchange for the prize of virginity; and, by contrast, the unmarried woman is debarred from maternity. Every woman, Mina argues, has the right to bear children; and indeed, superior women have a duty to do so. She concludes, therefore, that the way forward is for women to destroy in themselves 'the desire to be loved'. In addition, they must defy superstition and understand that 'the impurity of sex' is another illusion; the only impurity is in the mental attitude taken towards it.[11]

Individualist, original and radical with respect to feminism and to aesthetics, Mina Loy ventured in the same vein into psychology and cultural politics. Her 'Auto-Facial-Construction', published in 1919, intends to instruct intelligent and patient readers 'to become masters of their facial destiny' by paying attention to controlling facial muscles and other physiognomic structures.[12] (In her old age, she refused to see anyone, because she couldn't bear people to see how she'd aged.)

In 1920 she produced 'International Psycho-Democracy', defined as 'A movement to focus . . . human reason on The Conscious Direction of Evolution . . . to replace the cataclysmic factor in social evolution *war*. An absolute, constructive and liberating ideal put to the will of mankind for acceptance or rejection.'[13]

The anarchic originality that fed all these themes is present in all aspects of Mina's verse: tone, images, subject matter and address. These lines, for example, from 'Apology of Genius',[14] provide an apologia; but they neither excuse the artist's authority nor placate the non-genius audience:

> Ostracized as we are with God
>> The watchers of the civilized wastes
>> reverse their signals on our track
>
>> Lepers of the moon
>> all magically diseased
>> we come among you
>> innocent
>> of our luminous sores
>
>> unknowing
>> how perturbing lights
>> our spirit
>> on the passion of Man

until you turn on us your smooth fools' faces
like buttocks bared in aboriginal mockeries

We are the sacerdotal clowns
who feed upon the wind and stars
and pulverous pastures of poverty

Our wills are formed
by curious disciplines
beyond your laws

You may give birth to us
or marry us
the chances of your flesh
are not our destiny –

The cuirass of the soul
still shines –
And we are unaware
if you confuse
such brief
corrosion with possession

In the raw caverns of the Increate
we forge the dusk of Chaos
to that imperious jewelry of the Universe
        – The Beautiful –
While to your eyes
        A delicate crop
of criminal mystic immortelles
stands to the censor's scythe.

With equal confidence of both experience and utterance, Mina Loy
tackles subjects most women poets have shunned until much more
recent times. In 'Parturition',[15] for example, we find the following
lines:

I am the centre
Of a circle of pain
Exceeding its boundaries in every direction
The business of the bland sun
Has no affair with me
In my congested cosmos of agony . . .

        The irresponsibility of the male

Leaves woman her superior Inferiority.

He is running upstairs
I am climbing a distorted mountain of agony
Incidentally with the exhaustion of control
I reach the summit
And gradually subside into anticipation of
Repose
Which never comes.
For another mountain is growing up
Which   goaded by the unavoidable
I must traverse
Traversing myself

Something in the delirium of night hours
Confuses while intensifying sensibility
Blurring spatial contours
So aiding elusion of the circumscribed
That the gurgling of a crucified wild beast
Comes from so far away
And the foam on the stretched muscles of a mouth
Is no part of myself
There is a climax in sensibility
When pain surpassing itself
Becomes exotic
And the ego succeeds in unifying the positive and
      negative poles of sensation
Uniting the opposing and resisting forces
In lascivious revelation . . .

The next morning
Each woman-of-the-people
Tiptoeing the red pile of the carpet
Doing hushed service
Each woman-of-the-people
Wearing a halo
A ludicrous little halo
Of which she is sublimely unaware

I once heard in church
God made them

Mina Loy is among the most unfairly neglected of the women

modernists. Her writing is not only suffused with integrity and vitality, but is also radically focused. Exceptionally for her time, she never compromised the perceptions and insights that came to her woman's eye; nor did she flinch from the knowledge gained from her experiences, that convinced her of the organic connections between sexuality, creativity and the dominance of men. True to her own principle, she did her best to destroy her desire to be loved.

Her great friend Djuna Barnes published her first book slightly earlier. *The Book of Repulsive Women: 8 Rhythms and 5 Drawings* was brought out by Guido Bruno, the literary entrepreneur of Greenwich Village, in November 1915. It was the sixth of his Chap Books series. The book's dedication reads:

> To Mother   who was more or less like All mothers,
> but she was mine, – and so – she excelled

The 'repulsiveness' of women refers to their capacity to bond together (the word 'lesbian' never appears); and the poems follow the dismal female path from poverty to death. Here is one extract, from 'From Fifth Avenue Up':

> Someday beneath some hard
> Capricious star,
> Spreading its light a little
> Over far,
> We'll know you for the woman
> That you are . . .
>
> See you sagging down with bulging
> Hair to sip,
> The dappled damp from some vague
> Under lip,
> Your soft saliva, loosed
> With orgy, drip.[16]

The original 15 cents cover price rose dramatically to 50 cents once the collection gained underground notoriety. It remained underground; was never publicly reviewed; and wasn't mentioned in print for half a century.

Djuna and her work were well known nonetheless, within the bohemian network of Greenwich Village. Before long, her stories, poems, plays and drawings were appearing in the little magazines, especially in *The Dial* and *The Little Review*. Some work appeared, too, in more commercial magazines. Between 1919 and 1920 three of her plays were performed by the Provincetown Players and were reviewed.

In 1923, Boni and Liveright published *A Book*: a collection of stories, drawings, poems and plays worked on during the previous eight or nine years. Among the collection's 20 poems, 11 can be sequentially read as the story of Djuna's love for Mary Pyne who'd died in 1915. The longest of these, 'Six Songs of Khalidine', is dedicated to Mary Pyne, and was rejected by Harriet Monroe for publication in *Poetry*.

A Book drew reviews from – among others – the *Chicago Literary Times* and *The Nation*. Floyd Dell, a practising novelist, wrote an unusually perceptive review for *The Nation*, focusing some of the more taxing problems introduced by the writing and reading of modernism:

> Djuna Barnes is one of those writers, of a recent school, who defiantly refuse to find any sort of significance in the rank welter of life . . . if one's sense of life is so profoundly different from that of most people as to be self-condemned to unintelligibility, there is no reason why one should not get a little fun out of it by mystifying the bourgeois. Literature depends so essentially on a community of interest between writers and readers, and the stray writer who fails to feel such a bond is so decidedly out of luck that even reprisals in the form of practical jokes must be forgiven . . .
>
> The whole book, when one has ceased to ponder its unintelligibilities, leaves a sense of the writer's deep temperamental sympathy with the simple and mindless lives of the beasts: it is in dealing with these lives, and with the lives of men and women in moods which approach such simplicity and mindlessness, that she attains a momentary but genuine power.[17]

In 1928, the year of the publication and prosecution of Radclyffe Hall's *Well of Loneliness*, Liveright in New York published Djuna's first novel, *Ryder*, which became a brief best-seller in America. Unlike Radclyffe Hall's explicit, melodramatic narrative, Djuna Barnes makes her lesbian themes and preoccupations hidden and obscure. More dominant is her absorption with linguistic and literary experiment. She acknowledges the influence of Joyce, finding him the greatest contemporary writer; and in *Ryder* attempts a pyrotechnical display of modes and traditions treated in wry, parodic or ironic styles. In the same year, in Paris, her *Ladies*

Almanack by a Lady of Fashion appeared anonymously. Written in a light vein, this had been intended for fun rather than for publication; but various plans to have it printed were made. Edward Titus at his Black Manikin Press was to produce it; but without giving any assurance of distribution, he asked Djuna not only to fund the printing, but also to yield both wholesale and retail rights. Then McAlmon, with whom she was on very friendly terms, offered to pay for the printing, thus making the book a Contact publication. Djuna and two of her friends paid for the drawings and hand-coloured the illustrations in 50 special copies. She sold all the books herself, charging $10 for the uncoloured copies, $25 for the hand-coloured ones and $50 for each of the 10 hand-coloured and signed copies.[18] There were 1,050 copies printed altogether; and the total number of pen-and-ink drawings was 22.[19]

The text presents a society of lesbian women, a 'cultural aristocracy' with rituals and credos, and erotic intrigues, clearly derived from the Natalie Barney salon (who are given 'straight' treatment in *The Well of Loneliness*). Other characters are derived from the painter Romaine Brooks; Radclyffe Hall's lover Una Troubridge; Hall herself; and *New Yorker* writer Janet Flanner. Mina Loy, the 'token heterosexual' in Barney's circle[20] is also characterised. The book's intention is to confront the anomalies of sexual identity in the vocabulary and diction of neo-classicism:

> Virtually plotless, the narrative records the mock sainthood of its heroine, Evangeline Musset, throughout the twelve months of the almanack year. Sometimes the book reads as a Sapphic manifesto, arguing the prerogatives of women in the social, patriarchal world from which they are excluded. At other times it appears to delight in verbal wit and frivolity for their own sake. Amid much laughter, however, there is lamentation, for the condition of these women is the human condition of 'loneliness estranged'.[21]

As with *The Book of Repulsive Women*, the *Ladies Almanack* gained an underground notoriety and wasn't republished until 1972. In 1949 there was a brief attempt to re-issue it. McAlmon wrote to Djuna:

> I think now it was an error for you not to have had it published under your name and The Contact Editions, but that could be remedied by pasting printed slips on the inside cover of the book.

That again is up to you. In the meantime, let them stay at the Mill house at Hours if you like.[22]

He informed her, too, that Bill Bird had told him 'the only Contact books at the Mill are Djuna's Ladies Almanac [sic] of which there is a large bale which must contain 500 to 100 [sic] copies.' Despite this prompting, however, Djuna didn't agree to a re-issue. Even so, the book was read and re-read; and as late as 1962, Natalie Barney wrote to her, 'Your "Ladies almanack" is a constant joy to me, and the rescuing scene is still valid!'[23]

The *Almanack*'s preface makes its subject matter perfectly clear:

Now this be a Tale of as fine a Wench as ever wet Bed, she who was called Evangeline Musset and who was in her Heart one Grand Red Cross for the Pursuance, the Relief and the Distraction, of such Girls as in their Hinder Parts, and their Fore Parts, and in whatsoever Parts did suffer them most, lament Cruelly . . . why is it that no Philosopher of whatever Sort, has discovered, amid the nice Herbage of his Garden, one that will content that Part, but that from the day that we were indifferent Matter, to this wherein we are Imperial Personages of the divine human Race, no thing so solaces it as other Parts as inflamed, or with the Consolation every Woman has at her Finger Tips, or at the very Hang of her Tongue? . . .

It has been noted by some and several, that Women have in them the Pip of Romanticism so well grown and fat of Sensibility, that they, upon reaching an uncertain Age, discard Duster, Offspring and Spouse, and a little after are seen leaning, all of a limp, on a Pillar of Bathos . . .

The mannered rivalry is sustained throughout the entries for each of the months of the year, each pointing its 'moral' by making fun of a lesbian notable. 'March' presents the would-be-married pair Una Troubridge and Radclyffe Hall (known to all as 'John'), who, despite being loyal Catholics, derived comfort and fascination from spiritualism; who enjoyed a privileged way of life owing to Radclyffe Hall's inherited wealth; who were conservative and traditionalist in values and taste. Here is part of Djuna's satirical view of them:

Among such Dames of which we write, were two British Women. One was called Lady Buck-and-Balk, and the other plain Tilly-Tweed-In-Blood. Lady Buck-and-Balk sported a Monocle and believed in Spirits. Tilly-Tweed-In-Blood sported a Stetson and believed in Marriage. They came to the Temple of the Good Dame Musset, and they sat down to Tea, and this is what they said:

'Just because woman falls, in this Age, to Woman, does that mean that we are not to recognize Morals? What has England done to legalize these Passions? Nothing! Should she not be brought to Task, that never once through her gloomy Weather have two dear Doves been seen approaching in their bridal Laces, to pace, in stately Splendor up the Altar Aisle, there to be United in Similarity, under mutual Vows of Loving, Honouring, and Obeying, while the One and the Other fumble in that nice Temerity, for the equal gold Bands that shall make of one a Wife, and the other a Bride?[24]

It is for her masterpiece, *Nightwood*, though, that Djuna Barnes is best known to literary history. Published by Faber in 1936, the text was written between 1931 and 1934, mostly at Peggy Guggenheim's English country house, Hayford Hall. The tense, associational style of this experimental novel has been much lauded and much despised, for its now-familiar modernist traits. But it can be read, too, as a *roman à clef* about the relationship with Thelma Wood that Djuna mourned; and about the Paris of the twenties they both knew. The book is dedicated to Peggy Guggenheim and her lover, John Holms.

The writer Emily Holmes Coleman, a friend both of Djuna and of Peggy Guggenheim, was a frequent visitor to Hayford Hall; and became a prime mover in the publication of *Nightwood*. She persuaded T.S. Eliot to take it for Faber (while at the same time, John Holms pushed his friend Edwin Muir to speak for the book to Faber). Eliot ended up writing an Introduction, which assured the novel's reputation.

The narrative centres on the effect of a woman, Robin Vote (Thelma Wood) on the lives of four people who meet in Paris. After marrying Felix Volkbein, a phony baron, and bearing his child, Robin leaves him for Nora Flood (Djuna Barnes), an American journalist in Europe. Nora eventually loses Robin to the despicable Jenny Petherbridge, another lesbian.

Abandoned, Nora turns to Matthew O'Connor (Dan Mahoney) in her distraught depression. At the end of the novel, Robin returns to confront Nora at a chapel on her American estate, but the inarticulate encounter brings no resolution.

Nightwood, like her 1928 publications, shows Djuna Barnes rebelling against the traditional chronology of linear plot development. The book is divided into eight sections, which are discontinuous in time and place; indeed, the sense of time is lost altogether when the characters enter the mysteries of night and sleeping. As Eliot's introduction suggested, the appeal of such a book would perhaps chiefly be to readers of poetry.

The novel attracted a huge critical literature (which is still mounting); but it never made Djuna much money. She lived in near poverty for most of the latter half of her life, sustained by Janet Flanner, Natalie Barney, Peggy Guggenheim and other friends.

Nightwood is still remembered and in print. The work of Mary Butts, on the other hand, is hardly remembered at all. Her collection of short fiction, *Speed the Plough*, published in 1923 by Chapman & Hall in London, brought together work written over the previous decade; but it received hardly any attention and sold less than 200 copies. She'd been married to the writer John Rodker, who contributed regularly to both *The New Freewoman* and *The Egoist*. Mary, too, contributed to *The Egoist*; and knew Pound, Harriet Weaver and others attached to the *Egoist* circle. She left Rodker in 1919 after falling in love with Cecil Maitland, a young, dissipated Scot with whom she went to live in Paris.

Douglas Goldring, a young English writer who was a friend of Pound, liked her stories and pushed her to collect them for single-volume publication. He introduced her to Alec Waugh, who persuaded Chapman & Hall to publish the book. Despite its disappointing reception, other of her stories were appearing regularly in *The Little Review*, which serialised her novel *Ashe of Rings* during 1921. In 1925 McAlmon's Contact Editions published the novel in Paris and in 1933 it was reprinted in London by Wishart.

During her time in Paris, Mary became friendly with H.D., Bryher, McAlmon, Sylvia Beach and Djuna Barnes. Ford Madox Ford and Ezra Pound were particular advocates of her work. But her interests were not straightforwardly literary. She and Maitland became involved with Aleister Crowley, a black magic proponent and practitioner, joining him in occult rites and spending time on his island Cefalu, where rituals were performed under his orders. The preoccupations encouraged by Crowley provided thematic material for much of her work, which evidences occult overtones, mysterious signs and symbols, and a sense of strange powers.

Some of Mary Butts' work shows a preoccupation with incest, a reflection, perhaps, of her intense relationship with her brother Tony, who – under the pseudonym William Darfey – wrote a novel called *Curious Relations* in 1945. Mary's *Ashe of Rings* presents a range of rituals and machinations that include witchcraft, incest, arcane deities, adultery, nepotism and spiritualism. Such preoccupations and their connotations of power and insight are characteristic, too, of her shorter work. The principal in her short story 'Deosil', for instance, reflects:

> He knew, if any man living knew he knew, that sometimes things were improved, or rather that they were changed, and that in individual action there were moments of a peculiar quality that expressed the state in which he knew the whole earth could live all the time, and settle the hash of time, progress and morality once and for ever. What he wanted to happen was for some man to say a word of power which should evoke this state, everywhere, not by any process, but in the twinkling of an eye. This is magic. Lovers did it, especially his lovers, and saints, when he and one or two men he knew were being saints, with a woman or so about to encourage them, at night, in a smoky room. There were moments too, under the hills, breaking-in horses when it came, the moment of pure being, the co-ordination of power.[25]

It becomes clear as the story proceeds, though, that this principal – Dick Tressider – is more mystic anti-hero than hero, destined to submit to the ordinary, rather than to achieve summits of insight. Equally (and perhaps more easily) in her poems, the same issues prevail. The following lines, from 'Pythian Ode', are as good an example as any:

> They filled the bowl with wine.
> Wine is not Apollo's drink.
> We are here to observe the transition
> From fact to reality.
>
> In. In. In. There are things which to
> display is the only way to hide. That
> ambiguous hint especially we call the divine mind.
> It drifted up through a crack in a stone, and
> out from the mouth of a woman.
> The wind that blows and blows crooked.
> There was the Pythia, and under her a three-legged
> stool,
> a lid on the earth's mystery.

> A stone wreathed in raw wool
> Not a portrait statue of the god.[26]

Apollo 'gilt the earth, but on its navel the Pythia turned, sick with laurel, sick with ecstasy [sic]', an ecstasy Apollo has 'ordered' to 'make men better in their cities'. They are made better; but Delphi becomes 'a little old town with a too large cathedral./A ruin, a quarry.'

Ashe of Rings is set in an animate English landscape, rather than a classical one. Blood members of the ancient family Ashe share mysteries with their house and its great 'Rings' of earthworks. Stylistically, the prose is spare and self-consciously crafted; inner and exterior monologue are fluidly interwoven; narrative is made to depend on the inherent logic of the emotional and spiritual situations the characters enact. Anthony Ashe, in his old age, marries Melitta to beget an heir. After the birth of their daughter, Vanna Elizabeth, Melitta begins an affair with a neighbour, Sir Morice Amburton:

> While the rain streamed over and sluiced the further valley and the sun spangled the wood on the Rings, Anthony found them. From behind he skirted them; came and stood and looked at them.
>
> 'Thank God you know,' said Melitta.
>
> 'Good God!' said Morice Amburton.
>
> 'Here?' said Anthony Ashe.
>
> She snatched her hat. Morice said:
>
> 'We have nothing to be ashamed of, Ashe. You must see that. We owe you every apology, but I intend to make Mrs Ashe my wife. Will you arrange for a divorce?'
>
> 'You've had her. You can have her. But why here?' It had seemed convenient to them.
>
> – 'Leave this place. Any other part of my grounds are at your disposal.' . . .
>
> They got up, and went down the hill. He watched them over the Rings, and withdrew into the wood. They felt their backs naked while his eyes followed them. He brought clean leaves to cover the place where they had lain. A torn twig he broke off . . . An idea made him pause. On a beech-trunk he scored a strip.
>
> This, too, had its place in the cycles.[27]

Years later, Elizabeth – whom her father had called 'Van' – begins an affair with a Russian painter called Serge who is avoiding the draft and who has previously been the lover of her friend Judy. Van muses:

> Both Serge and she were free in their sorrows; only they could not approach each other because of Serge's nature and her own. She could cry and fake a victory over him; but true liberty did not allow that. They had passed into another stage in the association of two similar, slightly dissimilar animals. No need to make such a fuss, yet it was dreary. She loved him; but without the illusion that love would alter him. She also knew herself to be as unalterable. It was good perhaps that she should have vision and Serge detachment . . .
>
> They were close up, kissing one another, violently, repeatedly, tears running down, salting their lips. Hers she caught on her tongue, but his fell straight, lead plummets, and rolled off his chin, warm pearls, bitter to taste.
>
> 'Your tears are heavy.' He nodded and shook his head. They walked together, slowly, to the broken sofa, and crept down on to it, side by side, trying to dry one another's tears.[28]

Oswell Blakeston, who knew, liked and admired Mary Butts, finds in her work the capacity to 'make us feel a permanent world of values behind the impermanent';[29] and indeed, critical acclaim greeted her third novel *Death of Felicity Taverner*, published by Wishart in 1932. Bryher was a constant supporter, too; and published short stories and other pieces in *Life and Letters To-day* after she'd taken the journal over in 1935. After Mary's untimely death from a ruptured appendix, Bryher collected and published her *Last Stories* in 1938.

All the writers we've considered wrote vastly more than we've been able to mention; all, whether they enjoyed some success, or none, from their various books, have been unjustly neglected; and all display a battery of fierce, exotic and heterogeneous talents. These modernist women not only broke the moulds of traditional forms, but also broke open traditional notions of what women are like, are supposed to be like, are supposed to think and perceive. We've ignored their achievements at our own cost, since they offer a gift of life; but they, noticed or not, stand as bravely now in their published work, as they did when they wrote. For them, everything was new; everything could be made; everything mattered.

Endnote

Experiments are conducted, in the main, in order to solve problems. The women modernists we've surveyed – all too briefly – weren't neurotics or dilettantes; they didn't experiment out of idleness or *ennui*, but were driven by deep frustrations with the status quo. The vast amount of written materials they produced testify to the seriousness and integrity of their pursuit of truth; their experimental approach to the central relationships and practical problems of their lives, conducted with equal fervour and energy, is characterised equally by a commitment to the truth.

Of major significance to their development as writers is the inevitable ambivalence caused by that problematic noun-made-adjective, 'woman'. Is a female writer a 'woman' in her living and – somehow separately – a 'writer' in the same way as so many men have been writers? Or is she a 'woman writer'? How can she find out? What follows from the one identity or the other? Does it change the way she writes? Or might it change the way she lives? Or both?

It seems clear that for the modernist women, the solution to the problem had to be acted out rather than theoretically derived. The need to find emotional satisfaction had somehow to be balanced against the need to pursue independence of vision. We might think, for instance, that H.D. married Aldington in a blaze of passion; and leave it at that. It's also true, however, that she married Aldington after a storm of despair and grief after the loss of Frances Gregg and Pound. Further, Aldington wasn't the father of her child; so although she was – for a time – both wife and mother, the two roles were not integrated in relation to the same man. Dorothy Richardson solved her maternal needs even more spectacularly. First as a result of her affair with Wells, she faced becoming an unmarried mother. Then she rejected several offers of marriage, most importantly, that of Benjamin Grad. Next she persuaded Grad and her passionate friend, Veronica Leslie-Jones, to marry each other, with the explicit understanding between all three that a child of the marriage would in some way be hers. Still later, she married a man many years her junior.

Attitudes towards women were less tormented. H.D. survived her passionate attachments to Frances Gregg and Brigit Patmore partly by transforming them into explosive triangular relationships with men: Pound became infatuated with Frances; and H.D. married Brigit's lover, Aldington. Later, her permanent partner, Bryher, married Kenneth Macpherson in order to facilitate H.D.'s attachment to him. Dorothy Richardson's *alter ego*, Miriam, directly juxtaposes the sexual dynamic between herself and Hypo Wilson, with the 'being together' of herself and Amabel, finding sexual contact typical of the first and irrelevant to the second. She grapples with wanting to discover what love is like when it's generated from a female context and fulfils a specifically female need. A later relationship, with a new character called Jean, gives Miriam her 'clue to the nature of reality': knowing that her friend exists, is enough, that 'in separation we should not be parted'.[1] By the end of *Pilgrimage* it's evident to the reader that Miriam discovers the roots of her identity as a woman through her love for other women. Such relationships can exclude the world of men and can allow feelings between women which are independent of men's images of them.

Both H.D. and Richardson experienced with women a particularity of bonding which they expressed often with the analogy of mirrors; the woman intimate can both hold up the self to the self, as well as use her friend for the same purpose, each thus becoming both seer and mirror. The resulting sense of recognition powerfully merges each woman's inner and exterior realities. For Richardson, the essential characteristic of women was 'egoism'. A 'womanly woman'

lives, all her life in the deep current of eternity, an individual, self-centred . . . Because she thinks flowingly, with her feelings, she is relatively indifferent to the fashions of men, to the momentary arts, religions, philosophies, and sciences, valuing them only in so far as she is aware of their importance in the evolution of the beloved . . . Only completely self-centred consciousness can attain to unselfishness – the celebrated unselfishness of the womanly woman.[2]

Other modernists made less effort to understand the claims of men. The straightforwardly lesbian women chose to develop to the fullest extent possible, their attachments to other women. Some made commitments to permanent partnerships: Amy Lowell, Gertrude Stein and Sylvia Beach, for example. Others lived more covertly, leaving us to speculate about the obscurities pertaining to relationships such as Margaret Anderson's with Jane Heap, or Harriet Weaver's with Dora Marsden. There are, too, tempestuous, short-lived unions, such as that between Djuna Barnes and Thelma Wood, taking place either in a life otherwise taken up with a score of casual relationships, or with volatile relationships with men, or with seclusion and celibacy. Djuna Barnes – before and after Thelma Wood – passed through all these experiences.

More important, though, than the kinds of lesbian lives modernist writers led, are the effects on their work which lesbian experience confers. For writers, the possibility of close identification, unstinting support and the practical expediting of social and domestic life can provide a stability and a haven of time and space in which to work, which more typically only male writers can enjoy. Ada Russell made sure that Amy Lowell could work in peace, undisturbed by domestic planning; and, too, took on the roles of secretary, confidante and critic. Alice Toklas believed utterly in Gertrude Stein's genius; as did Bryher in H.D.'s. Adrienne Monnier, though she read no English, gave full support to Sylvia Beach's labours for Joyce in particular and for the other writers she wanted to help. It's true that some women living with men have also had support. Leonard Woolf provided protection to Virginia; Lewes gave the support George Eliot needed. Dorothy Richardson's husband Alan Odle, though no literary critic, admired her enormously and had no wish to deflect or distract her. But on the whole, women writers are few in number who can – or ever could – depend on a man for the constant support writers need. Male writers have almost automatically derived such support from the women close to them, whether it is intense and stormy, like the Lawrences, or conventionally wifely, like the Joyces. Katherine

Mansfield, for example, had to encourage Murry, rather than he her work, even when she was terminally ill; and for her own writing she called on her friend Ida Baker, whom she addressed as her 'wife'. As well as the close identification experienced by all women in lesbian partnerships, lesbian writers are in a position to depend on another woman for the loyalty, faith, encouragement and solace which women are socialised to give.

It's as true of the lesbian modernists as of any other lesbian women that lesbian lives can't be understood in terms of the simple notion of 'sexual orientation'. In instance after instance, H.D.'s forthright declaration that men fail her is echoed by other women who 'show themselves quite capable of sexual and/or emotional congress with men. The point is not whether a woman can or can't make adequate relationships with men, but rather that she can and does make significant relationships with women; and that it is in such relationships that she is free to be herself, to take on or to deny socio-sexual roles, and to establish her own emotional authority over the substance of both her life and her work.

It's hardly surprising, given the hermetic nature of the subject in the early years of the century, that Bryher (and others) found comfort in the theories of Havelock Ellis, since identities and behaviours need naming and placing in order to be deemed to exist at all. Havelock Ellis, Freud, and other theorists giving structural explanations of human sexuality offered – at the very least – a place in nature to lesbian women. It's not surprising, either, that now – two-thirds of a century later and with the benefit of hindsight – contemporary feminism and the reclaiming of women's history demonstrate the inadequacy of notions like 'inversion' and 'Electra complex'. Quite simply, women chose (as they still do) to partner each other because it made sense to do so. Writers, in particular, must seek a personal environment where the claim to imaginative vision isn't constantly subverted by the expectation to be womanly. Those who don't choose the lesbian option in quest of freedom nevertheless find conventional heterosexuality insupportable.

Men fail creative women because society decrees that they must. It isn't only sex women may want from each other; it's the full range of intelligence and feeling giving the connection to experience which every writer craves. In the case of women, the challenge to sexual convention is the most radical challenge that can be made, given that social expectation stipulates the female role and function to be fundamentally a sexual one. Few would dream of condemning a male writer as a failure, both as a man and as a citizen, if he were not a husband and father; but the woman writer, by contrast, risks being dismissed as an eccentric if she doesn't choose to become a wife and mother. Endless speculation about the sexual sanity of Virginia Woolf has pervaded judgment of her fiction in a way that's never happened to the fiction of Joyce and Lawrence (two much more obvious contenders for such speculation). It's precisely because women writers have had their work and lives judged according to the sexual double standard that it has been of crucial importance to them to challenge that standard in their daily living, as well as in their literary experiments.

For women whose intelligence and need for autonomy precluded a life based on conventional heterosexuality, but for whom – too – open sexual experimentation was too problematic to pursue, there were choices other than seclusion and isolation. For them it was always evident that there is more to life than sex, however society might insist that a woman is primarily a sexual creature. Because women's destinies are assumed to derive from their sexual roles and practices, it's clear that any woman who refuses sexual relationships is behaving as radically as her lesbian counterparts. The unattached woman – in whichever condition of chastity or celibacy she lives – demonstrates her independence both from the destiny laid before her and from those men who would have her fulfil it. Her choice may – and will – provoke from men derision, or pity, or even – sometimes – a sentimental adulation; but more importantly, their judgments of her sexuality will influence their judgments of her work and worth, as is the case with any woman whose life is not perceived to be conventionally heterosexual. Unattachment is, after all, as subversive of social expectation as is lesbianism.

Many women seem to have found the model offered by their parents sufficient to dissuade them from establishing anything similar. May Sinclair, whose shipowner father became bankrupt and alcoholic, had an unhappy and restless childhood, moving about from place to place with her mother and watching what resources there were being given to her four brothers so that they could live like gentlemen. She had no formal education, although an informal year spent under Dorothea Beale at Cheltenham Ladies College influenced her considerably. Despite great emotional turmoil between them, May Sinclair lived with her mother – nursing and caring for her – until her mother's death. In her turn, she was cared for by her housekeeper, cook and companion, Florence

Bartrop, for 27 years; until her own death. Harriet Weaver, who knew at first hand from her mother's strictures, the effects of unceasing adjustment, compromise and negotiation, learned to keep her thoughts to herself; but the experience seems to have made her ardent for freedom of expression and independence of mind. She did more for Dora Marsden than most intimates would dream of doing; but not even for Dora would she give up her privacy and independence to go and live with her. Harriet Weaver was exceptional in the respect and affection she drew from anyone associated with her; but she kept her distance and pursued a life made almost impregnable to the interference of others. Harriet Monroe, romantic and traditionalist though she may have been, was not seduced by idealism or respectability to join the ranks of conventional society, but found her pleasures and satisfactions in art and work. Marianne Moore, devoted to mother and brother both, did not write like an embittered 'spinster' and indeed enjoyed lifelong friendships which were both stimulating and satisfying.

Sometimes, after all, the best means of defence is defence. Modernist women – writers, editors, publishers, booksellers – who wanted to fulfil their own drives with as little compromise as possible, either eschewed sexual relationships with men altogether; or dallied with them; or chose the lesbian option; or did their best (as far as they dared) before seeing the writing on the wall and deciding to leave the battlefront. There were some, though – a minority, certainly – for whom the best means of defence was indeed, attack. For these women, their sense of sanity and autonomy demanded that they keep the battle joined until heterosexual relations underwent transformation. The debate about these strategies – defence or attack – raged in the pages of *The Freewoman* (as it rages still); and heterosexual women argued that the re-casting of roles between women and men was an essential condition of their emotional fulfilment. Whether their need derived from a dependent, conditioned response to the men society has fashioned for us; or from a courageous vision that the battle must be fought because something worthwhile can be won from it, is an issue still unresolved among feminists. In the network of women we've been considering, however, some went on trying to construct heterosexual alternatives to the norm. Brigit Patmore, Mary Butts and – in particular – Mina Loy, lived tempestuous lives in the process. Nor are their lives untypical of women bent on self-fulfilment and self-discovery for whom sexual relationships with men remain essential; but the trail of impulsive, explosive and fraught entanglements is daunting when it must co-exist with literary labour. It's tempting to wonder whether the energy necessary to the pursuit of adequate relationships might not, in a saner world, have been more enabling in the practice of the craft.

The modernist women discovered – and began to map – the organic connections between literary and social conventions; between what Mina Loy called 'the desire to be loved' and the independent moral authority required in the stance of an artist; between the traditional values inhering in nineteenth-century verse and fiction, and the traditional femininity required of respectable women. Their solution to the dilemmas and ambivalences arising from these connections was utterly radical. Some – owing to individual differences in temperament and circumstances – acted and reacted more covertly than others. All, however, eschewed the conventional modes of thought and feeling expected of women; and instead chose to follow the logic of their own most fundamental perceptions and experiences. This led, as we've seen, to continuous experimentation both in the substance of their actual lives and in the struggle for literature. The body of work they produced as a result is magnificent testimony to the courage of women who refuse to be content with their assigned identities and functions. It is testimony, too, to the total commitment women will give to shaping a literature – and therefore a world – in which the texture of women's experience is central. The modernist women – stunning, shocking, brilliant and versatile – gave everything they had in the effort to make their literature new.

Notes

Chapter 1   Another Bloomsbury?

1. Virginia Woolf, 'Romance and the Heart', *Nation and Athenaeum* Literary Supplement, 19 May 1923, p. 229.

Chapter 2   H.D.'s triangles

1. H.D., 'Eurydice', *Collected Poems* 1912–1944, edited by Louis L. Martz, New Directions, New York, 1983; Carcanet Press, Manchester, 1984, p. 55.
2. H.D., *End to Torment. A Memoir of Ezra Pound*, edited by Norman Holmes Pearson and Michael King. With the poems from 'Hilda's Book' by Ezra Pound. New Directions, New York, 1979; Carcanet Press, Manchester, 1980, p. 12.
3. Ezra Pound, 'Sancta Patrona Domina Caelae' in H.D., *End to Torment*, pp. 83–4.
4. *End to Torment*, pp. 15–16.
5. Ford Madox Ford, *Return to Yesterday*, Liveright, New York, 1972, pp. 356–7.
6. ibid.
7. H.D., 'Paint It Today', unpublished manuscript (Beinecke Library), pp. 6–9.
8. *End to Torment*, pp. 35–6.
9. H.D., *HERmione*, New Directions, New York, 1981; Virago, London, 1984, pp. 146–7, 179.
10. ibid., pp. 218–19.
11. Frances Gregg Wilkinson, unpublished memoirs (Oliver Wilkinson) pp. 1256, 1251.

12. *HERmione*, p. 219.
13. Frances Gregg Wilkinson, unpublished `manuscript poem (Oliver Wilkinson).
14. 'Paint it Today', ch. 3, p. 1.
15. Ezra Pound to May Sinclair, 29 September 1911 (University of Pennsylvania Library).
16. H.D. to Mrs Isabel Pound, postmarked 26 February 1912 (Beinecke Library).
17. Frances Gregg Wilkinson, unpublished memoirs (Oliver Wilkinson) pp. 1345–7.
18. ibid., pp. 1356–7.
19. H.D. to Mrs Isabel Pound, 26 February 1912 (Beinecke Library).
20. H.D. to Mrs Isabel Pound, 5 December 1912 (Beinecke Library).
21. Brigit Patmore, 1882–1965. Brigit Patmore, H.D. and Richard Aldington were very close during the early part of the Great War. Brigit appears as 'Morgan le Fay' in H.D.'s autobiographical novel *Bid me to Live*; and as 'Mavis' in the 'Murex' section of H.D.'s *Palimpsest*. H.D. appears as 'Helga' in Brigit's novel *No Tomorrow* (1929). Brigit's earlier novel *This Impassioned Onlooker* (1926) is dedicated to H.D. (calling her 'Belgarda') and contains, also, slightly disguised portrayals of her. Despite her strong feelings for H.D., and their long friendship, Brigit resumed her affair with Aldington in 1928 and Aldington left Dorothy Yorke for her. They lived together for ten years, until Aldington left Brigit for her daughter-in-law, Netta.
22. *End to Torment*, p. 18.
23. 'Paint It Today', ch. 3, p. 15.
24. *End to Torment*, pp. 8–9.
25. H.D. to Mrs Isabel Pound, 30 December 1912 (Beinecke Library).
26. Helen Doolittle, manuscript diary, 8 May 1913 (Beinecke Library).
27. ibid., 19 September 1913.
28. 'Paint It Today', ch. 4, p. 18.
29. H.D. to Mrs Pound, postmarked 18 October 1913 (Beinecke Library).
30. H.D. to Frances Gregg Wilkinson, n.d. (Oliver Wilkinson).
31. 'Paint It Today', ch. 5, p. 11.

32. Richard Aldington to Amy Lowell, 21 May 1915 (Houghton Library).
33. H.D., *Palimpsest*, Southern Illinois University Press, Carbondale and Edwardsville, 1968, p. 99.
34. John Cournos, *Miranda Masters*, Alfred A. Knopf, New York, 1926.
35. H.D., 'Eros', part V, *Collected Poems*, pp. 317–18.
36. H.D., *Bid Me to Live*, Black Swan Books, Redding Ridge, Conn., 1983; Virago, London, 1984, p. 99.
37. ibid., p. 56.
38. ibid., p. 58.
39. ibid., p. 78.
40. ibid., p. 81.
41. Cecil Gray to H.D., 12 March 1918 (British Library).

Chapter 3   Enter Bryher

1. H.D. to Bryher, postmarked 13 July 1918 (Beinecke Library).
2. Bryher to Amy Lowell, 14 September 1917 (Houghton Library).
3. Bryher, *The Heart to Artemis*, Harcourt, Brace & World, New York, 1962, p. 143.
4. ibid., pp. 151–2.
5. ibid., p. 152.
6. ibid., pp. 152–3.
7. ibid., p. 165.
8. Bryher to Amy Lowell, 14 September 1917 (Houghton Library).
9. Bryher to Amy Lowell, 15 December 1917 (Houghton Library).
10. Bryher to Amy Lowell, 12 August 1918 (Houghton Library).
11. Bryher, *Two Selves*, Contact Publishing Co., Paris, 1923, p. 124.
12. ibid., p. 126.
13. Bryher to H.D., 22 December 1918 (Beinecke Library).
14. H.D., 'Asphodel', part II, p. 113 (Beinecke Library).
15. H.D. to Bryher, 12 November 1918 (Beinecke Library).
16. H.D. to Bryher, 19 December 1918 (Beinecke Library).
17. H.D. to Bryher, n.d. [late 1918] (Beinecke Library).
18. H.D. to Bryher, 14 February 1919 (Beinecke Library).
19. ibid.

20. Bryher to H.D., 20 March 1919 (Beinecke Library).
21. 'Asphodel', part II, p. 108.
22. Bryher to Brigit Patmore, 25 March 1919 (Beinecke Library).
23. 'Asphodel', part IV, p. 131.
24. ibid., p. 184.
25. For fuller accounts of the McAlmon/Bryher marriage, see: Barbara Guest, *Herself Defined. The Poet H.D. and her World*, Doubleday, New York, 1984; Collins, London, 1985; and Robert McAlmon, *Being Geniuses Together*, The Hogarth Press, London, 1984.
26. Bryher to H.D., [12] June 1923 (Beinecke Library).
27. Bryher to H.D., 14 June 1923 (Beinecke Library).
28. Bryher to Sylvia Beach, 3 January [1926?] (Beinecke Library).
29. Bryher to H.D., n.d. [1924?] (Beinecke Library).
30. For details of these marriage and divorces, see Barbara Guest, *Herself Defined*.
31. H.D., 'To Bryher', dedication in *Palimpsest*, Contact Publishing Co., Paris, 1926.
32. Alice B. Toklas to John Schaffner, 11 November 1961, in *Staying on Alone. Letters of Alice B. Toklas*, Liveright, New York, 1973, p. 406.

Chapter 4   Dorothy Richardson's life-style of writing

1. Dorothy Richardson, 'Data for Spanish Publisher', ed Joseph Prescott, *London Magazine* (6), June 1959, pp. 14–19.
2. Anthony West, *H.G. Wells: Aspects of a Life*, Hutchinson, London, 1984.
3. Dorothy Richardson, *Dawn's Left Hand* in *Pilgrimage*, vol. 4, Virago, London, 1979, pp. 230–33.
4. ibid., pp. 257–8.
5. Dorothy Richardson, *Oberland* (*Pilgrimage*, vol. 4), p. 93.
6. Dorothy Richardson, *The Tunnel* (*Pilgrimage*, vol. 2), p. 149.
7. Dorothy Richardson, 'Comments by a Layman', *The Dental Record*, XXXVIII (1), 1 January 1918, pp. 14–15.
8. 'Comments', *The Dental Record*, XXXVI (10), 2 October 1916, pp. 541–4.
9. Dorothy Richardson, *The Trap* (*Pilgrimage*, vol. 3), p. 495.
10. Dorothy Richardson to Peggy Kirkaldy, 14 October 1935 (Beinecke Library).
11. Dorothy Richardson, *Revolving Lights* (*Pilgrimage*, vol. 3), p. 303.

12. Dorothy Richardson, *Dawn's Left Hand* (*Pilgrimage*, vol. 4), p. 196.
13. ibid., p. 217.
14. ibid., p. 242.
15. Veronica Grad to Rose Odle, n.d. [1957] (Beinecke Library).
16. Dorothy Richardson, *Clear Horizon* (*Pilgrimage*, vol. 4), p. 285.
17. ibid., p. 292.
18. Veronica Grad to Rose Odle, n.d. [1957] (Beinecke Library).
19. ibid.
20. Dorothy Richardson to Peggy Kirkaldy, 12 February 1943 (Beinecke Library).
21. Dorothy Richardson to Pauline Marrian, 25 July 1952 (Beinecke Library).
22. Dorothy Richardson to Henry Savage, 6 January 1950 (Beinecke Library).

Chapter 5   Amy Lowell's garden

1. Amy Lowell, quoted in Jean Gould, *Amy. The World of Amy Lowell and the Imagist Movement*, Dodd, Mead & Co., New York, 1975, p. 43.
2. Amy Lowell, diary entry for 25 May 1889 (Houghton Library).
3. S. Foster Damon, *Amy Lowell, a Chronicle*, Houghton Mifflin Co., Boston, 1935, p. 121.
4. Amy Lowell to H.D., 16 February 1916 (Houghton Library).
5. Damon, op. cit., p. 138.
6. Amy Lowell to Eunice Tietjens, 5 June 1923 (Houghton Library).
7. Harriet Monroe to Amy Lowell, 24 June 1913 (Houghton Library).
8. Ezra Pound to Harriet Monroe, 13 August 1913 in *The Letters of Ezra Pound 1907–1941*, edited by D.D. Paige, Harcourt, Brace, New York, 1950, p. 22.
9. Gould, op. cit., p. 124.
10. Amy Lowell to D.H. Lawrence, quoted in Gould, op. cit., p. 309.
11. Amy Lowell to H.D., 23 November 1915 (Houghton Library).
12. ibid.
13. Amy Lowell to H.D., 6 February 1916 (Houghton Library).
14. Amy Lowell to H.D., 28 June 1916 (Houghton Library).
15. Amy Lowell, 'Christmas Eve', quoted in Lillian Faderman,

Surpassing the Love of Men, William Morrow, New York, 1981, p. 394.

16. Amy Lowell, 'Mise en Scène', 'The Garden by Moonlight', in her *Pictures of the Floating World*, Houghton Mifflin, Boston, 1919, pp. 42, 54.

17. Amy Lowell, 'Madonna of the Evening Flowers', in *Pictures of the Floating World*, pp. 45–6.

18. Damon, op. cit., p. 264.

19. Amy Lowell to Harriet Monroe, 13 January 1935 (Houghton Library).

20. Amy Lowell, 'April', in *Pictures of the Floating World*, p. 63.

21. Gould, op. cit., p. 119.

22. Damon, op. cit., p. 270.

23. Margaret Anderson to Amy Lowell, July 1914 (Houghton Library).

24. Damon, op. cit., p. 380.

25. Amy Lowell to Bryher, 14 November 1917 (Houghton Library).

26. Amy Lowell to Bryher, 4 November 1918 (Houghton Library).

27. ibid.

28. Bryher to Amy Lowell, 28 November 1918 (Houghton Library).

29. Bryher, *West*, Jonathan Cape, London, 1925, pp. 25–6.

30. Damon, op. cit., p. 701.

31. Gould, op. cit., p. 346.

32. Amy Lowell, 'In Excelsis' in her *What's O'Clock*, Houghton Mifflin, Boston, 1925, pp. 54–7.

Chapter 6   French connections

1. James R. Mellow, *Charmed Circle: Gertrude Stein & Company*, Avon Books, New York, 1975, p. 63.

2. ibid., p. 66

3. ibid., p. 65.

4. Gertrude Stein, *Fernhurst, Q.E.D., and Other Early Writings*, ed Leon Katz, Peter Owen, London, 1972, pp. 99–100.

5. Alice B. Toklas, *What is Remembered*, Holt, Rinehart & Winston, New York, 1963, pp. 23–4.

6. Linda Simon, *The Biography of Alice B. Toklas*, Doubleday, New York, 1977, p. 49.

7. ibid., p. 67.

8. ibid., p. 76.

9. ibid., p. 73.
10. Gertrude Stein, 'Ada' in her *Geography and Plays*, Four Seas, Boston, 1922, p. 200.
11. Gertrude Stein, 'Didn't Nelly and Lilly Love You' in her *As Fine as Melanctha*, Yale University Press, New Haven, 1954, pp. 221–52.
12. Lillian Faderman, *Surpassing the Love of Men*, William Morrow, New York, 1981, p. 403.
13. 'Didn't Nelly and Lilly Love You'.
14. ibid., p. 245.
15. See Faderman, op. cit., p. 402.
16. Gertrude Stein, 'As a Wife Has a Cow A Love Story', in *Selected Writings of Gertrude Stein*, edited by Carl van Vechten, Random House, New York, 1946, p. 482.
17. Bryher, *The Heart to Artemis*, Harcourt, Brace & World, New York, 1962, p. 211.
18. Gertrude Stein, 'A Sonatina Followed by Another', in her *Bee Time Vine and Other Pieces*, Yale University Press, New Haven, 1953, p. 8.
19. Alice B. Toklas, *What is Remembered*, Holt, Rinehart & Winston, New York, 1963.
20. Noel Riley Fitch, *Sylvia Beach and the Lost Generation*, W.W. Norton & Co., New York and London, 1983, p. [11].

Chapter 7   Djuna Barnes: 'A most extraordinary and unusual time of it'

1. Andrew Field, *Djuna*, G.P. Putnam's Sons, New York, 1983, p. 180.
2. ibid., p. 193.
3. Djuna Barnes, 'To the Dogs' in *A Book*, Boni & Liveright, New York, 1923, p. 45.
4. ibid., p. 47.
5. Robert Davis to Djuna Barnes, 30 June 1911 (University of Maryland Library).
6. Djuna Barnes, 'How It Feels To Be Forcibly Fed', *World Magazine* (New York), 6 September 1914.
7. Mabel Dodge Luhan, 1879–1962. American patron of writers and artists, she held a weekly salon in her New York apartment in the years before and during the Great War. She was a good friend of Gertrude Stein and Mina Loy, whom she had known in Florence and Paris before the First World War. See her

autobiography, *Intimate Memories*, Random House, New York, 1946.

8. Djuna Barnes to Courtenay Lemon, n.d. [1915] (University of Maryland Library).

9. Djuna Barnes, 'Six Songs of Khalidine' in *A Book*, pp. 145–6.

10. Edmund Wilson, *The Twenties*, edited by Leon Edel, Farrar, Strauss & Giroux, New York, 1975, p. 369.

11. ibid., p. 85.

12. ibid.

13. Djuna Barnes to Courtenay Lemon, postmarked 28 July 1919 (University of Maryland Library).

14. Djuna Barnes to Courtenay Lemon, n.d. [1919?] (University of Maryland Library).

15. Courtenay Lemon to Djuna Barnes, n.d. [1919?] (University of Maryland Library).

16. Margaret Anderson, *My Thirty Years' War*, Horizon Press, New York, 1969, p. 181.

17. Wilson, op. cit., p. 85.

18. Djuna Barnes to Margaret Anderson, n.d. [1964] (University of Maryland Library).

19. Field, op. cit., p. 60.

20. ibid., p. 61.

21. Robert McAlmon, *Post-Adolescence*, Contact Publishing Company, Paris, 1923, p. 23.

22. ibid., pp. 94–5.

23. Field, op. cit., p. 113.

24. Djuna Barnes, 'Farewell to Paris', unpublished manuscript (University of Maryland Library).

25. Robert McAlmon to Djuna Barnes, Christmas card, n.d. (University of Maryland Library).

26. Robert McAlmon to Djuna Barnes, 2 September 1952 (University of Maryland Library).

27. Thelma Wood to Djuna Barnes, 7 March [1922?] (University of Maryland Library).

28. Thelma Wood to Djuna Barnes, 23 March [1922?] (University of Maryland Library).

29. Thelma Wood to Djuna Barnes, n.d. [1922?] (University of Maryland Library).

30. Natalie Barney to Djuna Barnes, 13 January 1963 (University of Maryland Library).

31. Field, op. cit., p. 101.

32. John Glassco, *Memoirs of Montparnasse*, Oxford University Press, London, 1970, p. 39.
33. ibid., p. 43.
34. Djuna Barnes to Eleanor Fitzgerald, 10 May 1926 (University of Maryland Library).
35. Thelma Wood to Djuna Barnes, n.d. [1927?] (University of Maryland Library).
36. Field, op. cit., p. 152.
37. Thelma Wood to Djuna Barnes, 30 June [1930?] (University of Maryland Library).
38. Thelma Wood to Djuna Barnes, 5 August [1930?] (University of Maryland Library).
39. Field, op. cit., p. 162.
40. ibid., p. 18.
41. Djuna Barnes to Charles Henri Ford, n.d. [1933] (Humanities Research Center, University of Texas).
42. Field, op. cit., p. 209.
43. Djuna Barnes to Robert McAlmon, 27 December 1940 (Beinecke Library).
44. Djuna Barnes to Robert McAlmon, 29 October 1942 (Beinecke Library).
45. Field, op. cit., p. 220.
46. Natalie Barney to Djuna Barnes, 21 May 1963 (University of Maryland Library).
47. Djuna Barnes to Natalie Barney, 24 October 1966 (University of Maryland Library).
48. Djuna Barnes to Natalie Barney, 29 August 1965 (University of Maryland Library).
49. Djuna Barnes to Natalie Barney, 1 May 1965 (University of Maryland Library).
50. Djuna Barnes to Natalie Barney, 22 April 1966 (University of Maryland Library).

Chapter 8   Mary Butts, Mina Loy and the dead language of amor

[We are extremely grateful to Mina Loy's daughter, Joella Bayer, for information given to V.L. Smyers in a telephone interview on 22 March, 1987.]

1. Virgil Thomson, *Virgil Thomson*, Alfred A. Knopf, New York, 1966, p. 87.

2. Camilla Bagg, interview with Virginia Smyers, 13 December 1983.
3. ibid.
4. Cf. Robert McAlmon, 'History of Encounters', unpublished typescript (Beinecke Library).
5. Bryher, interview with Virginia Smyers, 18 December 1979.
6. Camilla Bagg, interview with Virginia Smyers, 13 December 1983; H.D.–Bryher correspondence (Beinecke Library); Norman Holmes Pearson papers (Beinecke Library).
7. Peggy Guggenheim, *Out of this Century*, Universe Books, New York, 1979, p. 73.
8. Robert McAlmon, 'History of Encounters'.
9. ibid.
10. Mary Butts, *Imaginary Letters*, Talonbooks, Vancouver, 1979.
11. Quoted in Hugh Ford, *Published in Paris. American and British Writers, Printers, and Publishers in Paris 1920–1939*, Pushcart Press, New York, 1980, p. 134.
12. Robin Blaser, 'Afterword' in Mary Butts, *Imaginary Letters*, p. 75.
13. Marianne Moore to Robert McAlmon, 28 July 1922 (Beinecke Library).
14. Thomson, op. cit., p. 87.
15. ibid., p. 88.
16. Blaser, op. cit., p. 65.
17. ibid., p. 75.
18. Oswell Blakeston, 'Dangerous Encounter', *Gay News*, 25 November–8 December 1982.
19. Oswell Blakeston, interview with Virginia Smyers, 28 December 1983.
20. Mary Butts to Angus Davidson, 30 August 1933 (Beinecke Library).
21. Mina Loy, *The Little Review*, spring 1929, p. 46.
22. Quoted in *The Last Lunar Baedeker* by Mina Loy, edited by Roger Conover, The Jargon Society, Highlands, North Carolina; 1982, Introduction, p. lxvi.
23. Filippo Tomasino Marinetti founded the Italian 'Futurist' movement in 1909.
24. Conover, op. cit., p. lxv.
25. ibid., p. xxxv.
26. Mina Loy to Mabel Dodge, 20 April [1913?] (Beinecke Library).

27. Mina Loy, 'Aphorisms on Futurism', *Last Lunar Baedeker*, pp. 272–4.
28. Mina Loy to Mabel Dodge, n.d. [1914?] from 54 Costa San Giorgio (Beinecke Library).
29. Mina Loy to Mabel Dodge, February 1914 (Beinecke Library).
30. Mina Loy to Mabel Dodge, 10 March [1914?] (Beinecke Library).
31. Mina Loy to Mabel Dodge, n.d. [1914?] (Beinecke Library).
32. Mina Loy, 'Feminist Manifesto', *The Last Lunar Baedeker*, pp. 269–71. These extracts are taken from the revised published version. The original draft is in the Beinecke Library with the Mabel Dodge Luhan papers.
33. Mina Loy to Mabel Dodge, 17 September [1914?] (Beinecke Library).
34. Mina Loy to Mabel Dodge, n.d. [1914?] (Beinecke Library).
35. Mina Loy to Mabel Dodge, n.d. [1915?] (Beinecke Library).
36. ibid.
37. Conover, op. cit., p. xli.
38. *New York Evening Sun*, 17 February 1917; quoted in Conover, op. cit., p. xliv.
39. Conover, op. cit., p. xlvii.
40. ibid., p. lii.
41. ibid., p. liii.
42. Arthur Cravan to Mina Loy, December 1917, quoted in Conover, op. cit., p. lviii.
43. Robert McAlmon, *Post-Adolescence*, Contact Publishing Company, Paris, 1923, pp. 21–2.
44. Mina Loy to Mabel Dodge, n.d. [1920] (Beinecke Library).
45. Mina Loy to Mabel Dodge, 3 July [1921?] (Beinecke Library).
46. Sylvia Beach, *Shakespeare & Company*, Faber & Faber, London, 1956, p. 113.
47. Andrew Field, *Djuna*, G.P. Putnam's Sons, New York, 1983, p. 126.
48. Harriet Monroe, 'The Editor in France', *Poetry*, XXIII, 1923, pp. 95–6.
49. Robert McAlmon, *Being Geniuses Together 1920–1930*, rev. edn, Doubleday, New York, 1968, p. 41.
50. Mina Loy, 'Gertrude Stein', in *The Last Lunar Baedeker*, p. 26.
51. Djuna Barnes to Mina Loy, 5 July 1930 (private collection).
52. Djuna Barnes to Mina Loy, 30 October 1930 (private

collection).
53. Djuna Barnes to Mina Loy, 5 July 1930 (private collection).
54. ibid.
55. Conover, op. cit., p. lxxvii.
56. ibid., p. lxxviii.
57. Mina Loy, 'Letters of the Unliving', *The Last Lunar Baedeker*, pp. 263–5.
58. Mina Loy, *The Little Review*, spring 1929, p. 46.

Chapter 9   Loners

1. Alfred Kreymborg, *Troubadour: An American Autobiography*, Sagamore Press, New York, 1957, p. 190.
2. Cf. correspondence between Mrs Moore, Marianne Moore and Warner Moore; and between Marianne Moore and Bryher, Marianne Moore and H.D., in the Rosenbach Library, Philadelphia.
3. The correspondence from Marianne Moore to Alyse Gregory is in the Beinecke Library, but may not be read until the year 2000.
4. Harriet Monroe, *A Poet's Life: Seventy Years in a Changing World*, Macmillan, New York, 1938, p. 60.
5. ibid., p. 23.
6. ibid., pp. 35–6.
7. ibid., p. 58.
8. ibid., pp. 60–61.
9. ibid., p. 62.
10. ibid., p. 118.
11. ibid.
12. ibid., p. 119.
13. Harriet Monroe, *Chosen Poems*, Macmillan, New York, 1935, pp. 110–11.
14. *A Poet's Life*, pp. 185–6.
15. ibid., p. 317.
16. ibid., p. 217.
17. Amy Lowell to Harriet Monroe, February 1916 (Houghton Library).
18. *A Poet's Life*, p. 146.
19. Samuel Beckett to Sylvia Beach, 22 October 1961, quoted in Jane Lidderdale and Mary Nicholson, *Dear Miss Weaver*, Viking, New York, 1970, p. 455.
20. Lidderdale and Nicholson, op. cit., p. 33.

21. ibid., p. 37.
22. ibid., pp. 37–8.
23. ibid., p. 42.
24. ibid., p. 40.
25. ibid., p. 46.
26. *The Freewoman*, I (1), 23 November 1911.
27. Lidderdale and Nicholson, op. cit., p. 89.
28. Iris Barry, 'The Ezra Pound Period', *The Bookman* (New York), LXXIV (2), October 1931, pp. 165–6.
29. ibid., p. 168.
30. See Lidderdale and Nicholson, op. cit., for details.
31. ibid., p. 169.
32. ibid., p. 178.
33. Robert McAlmon, *Being Geniuses Together 1920–1930*, rev. edn, Doubleday, New York, 1968, p. 89.
34. Harriet Weaver to Sylvia Beach, 12 November 1924 (University College London Library).
35. Harriet Weaver to Bryher, 9 October 1924 (Beinecke Library).
36. Lidderdale and Nicholson, op. cit., p. 251.
37. Harriet Weaver to Sylvia Beach, 11 April 1925 (University College London Library).
38. Harriet Weaver to Sylvia Beach, 22 June 1925 (University College London Library).
39. ibid.
40. Harriet Weaver to Sylvia Beach, 14 June 1926 (University College London Library).
41. Lidderdale and Nicholson, op. cit., p. 282.
42. Harriet Weaver to Sylvia Beach, 18 October 1928 (University College London Library).
43. Lidderdale and Nicholson, op. cit., p. 284.
44. Harriet Weaver to Sylvia Beach, 9 July 1937 (University College London Library).
45. Dora Marsden to Harriet Weaver, quoted in Lidderdale and Nicholson, op. cit., p. 449.
46. ibid.

Chapter 10 'The stand of the individual against immensities' – Periodical publishing I

1. Harriet Monroe, 'Poet's Circular', quoted in Daniel Cahill, *Harriet Monroe*, Twayne Publishers, New York, 1973, p. 43.
2. Ezra Pound to Harriet Monroe, n.d. [October 1912] in *The*

Letters of Ezra Pound 1907–1941, edited by D.D. Paige, Harcourt, Brace, New York, 1950, p. 11.

3. Ezra Pound to Harriet Monroe, n.d. [Jan/Feb 1914] quoted in Ellen Williams, *Harriet Monroe and the Poetry Renaissance, The First Ten Years of Poetry, 1912–22* University of Illinois Press, Urbana, 1977, p. 95.

4. Ezra Pound to Harriet Monroe, 7 November 1913, in Paige (ed.), op. cit., p. 24.

5. Amy Lowell to Harriet Monroe, 16 February 1914 (Houghton Library).

6. Richard Aldington to Amy Lowell, 8 July 1915 (Houghton Library).

7. Amy Lowell to H.D., 6 February 1916 (Houghton Library).

8. Harriet Monroe to Ezra Pound, 25 November 1918 (Beinecke Library).

9. Amy Lowell to H.D., 3 February 1920 (Houghton Library).

10. Harriet Monroe, quoted in Cahill, op. cit., p. 356.

11. ibid., pp. 357–8.

12. ibid., p. 411.

13. Harriet Weaver, undated typescript (Harriet Shaw Weaver papers, British Library)

14. Les Garner, *Stepping Stones to Women's Liberty*, Heinemann Educational Books, London, 1984, p. 65.

15. Undated circular, headed 'The New Freewoman' (Harriet Shaw Weaver papers, British Library)

16. Harriet Weaver, undated typescript (Harriet Shaw Weaver papers, British Library).

17. Jane Lidderdale and Mary Nicholson, *Dear Miss Weaver*, Viking, New York, 1970, p. 460.

18. Ezra Pound to Harriet Monroe, 13 August 1913, in Paige (ed.), op. cit., p. 22.

19. Ezra Pound to Dora Marsden, n.d. [*c.* July 1913] quoted in Lidderdale and Nicholson, op. cit., p. 67.

20. Ezra Pound to Amy Lowell, 23 February 1914, in Paige (ed.), op. cit., pp. 31–2.

21. Ezra Pound to Amy Lowell, 18 March 1914, in Paige (ed.), op. cit., p. 33.

22. H.D. to Amy Lowell, 27 April 1915 (Houghton Library).

Chapter 11 'Life for Art's sake' – Periodical publishing II

1. Richard Aldington to Amy Lowell, 26 December 1914 (Houghton Library).
2. Richard Aldington to Amy Lowell, 11 June 1916 (Houghton Library).
3. H.D. to Marianne Moore, 3 September 1916 (Rosenbach Library).
4. Margaret Anderson, 'Announcement', *The Little Review*, March 1914, pp. 1–2.
5. Margaret Anderson (ed.), *The Little Review Anthology*, Hermitage House, New York, 1953, p. 11.
6. Ezra Pound to Margaret Anderson, n.d. [January? 1917] in Paige (ed.), op. cit., pp. 106–7.
7. Ezra Pound to John Quinn, 18 April 1917, in Paige (ed.), p. 109.
8. Ezra Pound to Margaret Anderson, n.d. [May 1917] in Paige (ed.), p. 111.
9. Amy Lowell to H.D., 14 July 1917 (Houghton Library).
10. Amy Lowell to Margaret Anderson, 10 April 1916 (Houghton Library).
11. H.D. to Amy Lowell, 10 August 1917 (Houghton Library).
12. Amy Lowell to H.D., 22 August 1917 (Houghton Library).
13. H.D. to Amy Lowell, 19 September 1917 (Houghton Library).
14. Amy Lowell to H.D., 15 October 1917 (Houghton Library).
15. Ezra Pound to Margaret Anderson, n.d. [December 1917] in Paige (ed.), p. 126.
16. Ezra Pound to Margaret Anderson, n.d. [January 1918] in Paige (ed.), pp. 129–30.
17. Frederick J. Hoffman and Charles Allen, *The Little Magazine*, Princeton University Press, Princeton, NJ, 1946, pp. 57–60.
18. Edited by Alfred Kreymborg, including poems by T.S. Eliot and William Carlos Williams.
19. These articles appeared in the following issues of *The Little Review*:

    Amy Lowell, 'Letter from London', October 1914, pp. 6–9.

    Margaret Anderson's review of Amy Lowell's *Sword Blades and Poppy Seed*, December 1914, pp. 29–30.

    Harriet Monroe's *You and I* reviewed, December 1914, pp. 23–4.

    Richard Aldington on H.D., March 1915, pp. 22–5.

Amy Lowell and J.G. Fletcher on *Some Imagist Poets*, March 1915, pp. 27–35.

F.S. Flint on Amy Lowell, January–February 1916, pp. 16–17.

J.G. Fletcher on H.D., June–July 1916.

Some Imagist Poets reviewed June-July 1916, pp. 26–31.

'The Vers Libre Contest', April 1917.

Ezra Pound on Marianne Moore, March 1918, pp. 54–8.

Reviews of Dorothy Richardson by John Rodker, September 1919, pp. 40–41; by William Carlos Williams, September 1919, pp. 36–9; by Robert McAlmon, autumn 1924, p. 48.

Mina Loy on John Rodker, September–December 1920, pp. 56–7.

Mary Butts on *The Poets' Translation Series*, January–March 1921, pp. 45–7.

Gertrude Stein on Jane Heap, spring 1929, pp. 9–10.

20. Marianne Moore, 'Interview with Donald Hall', *A Marianne Moore Reader*, Viking, New York, 1965, p. 266.

21. Ford Madox Ford, quoted in Bernard J. Poli, *Ford Madox Ford and The Transatlantic Review*, Syracuse University Press, Syracuse 1967, p. 37.

22. ibid., pp. 116–17.

23. Bryher, *The Heart to Artemis*, Harcourt, Brace & World, New York, 1962, pp. 245–6.

24. Dorothy Richardson to Bryher, 1 July [1927] (Beinecke Library).

25. Dorothy Richardson to Bryher, n.d. [1927] (Beinecke Library).

Chapter 12   'The public is a stupid beast' – Book publishing I

1. Amy Lowell to Harriet Monroe, 15 September 1914 (Houghton Library).

2. ibid.

3. Cf. S. Foster Damon, *Amy Lowell*, Houghton Mifflin, Boston, 1935.

4. Amy Lowell to H.D., 6 February 1916 (Houghton Library).

5. H.D. to Amy Lowell, 7 October 1915 (Houghton Library).

6. Amy Lowell to H.D., 23 November 1915 (Houghton Library).

7. H.D. to Amy Lowell, n.d. [February 1916] (Houghton Library).

8. Amy Lowell to H.D., 6 February 1916 (Houghton Library).

9. Amy Lowell to H.D., 2 January 1917 (Houghton Library).

10. Bryher to Amy Lowell, 15 December 1917 (Houghton Library).

11. Robert McAlmon, 'Forewarned as Regards H.D.'s Prose', in H.D., *Palimpsest*, Southern Illinois University Press, Carbondale and Edwardsville, 1968, p. 244.

12. Louise Morgan, review of *Palimpsest* in *The Outlook* (London), quoted in Hugh Ford, *Published in Paris*, Pushcart Press, New York, 1980, p. 72.

13. Alyse Gregory, 'A Poet's Novel', *The Dial*, 82 (5), May 1927.

14. H.D., 'Notes on Recent Writing', in her *Bid Me to Live*, Black Swan Books, Redding Ridge, Conn., 1983, pp. 204–05.

15. H.D. to Marianne Moore, postmarked 7 September 1915 (Rosenbach Library).

16. H.D. to Marianne Moore, 3 September [1916] (Rosenbach Library).

17. H.D. to Marianne Moore, postmarked 29 August 1917 (Rosenbach Library).

18. Ezra Pound to Marianne Moore, 16 December 1918, in *The Letters of Ezra Pound 1907–1941*, edited by D.D. Paige, Harcourt, Brace, New York, 1950, pp. 143–4.

19. Marianne Moore to Ezra Pound, 9 January 1919, in Charles Tomlinson (ed.), *Marianne Moore: A Collection of Critical Essays*, Prentice-Hall, Englewood Cliffs, NJ, 1969, pp. 16–18.

20. H.D. to Marianne Moore, 6 July [1920] (Rosenbach Library).

21. Bryher to Marianne Moore, 24 September 1920 (Rosenbach Library).

22. Marianne Moore to Bryher, 15 October 1920 (Beinecke Library).

23. Cf. Jane Lidderdale and Mary Nicholson, *Dear Miss Weaver*, Viking, New York, 1970, pp. 177, 240, 461, 464.

24. Harriet Monroe, 'A Symposium on Marianne Moore', *Poetry*, XIX (4) January 1922.

25. Marianne Moore to H.D., 3 May 1921 (Beinecke Library).

26. H.D. to Marianne Moore, 9 July 1921 (Rosenbach Library).

27. Marianne Moore to Bryher, 7 July 1921 (Beinecke Library).

28. Marianne Moore, *A Marianne Moore Reader* Viking, New York, 1965, p. 258.

29. Bryher, *The Heart to Artemis*, Harcourt, Brace & World, New York, 1962, p. 168.

30. Amy Lowell to Bryher, 13 June 1918 (Houghton Library).

31. Bryher, *The Heart to Artemis*, p. 238.
32. Dorothy Richardson to S.S. Koteliansky, 11 December 1933 (British Library).
33. Dorothy Richardson to S.S. Koteliansky, 8 August [1934] (British Library).
34. Dorothy Richardson to Bernice Elliott, 27 February 1949 (Beinecke Library).
35. Dorothy Richardson to Peggy Kirkaldy, 14 February 1943 (Beinecke Library).
36. Dorothy Richardson, 'Women in the Arts', *Vanity Fair*, May 1925.
37. Dorothy Richardson to Rose Odle, 27 November 1949 (Beinecke Library).
38. Dorothy Richardson to Henry Savage, 11 March 1950 (Beinecke Library).
39. *Minneapolis Journal*, 1 December 1912.
40. Louis Untermeyer, *Chicago Evening Post*, 14 February 1913.
41. Damon, op. cit., p. 262.
42. Bryher to Amy Lowell, 14 September 1917 (Houghton Library).
43. Amy Lowell to Bryher, 29 June 1918 (Houghton Library).
44. Amy Lowell to H.D., 13 August 1918 (Houghton Library).
45. Bryher, *The Heart to Artemis*, p. 182.
46. Bryher to Amy Lowell, 15 October 1918 (Houghton Library).
47. Bryher, *The Heart to Artemis*, pp. 193–4.
48. ibid., p. 194.
49. Marianne Moore to Bryher, 29 November 1920 and 3 May 1921 (Beinecke Library).
50. *The Nation*, 112, 2 February 1921, p. 188.
51. Dorothy Richardson to Bryher, n.d. [1923] (Beinecke Library).
52. See the Robert McAlmon–Norman Holmes Pearson correspondence in Beinecke Library.

Chapter 13   'There is a climax in sensibility' – Book publishing II

1. Donald Gallup, 'The Making of The Making of Americans', in Gertrude Stein's *Fernhurst, Q.E.D., and Other Early Writings*, edited by Leon Katz, Peter Owen, London, 1972, pp. 175–214; this article provides full details of the publishing history which we've summarised here.

2. McAlmon gives his own account of this fiasco in his *Being Geniuses Together*, rev. edn, Doubleday, New York, 1968, pp. 206–7.
3. Robert McAlmon to Gertrude Stein, quoted in Gallup, op. cit., pp 210–11.
4. McAlmon, *Being Geniuses Together*, p. 142.
5. Gallup, op. cit., p. 211.
6. Mina Loy in *The Transatlantic Review*, II (3), September 1924, p. 306.
7. Mina Loy in *The Transatlantic Review*, II (4), October 1924, pp. 429–30.
8. Gertrude Stein, *The Making of Americans*, Peter Owen, London, 1968, p. 193.
9. Gertrude Stein, 'Capital, Capitals', *This Quarter*, I (1), 1924, pp. 13, 23.
10. Yvor Winters, 'Mina Loy', *The Dial*, 8, June 1926, pp. 496–9.
11. Mina Loy, 'Feminist Manifesto' in *The Last Lunar Baedeker*, edited by Roger Conover, The Jargon Society, Highlands, North Carolina, 1982, pp. 269–71.
12. Mina Loy, 'Auto-Facial-Construction' in ibid., pp. 283–4.
13. Mina Loy, 'International Psycho-Democracy', in ibid., pp. 276–82.
14. Mina Loy, 'Apology of Genius', in ibid., pp. 4–5.
15. Mina Loy, 'Parturition', in ibid., pp. 67–71.
16. Djuna Barnes, 'From Fifth Avenue Up', in *The Book of Repulsive Women*, Bruno Chap Books, New York, 1915, pp. 91–2.
17. Floyd Dell, *The Nation* (New York) CXVIII, 2 January 1924, pp. 14–15.
18. Hugh Ford, *Published in Paris*, Pushcart Press, Yonkers, NY, 1980, p. 132.
19. Andrew Field, *Djuna*, G.P. Putnam's Sons, New York, 1983, p. 125.
20. ibid., p. 126.
21. Louis F. Kannenstine, 'Djuna Barnes', in Karen Rood (ed.), *American Writers in Paris 1920–1939*, Gale Research Co., Detroit, Mich., 1980, pp. 19–20.
22. Robert McAlmon to Djuna Barnes, 4 December 1949 (University of Maryland Library).
23. Natalie Barney to Djuna Barnes, 21 July 1962 (University of Maryland Library).

24. *Ladies Almanack*, privately printed, Paris, 1928, p. 19.
25. Mary Butts, 'Deosil', *The Transatlantic Review*, II (3), September 1924, p. 41.
26. Mary Butts, 'Pythian Ode', in ibid., p. 236.
27. Mary Butts, *Ashe of Rings*, Wishart, London, 1933, pp. 51–2.
28. ibid., pp. 152–3.
29. Oswell Blakeston, 'Dangerous Encounter', *Gay News*, 25 November–8 December 1982.

Endnote

1. Dorothy Richardson, *March Moonlight* (*Pilgrimage*, vol. 4, Virago, London, 1979), p. 612.
2. Dorothy Richardson, 'Women and the Future: A Trembling of the Veil Before the Eternal Mystery of "La Gioconda" [*sic*]', *Vanity Fair* (New York), XXII, April 1924, pp. 39–40.

Bibliography

Section A   Unpublished sources

BEINECKE RARE BOOK AND MANUSCRIPT LIBRARY, Yale University, New Haven, Conn.

Beinecke Library is the major repository for the following writers' papers and correspondence: Bryher; H.D.; Mina Loy; Robert McAlmon; Ezra Pound; Dorothy Richardson; Gertrude Stein. It holds also some Mary Butts papers and correspondence; and the Mabel Dodge Luhan papers.

THE BRITISH LIBRARY, London

The Manuscripts Division of The British Library holds the Harriet Shaw Weaver papers, including the archive of *The New Freewoman* and *The Egoist*. It holds also some Dorothy Richardson correspondence.

THE GOLDA MEIR LIBRARY, University of Wisconsin, Milwaukee, Wisconsin.

The Golda Meir Library holds the archive of *The Little Review*.

HOUGHTON LIBRARY, Harvard University, Cambridge, Massachusetts.

Houghton Library holds the Amy Lowell papers, including carbon copies of her own letters, as well as correspondence addressed to her.

MCKELDIN LIBRARY, University of Maryland, College Park, Maryland.

McKeldin Library holds the Djuna Barnes papers.

THE REGENSTEIN LIBRARY, University of Chicago, Chicago, Illinois.

The Regenstein Library holds the *Poetry* magazine archive, as well as the personal papers of Harriet Monroe.

THE ROSENBACH MUSEUM AND LIBRARY, Philadelphia, Pennsylvania.

The Rosenbach Library is the major repository for Marianne Moore's papers.

UNIVERSITY COLLEGE, LONDON, LIBRARY.

University College Library holds copies of the correspondence from Harriet Shaw Weaver to Sylvia Beach. The originals are held in the Princeton University Library, Princeton, NJ.

Some unpublished materials used in research for this book are in private hands. We are grateful to the following people for sharing with us either papers or reminiscences, or both: Mrs Camilla Bagg, Mrs Joella Bayer, the late Oswell Blakeston, the late Winifred Bryher, Mr Roger Conover, Miss Jane Lidderdale, Miss Pauline Marrian, Mrs Sheena Odle, Mrs Perdita Schaffner, the late Owen Wadsworth, Mr Oliver Wilkinson.

Section B   Select bibliography of published works by modernist women

(When several editions of a work have been published, we give the first edition and the most recent edition we are aware of at the time of writing)

Djuna Barnes 1892–1982
The Book of Repulsive Women: 8 Rhythms and 5 Drawings, Bruno Chap Books, New York, 1915, Alicat Bookshop Press, Yonkers, New York, 1948.
A Book, Boni & Liveright, New York, 1923; Faber & Faber, London, 1958.
Ladies Almanack, privately printed, Paris, 1928; Harper & Row, New York, 1972.
Ryder, Liveright, New York, 1928; St Martin's Press, New York, 1979.

A Night among the Horses, Liveright, New York, 1929.

Nightwood, Faber & Faber, London, 1936; Harcourt, Brace, New York, 1937 (currently in print).

The Antiphon, Farrar, Straus & Cudahy, New York, 1958; Faber & Faber, London, 1958.

Selected Works of Djuna Barnes. Spillway, The Antiphon, Nightwood, Farrar, Straus & Cudahy, New York, 1962; Faber & Faber, London, 1980 (currently in print).

Creatures in an Alphabet, The Dial Press, New York, 1982.

Smoke and Other Early Stories, ed Douglas Messerli, Sun & Moon Press, College Park, Md., 1983; Virago Press, London, 1985.

I Could Never be Lonely Without a Husband, Interviews edited by Alyce Barry, Sun & Moon Press, College Park, Md., 1985; Virago Press, London, 1987.

Bryher 1894–1983

Amy Lowell: A Critical Appreciation, Eyre & Spottiswoode, London, 1918.

Development: A Novel, Constable, London, 1920; Macmillan, New York, 1920.

Two Selves, Contact Publishing Co., Paris, 1923.

West, Jonathan Cape, London, 1925.

Civilians, Pool Publications, Territet, 1927.

Film Problems of Soviet Russia, Pool Publications, Territet, 1929.

Paris 1900, trans. Sylvia Beach and Adrienne Monnier, La Maison des Amis des Livres, Paris, 1938.

Beowulf, Pantheon, New York, 1952.

The Fourteenth of October, Pantheon, New York, 1952; Collins, London, 1954; Penguin, Harmondsworth, 1964.

The Player's Boy, Pantheon, New York, 1953; Collins, London, 1957.

Roman Wall, Pantheon, New York, 1954; Collins, London, 1955.

Gate to the Sea, Pantheon, New York, 1958; Collins, London, 1959.

Ruan, Pantheon, New York, 1960; Collins, London, 1961.

The Heart to Artemis: A Writer's Memoirs, Harcourt, Brace & World, New York, 1962; Collins, London, 1963.

The Coin of Carthage, Harcourt, Brace & World, New York, 1963; Collins, London, 1964; Harcourt, Brace, New York, 1974.

Visa for Avalon, Harcourt, Brace & World, New York, 1965.

This January Tale, Harcourt, Brace & World, New York, 1966.

The Colors of Vaud, Harcourt, Brace & World, New York, 1969.
The Days of Mars: A Memoir, 1940–1946, Harcourt, Brace & World, New York, 1972; Marion Boyars, London, 1981.

Mary Butts 1890–1937
Speed the Plough and Other Stories, Chapman & Hall, London, 1923.
Ashe of Rings, Contact Publishing Co., Paris, 1925; Wishart, London, 1933.
Armed with Madness, Wishart, London, 1928; Albert & Charles Boni, New York, 1928.
Imaginary Letters, E.W. Titus, Paris, 1928; Talonbooks, Vancouver, 1979.
Death of Felicity Taverner, Wishart, London, 1932.
Several Occasions, Wishart, London, 1932.
The Macedonian, Heinemann, London, 1933.
Scenes from the Life of Cleopatra, Heinemann, London, 1935; Ecco Press, New York, 1984.
The Crystal Cabinet, My Childhood at Salterns, Methuen, London, 1937.
Last Stories, Brendin Publishing Co., London, 1938.

H.D. 1886–1961
Sea Garden, Constable, London, 1916; Houghton Mifflin, Boston, 1916; St James Press, London, 1975; St Martin's Press, New York, 1975.
Hymen, The Egoist Press, London, 1921; Henry Holt & Co., New York, 1921.
Heliodora and Other Poems, Houghton Mifflin, Boston, 1924; Jonathan Cape, London, 1924.
Collected Poems of H.D., Boni & Liveright, New York, 1925; 1940.
Palimpsest, Contact Publishing Co., Paris, 1926; Houghton Mifflin, Boston, 1926; rev. edn, Southern Illinois University Press, Carbondale and Edwardsville, 1968.
Hippolytus Temporizes, Houghton Mifflin, Boston, 1927; Black Swan Books, Redding Ridge, Conn., 1985.
Hedylus, Houghton Mifflin, Boston, 1928; Basil Blackwell, Oxford, 1928; new edn, Black Swan Books, Redding Ridge, Conn., 1980; Carcanet Press, Manchester, 1980.

Nights, (by John Helforth, pseud.) Privately printed, Dijon, France, 1935; New Directions, New York, 1986.

Euripides' Ion, Chatto & Windus, London, 1937; Houghton Mifflin, Boston, 1937; Black Swan Books, Redding Ridge, Conn., 1986.

Tribute to Freud, Pantheon, New York, 1956; new edn, David R. Godine, Boston, 1974; Carcanet, Manchester, 1985.

Bid Me to Live, Grove Press, New York, 1960; Black Swan Books, Redding Ridge, Conn., 1983; Virago, London, 1984.

Helen in Egypt, Grove Press, New York, 1961; Carcanet Press, Manchester, 1985.

Hermetic Definition, New Directions, New York, 1972; Carcanet Press, Manchester, 1972.

Trilogy, New Directions, New York, 1973; Carcanet Press, Manchester, 1973.

End to Torment. A Memoir of Ezra Pound, ed Norman Holmes Pearson and Michael King. With the poems from *'Hilda's Book'* by Ezra Pound. New Directions, New York, 1979; Carcanet Press, Manchester, 1980.

HERmione, New Directions, New York, 1981; Virago, London, 1984.

The Gift, New Directions, New York, 1982; Virago, London, 1984.

Collected Poems 1912–1944, ed Louis L. Martz, New Directions, New York, 1983; Carcanet Press, Manchester, 1984.

Amy Lowell 1874–1925

A Dome of Many-Coloured Glass, Houghton Mifflin, Boston, 1912.

Sword Blades and Poppy Seed, Macmillan, New York and London, 1914.

Six French Poets, Macmillan, New York and London, 1915.

Men, Women and Ghosts, Macmillan, New York and London, 1916.

Tendencies in Modern American Poetry, Macmillan, New York, 1917.

Can Grande's Castle, Macmillan, New York and London, 1918.

Pictures of the Floating World, Houghton Mifflin, Boston, 1919.

Legends, Houghton Mifflin, Boston, 1922.

What's O'Clock, Houghton Mifflin, Boston, 1925.

John Keats, Houghton Mifflin, Boston, 1925.

Ballads for Sale, Houghton Mifflin, Boston, 1927.

Complete Poetical Works, Houghton Mifflin, Boston, 1955 (currently in print).
A Shard of Silence: Selected Poems of Amy Lowell, ed G.R. Ruihley, Twayne Publishers, New York, 1957.

Anthologies edited by Amy Lowell:
Some Imagist Poets, Houghton Mifflin, Boston: vol. I, 1915; vol. II, 1916; vol. III, 1917.
A Miscellany of American Poetry (with Louis Untermeyer), Alfred Harcourt, New York, 1917.
A Miscellany of American Poetry (vol. II), Alfred Harcourt, New York, 1918.

Mina Loy 1882–1966
Lunar Baedecker [*sic*], Contact Publishing Co., Paris, 1923.
Lunar Baedeker & Time-tables, Jonathan Williams, Highlands, North Carolina, 1958.
The Last Lunar Baedeker, ed Roger Conover, The Jargon Society, Highlands, North Carolina, 1982; Carcanet Press, Manchester, 1985.

Harriet Monroe 1860–1936
Valeria and Other Poems, De Vinne Press, Chicago, 1891.
John Wellborn Root: A Study of his Life and Work, Houghton Mifflin, Boston, 1896.
Poets and their Art, Macmillan, New York, 1926.
Chosen Poems: A Selection from My Books of Verse, Macmillan, New York, 1935.
A Poet's Life: Seventy Years in a Changing World, Macmillan, New York, 1938.

Marianne Moore 1887–1972
Poems, The Egoist Press, London, 1921.
Observations, The Dial Press, New York, 1924.
Selected Poems, Macmillan, New York, 1935; Faber & Faber, London, 1935.
The Pangolin And Other Verse, Brendin Publishing Co., London, 1936.

Predilections, Viking, New York, 1955; Faber & Faber, London, 1956.

A Marianne Moore Reader, Viking, New York, 1965.

The Complete Poems, Macmillan and Viking, New York, 1967; Faber & Faber, London, 1968; Viking, New York, 1981.

The Complete Prose, ed Patricia C. Willis, Viking, New York, 1986; Faber & Faber, London, 1987.

Dorothy Richardson 1873–1957
Pilgrimage, first editions:
  Pointed Roofs, Duckworth, London, 1915.
  Backwater, Duckworth, London, 1916.
  Honeycomb, Duckworth, London, 1917.
  The Tunnel, Duckworth, London, 1919.
  Interim, Duckworth, London, 1919.
  Deadlock, Duckworth, London, 1921.
  Revolving Lights, Duckworth, London, 1923.
  The Trap, Duckworth, London, 1925.
  Oberland, Duckworth, London, 1927.
  Dawn's Left Hand, Duckworth, London, 1931.
  Clear Horizon, Duckworth, London, 1935.

Collected editions:
  Pilgrimage (including *Dimple Hill*), 4 vols, J.M. Dent and Cresset Press, London; Alfred A. Knopf, New York, 1938.
  Pilgrimage (including *March Moonlight*), 4 vols, J.M. Dent & Sons, London; Alfred A. Knopf, 1967.
  Pilgrimage, 4 vols, Virago Press, London, 1979.

Gertrude Stein 1874–1946
Three Lives, The Grafton Press, New York, 1909; Peter Owen, London, 1970; Penguin, Harmondsworth, 1979.

Tender Buttons, Claire Marie, New York, 1914; Haskell House, New York, 1982.

Geography and Plays, The Four Seas Co., Boston, 1922; Haskell House, New York, 1982.

The Making of Americans, Contact Editions, Paris, 1925; Something Else Press, New York, 1952; Peter Owen, London, 1968.

Before The Flowers Of Friendship Faded Friendship Faded, Plain Edition, Paris, 1931.

The Autobiography of Alice B. Toklas, Harcourt Brace, New York, 1933; Penguin, Harmondsworth, 1986.

Everybody's Autobiography, Random House, New York, 1937; Virago, London, 1985.

Paris France, Batsford, London, 1940; Brilliance Books, London, 1983.

Selected Writings of Gertrude Stein, ed Carl van Vechten, Random House, New York, 1946 (currently in print).

Blood on the Dining Room Floor, Banyan Press, New York, 1948; Virago, London, 1985.

Bee Time Vine and Other Pieces, 1913–1927, Yale University Press, New Haven, 1953; Books for Libraries Press, Freeport, New York, 1969.

Fernhurst, Q.E.D., and Other Early Writings, ed Leon Katz, appendix by Donald Gallup, Liveright, New York, 1971; Peter Owen, London, 1972.

Gertrude Stein: Writings and Lectures 1909–1945, ed Patricia Meyerowitz, Peter Owen, London, 1967; Penguin, Baltimore, 1971 as *Look At Me Now And Here I Am*.

Section C   Selected 'little magazines'

Broom; An International Magazine of the Arts, Rome, Berlin, New York, November 1921 to January 1924, monthly. Edited by Harold Loeb, with Alfred Kreymborg 1921–2. Reprinted Kraus Reprint Corp., New York, 1967.

Bruno's Weekly, New York, July 1915 to September 1916. Edited by Guido Bruno.

Close-up. An International Magazine Devoted to Film Art, Territet, Switzerland, July 1927 to December 1933, monthly and quarterly. Edited by Kenneth Macpherson and Bryher. Reprinted Arno Press, New York, 1971.

Contact, an American Quarterly Review, New York, December 1920 to June 1923, irregular. Edited by William Carlos Williams and Robert McAlmon. Reprinted Kraus Reprint Corp., New York, 1967.

The Dial, New York, vols 68–86, 1920–9, monthly. Edited by Scofield Thayer, with Marianne Moore 1925–9.

The Egoist, London, 1914–19, monthly. Continuation of *The New Freewoman*, q.v. Edited by Dora Marsden (1914) and Harriet Shaw Weaver (1914–19). Reprinted Kraus Reprint Corp., New York, 1967.

The Freewoman. A Weekly Feminist Review, London, 23 November 1911 to 10 October 1912. Edited by Dora Marsden.

The Glebe, New York, 1913–14, irregular. Edited by Alfred Kreymborg. Reprinted Kraus Reprint Corp., New York, 1967.

Life and Letters To-day, London, 1933–50, quarterly and monthly. Edited by Robert Herring and Bryher.

The Little Review, Chicago, New York, Paris, 1914–29, irregular. Edited by Margaret Anderson, with Jane Heap. Reprinted Kraus Reprint Corp., New York, 1967.

The New Freewoman, London, 1913, monthly. Continuation of *The Freewoman*, q.v. Edited by Dora Marsden. Superseded by *The Egoist*, q.v. Reprinted Kraus Reprint Corp., New York, 1967.

Others. A Magazine of the New Verse, Grantwood, NJ, July 1915 to July 1919, monthly. Edited by Alfred Kreymborg, with W. Saphir 1917–18. Reprinted Kraus Reprint Corp., New York, 1967.

Poetry. A Magazine of Verse, Chicago monthly. Edited 1912–35 by Harriet Monroe.

This Quarter, Paris, 1925–9, quarterly. Edited by Ernest Walsh and Ethel Moorhead. Reprinted Kraus Reprint Corp., New York, 1967.

The Transatlantic Review, Paris, January–December 1924, monthly. Edited by Ford Madox Ford.

transition, Paris, April 1927 to spring 1938, irregular. Edited by Eugene Jolas. Reprinted Kraus Reprint Corp., New York, 1967.

Section D   Works consulted or cited

Ackroyd, Peter, *Ezra Pound and His World*, Charles Scribner's Sons, New York, 1980.

Aldington, Richard, *Life for Life's Sake*, Viking, New York, 1941; Cassell, London, 1968.

Anderson, Margaret, *The Little Review Anthology*, Hermitage

House, New York, 1953; reprinted Horizon Press, New York, 1970.

My Thirty Years' War. The Autobiography. Beginnings and Battles to 1930, Horizon Press, New York, 1969.

Beach, Sylvia, *Shakespeare & Company*, Faber & Faber, London, 1956; Harcourt, Brace and Co., New York, 1959.

Boll, Theophilus E.M., *Miss May Sinclair: Novelist*, Fairleigh Dickinson University Press, Rutherford, NJ, 1973.

Brinnin, John M., *The Third Rose. Gertrude Stein and Her World*, Little, Brown, Boston, 1959.

Cahill, Daniel, *Harriet Monroe*, Twayne Publishers, New York, 1973.

Contact Collection of Contemporary Writers, Contact Publishing Co., Paris, 1925.

Costello, Bonnie, *Marianne Moore: Imaginary Possessions*, Harvard University Press, Cambridge, Mass., 1981.

Cournos, John, *Autobiography*, G.P. Putnam's Sons, New York, 1935.

Miranda Masters, Alfred A. Knopf, New York, 1926.

Crosby, Caresse, *The Passionate Years*, Dial, New York, 1953.

Damon, S. Foster, *Amy Lowell*, Houghton Mifflin, Boston, 1935; reprinted Archon Books, Hamden, Conn., 1966.

Delaney, Paul, *D.H. Lawrence's Nightmare. The Writer and His Circle in the Years of the Great War*, Basic Books, New York, 1978.

DuPlessis, Rachel Blau, *H.D.: The Career of that Struggle*, Harvester Press, Brighton; Indiana University Press, Bloomington, 1986.

Elwin, Malcolm, *The Life of Llewelyn Powys*, John Lane, The Bodley Head, London, 1946.

Faderman, Lillian, *Surpassing the Love of Men. Romantic Friendship and Love between Women from the Renaissance to the Present*, William Morrow, New York, 1981, The Women's Press, London, 1985.

Field, Andrew, *Djuna. The Life and Times of Djuna Barnes*, G.P. Putnam's Sons, New York, 1983; Secker & Warburg, London, 1983 (as *The Formidable Miss Barnes*).

Fitch, Noel Riley, *Sylvia Beach and the Lost Generation*, W.W. Norton & Co., New York and London, 1983.

Flanner, Janet, *Paris Was Yesterday 1925–1939*, Viking, New York, 1972.

Fletcher, John Gould, *Life Is My Song*, Farrar & Rinehart, New York, 1937.

Ford, Ford Madox, *Memories and Impressions*, Harper & Row, New York, 1911.

Return to Yesterday, Liveright, New York, 1972.

Ford, Hugh (ed.), *The Left Bank Revisited: Selections from the Paris Tribune 1917–34*, Pennsylvania State University Press, Pa., 1972.

Published in Paris. American and British Writers, Printers and Publishers in Paris 1920–1939, Pushcart Press, Yonkers, New York, 1980.

Friedberg, Anne, *Writing about Cinema: 'Close-up' 1927–1933*, University Microfilms, Ann Arbor, Mich., 1983.

Friedman, Susan, *Psyche Reborn: The Experience of H.D.*, Indiana University Press, Bloomington, 1981.

Fromm, Gloria G., *Dorothy Richardson, A Biography*, University of Illinois Press, Urbana and London, 1977.

Gallup, Donald, *The Flowers of Friendship: Letters Written to Gertrude Stein*, Alfred A. Knopf, New York, 1953.

Garner, Les, *Stepping Stones to Women's Liberty: Feminist Ideas in the Women's Suffrage Movement 1900–1918*, Heinemann Educational Books, London, 1984.

Gildzen, Alex (ed.), *A Festschrift for Djuna Barnes on her 80th Birthday*, Kent State University Libraries, Kent, Ohio, 1972.

Glassco, John, *Memoirs of Montparnasse*, Oxford University Press, London, 1970.

Goldring, Douglas, *The Nineteen Twenties: A General Survey and Some Personal Memories*, Nicholson & Watson, London, 1945.

South Lodge: Reminiscences of Violet Hunt, Ford Madox Ford and the English Review Circle, Constable, London, 1943.

Gould, Jean, Amy. *The World of Amy Lowell and the Imagist Movement*, Dodd, Mead & Co., New York, 1975.

Grant, Joy, *Harold Monro and the Poetry Bookshop*, Routledge & Kegan Paul, London, 1967.

Graves, Richard Perceval, *The Brothers Powys*, Routledge & Kegan Paul, London, Melbourne and Henley, 1983.

Gregory, Alyse, *The Day Is Gone*, E.P. Dutton & Co. Inc., New York, 1948.

Grosskurth, Phyllis, *Havelock Ellis. A Biography*, Alfred A. Knopf, New York, 1980.

Guest, Barbara, *Herself Defined. The Poet H.D. and her World*, Doubleday, New York, 1984; Collins, London, 1985.

Guggenheim, Peggy, *Out of this Century. Confessions of an Art Addict*, Universe Books, New York, 1979.

Haas, Robert Bartlett (ed.), *A Primer for the Gradual Understanding of Gertrude Stein*, Black Sparrow Press, Santa Barbara, Calif., 1976.

Hahn, Emily, *Lorenzo. D.H. Lawrence and the Women who Loved Him*, Lippincott, Phila. and New York, 1975.
Mabel: A Biography of Mabel Dodge Luhan, Houghton Mifflin, Boston, 1977.

Hanscombe, Gillian E., *The Art of Life: Dorothy Richardson and the Development of Feminist Consciousness*, Peter Owen, London, 1982; Ohio University Press, Athens, Ohio, 1983.

Hemingway, Ernest, *A Moveable Feast*, Scribner's, New York, 1964.

Hoffman, Frederick J. and Allen, Charles, *The Little Magazine*, Princeton University Press, Princeton, NJ, 1946.

Hunt, Violet, *The Flurried Years*, Hurst & Blachett, London, 1926.

Hutchins, Patricia, *Ezra Pound's Kensington: An Exploration 1885–1913*, Faber & Faber, London, 1965.

Joost, Nicholas, *Scofield Thayer and The Dial*, Southern Illinois University Press, Carbondale and Edwardsville, 1964.

Kenner, Hugh, *A Homemade World: The American Modernist Writers*, Knopf, New York, 1975.

King, Michael (ed.), *H.D. Woman and Poet*, National Poetry Society, Orano, Me., 1986.

Knoll, Robert, *Robert McAlmon: Expatriate Publisher and Writer*, University of Nebraska Studies No. 18, Lincoln, Nebraska, August 1957.

Kouidis, Virginia, *Mina Loy: American Modernist Poet*, Louisiana State University Press, Baton Rouge, La., 1980.

Kreymborg, Alfred, *Troubadour: An American Autobiography*, Sagamore Press Inc., New York, 1957.

Lawrence, D.H., *The Collected Letters*, ed Harry T. Moore, Viking, New York, 1962.

Lidderdale, Jane and Nicholson, Mary, *Dear Miss Weaver*. Harriet Shaw Weaver 1876–1961, Viking, New York, 1970.

Lindberg-Seyersted, Brita (ed.), *Pound/Ford. The Story of a Literary Friendship. The Correspondence between Ezra Pound and Ford Madox Ford and Their Writings about Each Other*,

Faber & Faber, London, 1982.

Luhan, Mabel Dodge, *Intimate Memories*, 4 vols, Harcourt, Brace, New York, 1933–7.

McAlmon, Robert, *Being Geniuses Together*, Secker & Warburg, London, 1938; rev. edn, Doubleday, New York, 1968; The Hogarth Press, London, 1984.

Post-Adolescence, Contact Publishing Co., Paris, 1923.

McMillan, Dougald, *transition 1927–38. The History of a Literary Era*, George Braziller, New York, 1976.

Mellow, James R., *Charmed Circle: Gertrude Stein & Company*, Avon Books, New York, 1975.

Messerli, Douglas, *Djuna Barnes: A Bibliography*, David Lewis, Rhinebeck, New York, 1975.

Mizener, Arthur, *The Saddest Story. A Biography of Ford Madox Ford*, World, New York, 1971.

Moore, Harry T., *The Intelligent Heart. The Story of D.H. Lawrence*, Farrar, Straus & Cudahy, New York, 1954.

Moore, Marianne, *A Marianne Moore Reader*, Viking, New York, 1959.

Norman, Charles, *Ezra Pound*, Macmillan, New York, 1960.

Parry, Albert, *Garrets and Pretenders*, Covici, Friede, New York, 1933.

Patmore, Brigit, *My Friends When Young*, Heinemann, London, 1968.

No Tomorrow, The Century Co., New York and London, 1929.

This Impassioned Onlooker, Robert Holden, London, 1926.

Plomer, William, *Museum Pieces*, Jonathan Cape, London, 1952.

Pocklington, G.R., and Foat, F.E.K., *The Story of W.H. Smith & Son . . . Rewritten and Brought up to Date . . .*, printed for private circulation, London, 1949.

Poli, Bernard J., *Ford Madox Ford and The Transatlantic Review*, Syracuse University Press, Syracuse, NY, 1967.

Pound, Ezra, *The Letters of Ezra Pound 1907–1941*, ed D.D. Paige, Harcourt, Brace, New York, 1950.

Powys, Llewelyn, *The Letters of Llewelyn Powys*, selected and edited by Louis Wilkinson, John Lane, The Bodley Head, London, 1943.

Ray, Man, *Self-Portrait*, Andre Deutsch, London, 1963.

Rood, Karen (ed.), *American Writers in Paris 1920–1939*, Gale Research Company, Detroit, Mich., 1980.

Secrest, Meryle, *Between Me and Life. A Biography of Romaine*

Brooks, Doubleday, New York, 1974.

Simon, Linda, *The Biography of Alice B. Toklas*, Doubleday, New York, 1977.

Smoller, Sanford J., *Adrift Among Geniuses. Robert McAlmon, Writer and Publisher of the Twenties*, Pennsylvania State University Press, University Park and London, 1975.

Stapleton, Laurence, *Marianne Moore. The Poet's Advance*, Princeton University Press, Princeton, NJ, 1978.

Stock, Noel, *The Life of Ezra Pound*, Routledge & Kegan Paul, London, 1970.

Thomson, Virgil, *Virgil Thomson*, Alfred A. Knopf, New York, 1966.

Toklas, Alice B., *Staying on Alone. Letters of Alice B. Toklas*, Liveright, New York, 1973.

What is Remembered, Holt, Rinehart & Winston, New York, 1963.

Tomlinson, Charles (ed.), *Marianne Moore. A Collection of Critical Essays*, Prentice-Hall, Englewood Cliffs, NJ, 1969.

West, Anthony, *H.G. Wells: Aspects of a Life*, Hutchinson, London, 1984.

Wickes, George, *The Amazon of Letters. The Life and Loves of Natalie Barney*, G.P. Putnam's Sons, New York, 1976.

Wilkinson, Louis, *The Buffoon*, Alfred A. Knopf, New York, 1916; Village Press, London, 1975.

Swan's Milk, Faber & Faber, London, 1934.

[Wilkinson, Louis] *Welsh Ambassadors: Powys Lives and Letters*, by Louis Marlow. With an Introduction by Kenneth Hopkins. Bertram Rota, London, 1971.

Williams, Ellen, *Harriet Monroe and the Poetry Renaissance: The First Ten Years of Poetry, 1912–22*, University of Illinois Press, Urbana, 1977.

Williams, William Carlos, *The Autobiography of William Carlos Williams*, Random House, New York, 1948; New Directions, New York, 1967.

Wilson, Edmund, *The Twenties. From Notebooks and Diaries of the Period*, ed Leon Edel, Farrar, Straus & Giroux, New York, 1975.

Index